The Counsellor's Handbook

The Counsellor's Handbook

A practical A–Z guide to professional and clinical practice

Second edition

Rowan Bayne, Ian Horton, Tony Merry, Elizabeth Noyes and Gladeana McMahon

Psychology Department, University of East London

First published in 1999 by:
Stanley Thornes (Publishers) Ltd

Reprinted in 2003 by:
Nelson Thornes Ltd
Delta Place
27 Bath Road
CHELTENHAM
GL53 7TH
United Kingdom

06 07 / 12 11 10 9 8

A catalogue record for this book is available from the British Library

ISBN 0 7487 3309 4

Page make-up by Acorn Bookwork, Salisbury, Wiltshire

Printed in Great Britain by Antony Rowe

Transferred to digital printing 2006

CONTENTS

___ Acknowledgements___

First Edition

We would like to thank all the people who have contributed to this book, particularly Susy Ajith and Ann Stapleton for their skill with word processing and for calmly making time in a busy office, and Rosemary Morris, our commissioning editor, for her quiet persistence and clear sense of boundaries. The book is dedicated to the students, past and present, on our Postgraduate Diploma in Therapeutic Counselling (Integrative).

Second Edition

For the second edition we owe a special thanks to Annette Rogers, our new secretary. Annette is coping with us and all the changes very positively, and is a welcome member of the counselling group at UEL. We would also like to thank Jane Bryant for her care, skill and enjoyment of her work.

Tables 3 and 4 are taken from *Counselling and Communications Skills for Medical and Health Practitioners*, with permission from the publishers, the British Psychological Society.

INTRODUCTION

This book is for counsellors and trainee counsellors. It offers ideas, evidence, arguments, information and occasionally advice on day-to-day aspects of counselling. We think of these as in four broad areas:

- Apparently peripheral aspects, like fees, furniture, holidays and smoking. Many books on counselling either ignore these or mention them only in passing. We treat them as important in their own right because they make effective counselling less likely if they are neglected, and because counsellors are sometimes concerned about them.

- Generic aspects, like boundaries, collusion, emotions and empathy. By 'generic' we mean not specific to a particular approach to counselling. For example, paraphrasing is a general skill (and included) while 'splitting' is specific to a particular approach (and not included).

- Clinical practice issues on which there is marked variation in practice, e.g. assessment, psychodiagnosis. For these we outline the main options and arguments.

- Techniques or strategies which are fairly general, or at least not specific to a particular approach to counselling e.g. life space diagrams, imagery. We want to emphasise that such techniques need to be used with sensitivity and care, taking both the client's needs and the counsellor's own experience into account. We say more about this in the entry on Experiments by clients

In this introduction we would like to say something about five things: the second edition; how we see the book being useful; how we wrote it; the terms 'counselling' and 'psychotherapy'; and feedback to us.

THE SECOND EDITION

For this second edition we have gained the energy and expertise of a new colleague and co-author, Gladeana, substantially revised more than half the entries, including some central ones (e.g. Empathy, Effectiveness, Multicultural counselling) and have added several new entries (e.g. Administration, Change, E-mail counselling, Loss and Non-verbal Communication).

USING THIS BOOK

The book is organised alphabetically, with the entries as their own index and cross-referenced so that everything we've written on a particular topic can be found and read quickly. We want counsellors with a pressing query or a vague disquiet to be able to find ideas that stimulate, crystallise, challenge or support their own theories, values and feelings. Further reading – longer discussions, research papers – is suggested for follow-up if desired. We hope that the book will be enjoyed in more leisurely, less-pressured moods too, but essentially it is a concise discussion of central, non-partisan elements of counselling with, where appropriate, practical guidelines.

HOW WE WROTE THE BOOK

The book started as a diploma staff development exercise, suggested by Rowan. We wrote lists of possible entries and then discussed how to proceed. We then chose about ten entries each to write first drafts for, with – surprisingly – no arguments about who was writing which entry. The drafts were edited by Rowan with Ian, and circulated, so that we all contributed to the final versions of some entries. Then we chose some more entries to write, deleted some from the list, added some more, and so on. The process was enjoyable and surprisingly easy. We've all suffered from writing but had found a method that suited us.

COUNSELLING AND PSYCHOTHERAPY

Some people argue that there is a difference between counselling and psychotherapy, but so far no one has been able to define with sufficient clarity what it is (Feltham, 1995a; Bond, 1996). In the BAC's words: 'There is no generally accepted distinction between counselling and psychotherapy. There are well founded traditions which use the terms interchangeably and others which distinguish between them' (British Association for Counselling, 1998, 3.3). Thorne (1992) dealt briskly with the distinctions which have been put forward, and with the 'dismal quest' for them. Rather, he hopes for a British Association for Counselling and Psychotherapy, based on the common elements in all approaches. We will use the terms counselling and psychotherapy and counsellor/ psychotherapist/therapist interchangeably.

FEEDBACK TO US

Finally, our experience and training, though diverse, hardly reflects the whole of counselling, and your favourite or most puzzling (and fairly general) concept or query may therefore be missing. If it is, please tell us. We would welcome comments on what we might have included, and on other aspects of the book. Our address is: Psychology Department, UEL, The Green, London E15 4LZ, UK.

ABUSE

(*See also*: Anger, Boundaries, Collusion, Counselling, Empathy, Post-traumatic stress disorder, Power, Sexual attraction, Touch)

Counselling the survivors of emotional, physical or sexual abuse requires great sensitivity. Both establishment of trust and exploration need to proceed at the client's own, often painfully slow, pace. Sometimes a large amount of previously unexpressed material pours out. Collusion of silence can be a hazard in this type of counselling; it is tempting to let clients avoid the painful expression of their past experience. Shillito-Clarke (1993, p.219) recommends the accounts in Walker (1992a) as a way of exploring reactions: 'I found it difficult to read without pausing between accounts or resorting to defensive strategies. In this respect, the book may prove an interesting testing ground for anyone interested in, but unsure of their ability to work with, survivors'.

Survivors of abuse sometimes suppress their emotions and memories to the point of forgetting about them altogether. In the USA, people with recently unearthed memories of sexual abuse have sued the alleged abusers for events that happened 20 or even 40 years earlier. Loftus (1993) discusses some of the problematic issues raised:

1. How common is it for memories of child abuse to be repressed?
2. How are jurors and judges likely to react to claims of repressed memories?
3. What are the memories like?
4. How authentic are they?

A major problem is that remembering things is a creative process: we simplify, shape and distort our memories (e.g. Loftus and Loftus, 1980). There are cases in which people were led to believe – by a therapist or therapy group – that they were abused and later reinterpreted these 'memories' as false.

Studies of counsellors and therapists whose clients report previously repressed memories conclude that the memories are seen as authentic because of accompanying symptoms, 'body memories' such as a rash, emotional pain and occasionally corroborating evidence from others (Loftus, 1993, p.523). On the other hand, cognitive psychologists generally regard 'repression', and therefore the idea of a 'recovered memory', with scepticism. One line of argument is that extremely painful events are remembered vividly by those who experienced them – e.g. children who have seen their parents murdered, survivors of concentration camps, victims and observers of catastrophes (Myers, 1998, p.428). However, it is also possible that prolonged, severe abuse leads to repressed memories.

Two practical implications for counsellors are to raise the possibility of abuse either with great care or not at all, and that using hypnosis or fantasy exercises to encourage memory is dangerous: they are more likely to increase confidence in what is recalled than its accuracy, however good the intentions of the counsellor or therapist. There are obvious costs, for the alleged survivors as well as those accused, of uncritically accepting false memories as facts.

However, as Walker (1996) points out, there are also many people 'with horribly clear recollections, often with no wish to accuse anybody, or to take legal action, but with a desperate need to try to heal their pain' (p.129). Her review and Draucker's (1992) book integrate ideas, practice and research on sexual abuse, and much of what they say is relevant to emotional and physical abuse and to counselling in general. Table 1 summarises some of Walker's practical conclusions.

For further detailed and balanced reviews of the evidence and arguments see, for example, Loftus (1993) and subsequent correspondence in the same journal (May 1994, pp.439–45) and Pope (1997) and following correspondence (September 1997, pp.987–1006).

Table 1

Responding to clients who may have been abused (adapted from Walker, 1996)

1. Tolerate, and work with, uncertainty. Try to balance the risks of (1) denying the level of abuse and its effects (particularly when the abuse is severe and horrifying) with (2) offering an explanation to relieve anxiety
2. Allow the client to set the pace in explaining her or his experiences. For example, if the client says 'bad things happened to me' the counsellor should respond at that level, not reframe the comment as 'abuse'. Use the term 'abuse' only if the client does. 'Many abuse survivors disclose hesitantly and gradually, otherwise it can be too much to bear' (Walker, 1996, p.135)
3. Try to respond calmly if memories are recovered, or appear to be recovered, in counselling
4. Help the client to think through any possible consequences of recovering memories such as legal action or confronting the abuser. A rapid response may be self-destructive
5. Be very cautious about the use of hypnosis in recovering 'buried memories'

ACCENTING

(*See also*: Concreteness, Empathy, Paraphrasing, Questions, Silence)

Accenting is the skill of saying back one or two of your client's words to help her or him clarify or explore more deeply. For example, client: 'I was fairly happy about that ...' Counsellor: 'Fairly happy.' It is best used sparingly.

ACCEPTANCE

(*See also*: Core conditions, Respect)

Most counsellors try to adopt a non-judgemental attitude towards their clients. The distinction between a client's actual behaviour and that client's impulses or fantasies is central. Most of us have experienced impulses or fantasies involving violent and/or destructive behaviour without acting on them. It can be very important for a client to know that he or she can give voice to these things without being judged or rejected for having them. The progress of counselling may get stuck if your client feels unable to express the dark side of their nature (if they have one), because they fear rejection or disapproval from you.

Most counsellors try to create a relationship in which their clients can explore both positively and negatively viewed aspects of themselves without the fear of (usually negative) evaluation of themselves as persons. *Positive* feelings or self-evaluations by clients also need to be accepted without evaluation. The acceptance of all feelings and impulses offers clients the opportunity (perhaps for the first time) to understand themselves as they currently are (Mearns and Thorne, 1988; Merry, 1995).

ACCREDITATION BY BAC, OF COUNSELLOR EDUCATION/TRAINING COURSES IN THE UK

(*See also*: Accreditation of individual counsellors, British Association for Counselling, Complaints, Counselling, Professionalism, Validation of counsellor education/training courses in the UK)

Over the past decade there has been an enormous expansion in the provision of counsellor education and training in the UK. It has become very difficult for people who want to train as counsellors, or for counsellors who want to undertake further training, to know which are likely to be good courses. Organisations wanting to employ counsellors are often ill-informed about the level and quality of training they should be seeking of their applicants. To help potential students, employers and clients to identify high standards of training, the British Association for Counselling (BAC) established the Courses Recognition Scheme. This validates in-depth training courses. 'In depth' is defined as one year full-time or two/three years part-time, to satisfy the minimum of 400 hours staff–student contact time.

The Courses Recognition Scheme (from 1997 The Courses Accreditation Scheme) was launched in 1988, after four years of consultation and research. Its aim is to recognise training programmes of very different orientations and traditions. The criteria and guidelines published in the booklet *The Recognition of Counsellor Training Courses* (British Association for Counselling, 1996) seek to preserve and enhance the independence of approaches while at the same time ensuring that adequate attention is paid to what are regarded as the core elements of training. Thus a course, whatever its rationale, must be able to satisfy the minimum criteria for each of nine core elements: admission, self-development, client work, supervision, skills training, theory, professional development, assessment and evaluation.

The minimum standards include providing in-depth training in a particular core theoretical model of counselling, appropriate balance among the academic, personal development and skill components consistent with that model, and completion by a student of not less than 100 hours of supervised client work during the course. The scheme also requires that courses be staffed by appropriately qualified and experienced practitioners, the majority of whom should be BAC-accredited counsellors or at least eligible for accreditation.

A further implication of being a BAC-accredited course is that the course is an organisational member of the BAC and thereby subject to its complaints and appeals procedures. This has an important function for 'consumer' protection, as a course can lose its recognised status for any breaches of codes of ethics and practice. The Courses Accreditation Scheme, like other forms of validation or accreditation, is concerned with design, development and provision of adequate resources, but (unlike them) is primarily concerned with preparation and delivery. It is especially interested in the ways in which feedback and evaluation are gathered from staff, students and external examiners and how this is used to modify and improve the programme.

Accreditation of a course is in several stages. The intention is to identify as early as possible those courses that are not suitable for the scheme: working through the entire procedure only to find the scheme is inappropriate for the particular course wastes both time and money. Course developers are strongly advised to arrange a consultation in order to clarify their eligibility for the scheme before preparing the substantial submission document. At the application stage each member of the BAC panel examines the document, often requesting further information or clarification. Once the panel is satisfied that the course meets the criteria on paper, they move into the visit stage and see the course in action. Panel members observe teaching sessions and supervision groups, talk to past and present students, examine written work, view the facilities and talk to members of staff. The Panel then decide whether to award Accredited status or whether certain conditions have first to be met. The course receives a full report. Representatives of accredited courses are required to consult with another recognised course throughout the five-year partnership stage, after which they must apply for re-accreditation.

The Courses Accreditation Scheme is essentially a peer evaluation scheme. Panels are drawn from core staff representatives of accredited courses to form the BAC Courses Accreditation Group (CAG), which is responsible for management and operation of the scheme. In this way the scheme receives continual feedback and is subject to modification and refinement – learning from the experience of those who have worked through the process. The CAG is ultimately accountable to the membership through the Management Committee of the BAC. In May 1998 there were 43 accredited courses, and the very large number of enquiries, requests for advice and consultations and the sales of the relevant BAC booklet, now in its third edition, indicate the impact of the scheme on counsellor education and training in the UK.

ACCREDITATION OF INDIVIDUAL COUNSELLORS BY THE BAC

(*See also*: Accreditation of counsellor training/education courses, Personal counselling for the counsellor, Personal growth for the counsellor, Professional development, Professionalism, Supervision)

An accredited counsellor is now commonly taken to be someone who has gained accreditation through the scheme introduced by the BAC in 1983. It is a form of peer appraisal for generic counsellors, based on a philosophy of counselling which integrates 900 hours of training and practice. The 900 hours includes 250 hours of theory, 200 hours of skills development and case discussion and 450 hours of supervised work with clients over a minimum period of three years. Alternatively, any of several specified combinations of formal units of training and experience of supervised counselling are needed. Evidence is required of serious and continuing commitment to professional and personal development, to consultation or supervision and to continuing in supervision for the period of accreditation. From October 1998, applicants are required to complete at least 40 hours of personal counselling or an equivalent activity consistent with their core theoretical model. The accreditation scheme is open to current members of BAC who assent to the BAC code of ethics. Applications, which must include case studies, a statement of counselling philosophy, and supervisor's and referee's reports, are judged without any face-to-face meeting. Counsellors who have successfully completed a BAC-accredited course have an easier task in that they complete only one case study and do not have to provide any training details.

Once accredited, the counsellor is required to undertake no fewer than 150 hours of counselling each year and 1.5 hours supervision each month. Unlike practice in other professional areas (e.g. social work and nursing) accreditation is for a five-year period only, after which counsellors must re-apply and demonstrate their continuing competence. Although the scheme was originally intended to protect the interests of the consumer, it is now used by many counsellors as a way of achieving professional status and is sometimes seen as an informal 'licence to practice'. Accredited counsellors can apply to join the United Kingdom Register of Counsellors as Registered Independent Counsellors. This is a voluntary register, but some form of statutory registration is currently being discussed, and seems inevitable at some point.

Granting of professional status usually depends on some form of certification by a professional body. However, many individual members of BAC are not eligible to apply as they are people using counselling skills at work rather than counsellors as defined by BAC. The effort of applying and the anxiety and potential embarrassment of being rejected are obvious disincentives. For some counsellors, any authorisation system, with its unavoidably judgemental element, and the trend towards professionalisation, are anathema.

The BAC scheme is now widely respected, with employers frequently asking for counsellors who are BAC accredited or at least eligible for accreditation. An external review (Foss, 1983) recommended that the scheme become more rigorous and that separate schemes are developed for accreditation of supervision and training courses. These have now been introduced.

ACTIVE LISTENING

See: Accenting, Empathy, Non-verbal communication, Paraphrasing, Questions, Silence, Summaries and 'moving interviews forward'

ADMINISTRATION

(See also: Accreditation, Business, Contract, Evaluation, Fees, Record keeping)

It is almost impossible for a counsellor to avoid administration. Administrative tasks may be limited to booking rooms, arranging appointments, keeping case notes, and writing letters to other professionals, although a counsellor may need a high degree of general and financial administrative skills (McMahon, 1994).

Administration can be seen as falling broadly within four categories.

1. General administration:

- Keeping an appointments diary for recording client appointments.
- Devising advertisements and placing them in appropriate places such as local papers and referral directories.
- Running a filing system to cater for documentation relating to items such as insurance, utilities, rent and information from professional associations such as the BAC and BPS.
- Using a telephone message service: an answering machine or call minder service which must be monitored on a regular basis.

2. Administration relating to client work:

- Producing a client information sheet outlining the service(s) offered and any relevant terms and conditions such as fees, cancellation policy and confidentiality.
- Keeping client details forms containing basic client details such as name, address, telephone numbers, doctor's details and a paragraph clearly outlining the client's consent to the terms and conditions of the counselling offered (McMahon, 1997; Sills, 1997).
- Producing client consent form(s), which may include forms outlining the client's permission for taping of counselling sessions, for their details to be used for the purposes of case studies or for therapeutic purposes such as permission for therapeutic touch to take place (Sills, 1997).
- Note-taking and recording supporting documentation requires the counsellor to have a reliable formula for recording case notes and for storing relevant documentation such as referral details, letters written to other professionals about the client, relevant therapeutic questionnaires and assessment material.
- Evaluation forms must be prepared to provide feedback to the counsellor of therapeutic outcome and client satisfaction.
- Keeping secure storage facilities to ensure that the ethical requirements for the protection of client confidentiality are met including registration under the Data Protection Act for all computer-based client records (British Association for Counselling, 1998).

3. Financial administration:

- Book-keeping skills will be required by counsellors in private practice for tasks such as entering income and expenditure, compiling profit and loss accounts, organising receipts, working out how much to put aside for income tax and reconciling bank statements (McMahon 1994; Syme, 1994).
- Invoicing systems, in addition to the provision of simple receipts, may be needed.

4. Professional administration:

- Accreditation schemes such as those currently offered by the BAC require the counsellor to complete a comprehensive application form. To be able to provide the relevant information for the initial application and for re-accreditation, the counsellor must keep reasonably accurate records of (amongst other things) the number of hours of training received (skills and theory), professional development activities, personal therapy, supervision received (and over what time) and number of hours of counselling undertaken per year.

ADVERTISING

(*See also*: Codes of ethics, Marketing)

In some professions, medicine for example, advertising of services is illegal. In counselling, it is both legal and professionally acceptable to advertise as long as you do not state or imply that you can cure people of any sickness, ill-health or disturbance. You can say that you can help with these problems and others like them, but you should not claim to be in possession of special knowledge or skills that guarantee any form of success. The British Code of Advertising Practice is available from the Advertising Standards Authority, Brook House, 2–16 Torrington Place, London WC1E 7HN (Tel: 0171-580 5555). It requires advertisements to be 'legal, decent, honest and truthful', and contains a clause stating that failure to substantiate any claims made, and to do so quickly, itself contravenes the Code.

It is advisable, therefore, to restrict advertising to straightforward statements of any areas you specialise in (such as stress or depression), the approach you use, and how potential clients can contact you. The costs of advertising can be claimed against tax, providing they are 'wholly and exclusively' incurred for the purpose of business.

Some counsellors advertise in their local press, in specialist magazines, in meeting places such as doctors' surgeries (provided that permission has been obtained from the doctors concerned), and drop-in and day centres. The BAC publishes an annual directory of counsellors and psychotherapists (which includes accredited and non-accredited members of BAC); a listing in this is a good way to get yourself known, but there can be up to 12 months to wait between providing

BAC with your details, and publication of the next directory. Local BAC branches also produce directories of counsellors.

If you produce any promotional literature (handouts, leaflets), be sure not to make claims that imply any guarantee of success. The BAC Code of Ethics states that, when announcing counselling services, counsellors should limit the information they give to name, address, telephone number, hours available, relevant qualifications, and a brief listing of the services offered. Care should also be taken not to indicate affiliation with an organisation in a manner which falsely implies accreditation, validation or sponsorship by that organisation.

ADVICE, GIVING

(*See also*: Challenge, Counselling, Empathy, Frame of reference, Information, Sued, being)

A basic aim of counselling is to support clients in taking responsibility for their decisions and being more independent. Generally, advice is inconsistent with this aim, and many counsellors therefore do not give advice. An exception is that if you suspect that a client is physically or mentally ill you should advise them to see their general practitioner (Cohen, 1992).

Not giving advice can be therapeutic in itself: it says, in effect, 'When you've explored what's troubling you, you'll see it more clearly and know what to do.' However, Lazarus offers a radically different view: 'I will often be fairly free with my advice', though he adds that he always phrases it 'This is the way I see it' (Dryden, 1991, p.60).

AGGRESSIVE AND VIOLENT CLIENTS

See: Anger, Violence and its prevention

ANGER, COPING WITH

(*See also*: Codes of ethics, Confidentiality, Emotions, Empathy, Ethical dilemmas, Experiments by clients, Furniture, Non-verbal communication, Sued, being, Touch, Violence and its prevention)

Some clients are so angry that you may feel, or actually be, threatened. In such cases empathy and – when your client is calm – an 'anger management' approach may be helpful. Novaco (1975) describes cognitive and behavioural techniques to help clients become aware of their arousal and of the thought patterns which lead to angry outbursts. By relaxing and learning to reconstrue those thoughts, the client may be helped to work towards more manageable behaviour.

A contract establishing the difference between 'feeling angry' and 'aggressive behaviour' (and agreeing not to behave aggressively during counselling), can clarify the situation and increase confidence. However, the inclusion of details on what will happen if the client becomes violent may either be useful or reduce trust, depending on the situation. All clients require recognition of their anger and a chance to talk about it, though for some the thought of talking about it is too threatening. It needs to be made explicit that *clients* can decide what is right for them: they are then more in control and less likely to feel threatened or to resort to violence.

How you respond to a potentially violent client if she or he becomes upset also needs to be established early on. Touch is risky and in some areas and cultures maintaining eye-contact may be interpreted as 'eyeballing' and responded to aggressively; in others, *not* looking can be seen as furtive and might cause unease and aggression. Comfortable 'personal space' also varies from person to person and culture to culture. You should be clear about these factors and agree that the client will take deep breaths and (literally) 'count to ten', or focus her or his attention 'out' – for example, by looking for all the things of a particular colour in the room. These strategies aid self-control, although a balance between self-control and clarifying emotions needs to be kept in mind.

ANGER, EXPRESSION OF

(*See also*: Emotions, Empathy, Experiments by clients, Journal, writing a)

Expression of anger is often encouraged in counselling, on the grounds that (1) suppressed emotions cause problems which are helped by the releasing of anger and/or (2) experiences are more likely to be understood and assimilated if spoken about, and that experiencing emotions facilitates this process. Some approaches see expression as vitally important; others see anger as a manifestation of depression or as an expression of fear, with fear as the emotion really needing to be expressed. In contrast, research on anger suggests that expressing it is usually unhelpful, and that the question of whether or not a person should express or suppress anger is better put as 'When does a person benefit from expressing anger? What kind of person? And, more subtly, 'When should an individual neither express nor suppress anger, but stop generating the emotion in the first place? Why does the same action (say, talking about one's anger) produce a feeling of communication in one circumstance and the opposite feeling in another?' (Tavris, 1984, p.172).

Tavris' general conclusion about expressing anger is that just 'releasing it' tends to consolidate the anger, exclude other emotions and make other people angrier too (Tavris, 1984, 1989). Anger can be expressed constructively, especially perhaps in counselling, but the view that not expressing it is stressful and that releasing it is healthy in a 'cathartic' way is too simple. Keinan *et al.* (1992) found that intense but infrequent expression of anger is associated with good physical health.

There are many ways of helping clients become more aware of their anger: empathy; experiential exercises (e.g. Ernst and Goodison, 1982); holding a conversation with it ('How long have you been there? What do you want?'); drawing it; writing to it. Sometimes more physical techniques, such as punching cushions, allow a non-verbal release of emotion and clearer understanding.

ANGER, IN COUNSELLORS

(*See also*: Immediacy, Self-disclosure by counsellors, Stress, Supervision)

Faced, in the session itself, with their own anger, counsellors are sometimes in a dilemma about whether to talk about it then or later. In other words, do you use the skills of self-disclosure or immediacy in the session, or wait until supervision? There is no easy answer; it depends on the circumstances. The first consideration is whether or not disclosing your anger will help your client. This is not as straightforward as it seems; what you might see as being helpful to your clients (in that you are letting them know their effect on people) they might see as unempathic, and the counselling could be disrupted. If in any doubt, it is better to discuss your angry response in supervision. There you can clarify whether you are picking up on your client's anger, or if it is your own anger which is being stimulated. It will then be possible to examine how you could enable your client to get in touch with her or his own anger while you talk about your feelings with your own counsellor.

ANSWERPHONE

(*See also*: Nuisance telephone calls)

Answering machines can make it easier for people to contact each other (and to avoid contact!), but they are very off-putting for some people, especially those who may be nervous about making contact with you in the first place. We suggest that saying when you will be available, if possible, and that giving your name rather than a number is more friendly (though some people prefer not to take this risk). For example: 'Hello. I'm usually available to answer the phone between ten and eleven each weekday morning, but if you'd prefer, please leave your name and a telephone number after the tone, and I will call you as soon as I can.'

ANXIETY

(*See also*: Depression, Emotions, Panic Attacks, Stress)

Anxiety is not simply about being too anxious; it is also about irrational worry and avoidance of situations that are the focus of this worry (Crino *et al.*, 1994). Although some anxiety is overt, it can also underlie depression, obsessions, hysteria, bodily symptoms and phobias. The American Psychiatric Association's DSM-IV outlines eleven different types of anxiety disorder (Frances, 1994). Counselling aims to help clients face up to anxiety through, for example, empathy, restructuring of thoughts, facing 'existential givens', or physically facing whatever is anxiety provoking. Some counsellors choose to use psychological assessment questionnaires such as the Beck Anxiety Inventory (BAI) to elicit the degree of anxiety (Weishaar, 1993). Such questionnaires, if completed before, during and after therapy can help to evaluate client progress. There is no clear evidence that one method is better than another, but some clients may prefer a particular approach. It may be helpful to give clients choice as part of the process of encouraging them to take responsibility – e.g. do they want to look at thoughts, feelings, or actions, or any combination of the three? The more extreme the anxiety the more likely it is that a variety of approaches is needed in its management (e.g. Hallam, 1992; van Deurzen, 1996).

APPROPRIATENESS OF COUNSELLING

See: Assessment, Contraindications for brief counselling, Referral

ASSERTIVENESS

(*See also*: Boundaries, Contract, negotiating a, Immediacy, Multiculturalism, Self-awareness, Sexual attraction, Stress, Thoughts, Values)

Assertiveness can be defined as 'being able to express and act on your rights as a person while respecting the same rights in others'. Three other levels of definition are in terms of the rights themselves, styles of behaviour and skills. Rakos (1991) reviews a variety of definitions and the problems associated with them. He draws attention to the distinction between assertiveness therapy (a more remedial approach, in clinical settings) and assertiveness training (for professional groups and the general public) (Rakos, 1991, p.187). Assertiveness training is for people who are already relatively assertive but who wish to develop particular skills and qualities further. Assertiveness therapy is 'a treatment of choice for most people with interpersonal difficulties' (Corey, 1991, p.305).

The terms used by Dickson (1987) for styles of behaviour which are *not* assertive are fairly standard: aggressive, passive and manipulative (indirectly aggressive). Lists of assertive rights vary more than the styles, but the left hand column of Table 2 is representative. The table's format, taken from Bond (1986), is unusual and makes explicit the 'respect for others' element in assertiveness.

Approaches to assertiveness training differ radically. In those which focus on skills, 'saying no' and 'making requests' are basic. Saying no includes the key skill, strongly supported by research (Rakos, 1991), of 'empathic assertion'. Other assertive skills are giving and receiving compliments, and giving and receiving criticism. Dickson's work (1987) is a practical source, and for both sexes despite its title. Assertiveness is most relevant to counsellors themselves in three ways: as part of such skills as negotiating a contract and immediacy, as a model to apply to problems with boundaries, and as one strategy for looking after themselves (Bayne, 1998a).

Table 2

Assertive rights

1. I have the right to be treated with respect	**and**	Others have the right to be treated with respect
2. I have the right to express my thoughts, opinions and values	**and**	Others have the right to express their thoughts, opinions and values
3. I have the right to express my feelings	**and**	Others have the right to express their feelings
4. I have the right to say 'No' without feeling guilty	**and**	Others have the right to say 'No' without feeling guilty
5. I have the right to be successful	**and**	Others have the right to be successful.
6. I have the right to make mistakes	**and**	Others have the right to make mistakes
7. I have the right to change my mind	**and**	Others have the right to change their minds
8. I have the right to say that I don't understand	**and**	Others have the right to say that they don't understand
9. I have the right to ask for what I want	**and**	Others have the right to ask for what they want
10. I have the right to decide for myself whether or not I am responsible for another person's problem	**and**	Others have the right to decide for themselves whether or not they are responsible for another person's problem
11. I have the right to choose not to assert myself	**and**	Others have the right to choose not to assert themselves

Assertive values are clearly for autonomy and against subservience. Cultural bias is therefore a problem. One solution is 'bicultural competence' (Rakos, 1991), when the person or group practise assertive skills for both the 'mainstream' culture and, where applicable, their own subculture and/or the subculture of clients, colleagues etc. Another solution is to emphasise individual style and self-awareness. Assertiveness training is then seen more as consciousness raising to allow greater choice, including whether or not to use skills to challenge a particular social context, than as prescribing how or when to use the skills.

ASSESSMENT

(*See also*: Beginnings, Challenge, Contract, negotiating a, Contraindications for brief counselling, Psychodiagnosis, Referral)

Counsellors vary radically in their attitudes towards assessment. Some counsellors use a range of assessment procedures which may involve lengthy intake interviews or case histories and diagnostic classification systems (e.g. DSM-IV or ICD-10). For others, the whole idea of assessment is anathema. They regard it as something 'done to the client', synonymous with the medical model of diagnosis, prescription and treatment in which the balance of power, responsibility and role of expert is held by the counsellor. While many counsellors prefer not to use any type of formal procedures and may avoid using the term 'assessment', few would argue with the need to obtain some information when starting work with each client.

Whatever your theoretical orientation, assessment will typically be concerned with one or more of the following objectives:

1. To help you and your client understand the nature of the client's presenting problem and related issues.

2. To identify the factors that may be associated with the problem and the client's experience or behaviour.

3. To determine the client's expectations and desired outcomes.

4. To collect baseline data that can be compared with subsequent data to evaluate progress.

5. To facilitate the client's learning and motivation by sharing the counsellor's view of the problem. This may in itself contribute to therapeutic change through increasing self-awareness.

6. To produce an initial assessment (formulation) which provides the counsellor a basis for (first) making a decision about whether to offer a counselling contract, to initiate referral or to suggest that counselling would not be appropriate and (second) to provide the basis for developing a therapeutic or counselling plan, including the length and pattern of contract. For detailed discussions of assessment in counselling, see Palmer and McMahon (1997).

Assessment categories

Various kinds of information can be gathered or areas explored during assessment:

1. Presenting problem – including affective (emotions, feelings, mood), somatic (body-related sensations), behavioural (what the client does or doesn't do) and cognitive (thoughts, beliefs, attitudes, values, images, fantasies, internal dialogue) elements.

2. Antecedents – factors that may have influenced or caused the presenting problem.

3. Consequences – factors which may be maintaining it, at least in part.

4. Previous attempts to solve or cope with the problem.

5. Client resources and strengths.

6. The frequency, duration and severity of the problem (i.e. how long or how often the problem occurs, when it first started and its effects).

ASSESSMENT FORMULATION

(*See also*: Contract, negotiating a, Expectations, clients', History taking, Information, giving, Psychodiagnosis, Referral)

An assessment formulation is an attempt to construct a picture of what is going on within the client and to describe and offer some explanation of the presenting problem, possible targets for change, and ideas about how you and your client might work together. It may include some tentative ideas about emerging themes or possible connections between the client's past and present behaviour and experience. Depending on your theoretical orientation, the formulation may hypothesise about the possible origin and development of the problem and why it persists.

The formulation integrates information from a variety of sources:

1. The client's account of the experience.
2. The client's developmental history and social context.
3. Your experience of the client.
4. Your own theoretical frameworks.

These sources may be supplemented by such techniques as:

- client diaries about the problem
- genograms, life-space diagrams
- psychological tests
- DSM-IV or ICD-10 classifications.

AVOIDANCE, BY CLIENTS

(*See also*: Boredom, Challenge, Denial, Empathy, Immediacy, Referral, Reluctant clients)

Sometimes clients avoid topics which they consciously do not want to talk about. When they do not say that they are doing this and just avoid the topic, it can make counselling difficult and frustrating. This problem may be overcome by agreeing (in the contract) that, if there is an area the client wishes not to talk about, they must make this clear and the counsellor will respect their wish. Once clients realise that their wishes are respected and that they can trust the counsellor, they are able to relax and usually quite quickly are able to talk about the area they were originally avoiding. However, we do *not* recommend expecting this outcome, or using the agreement as a manipulative technique.

When clients are unaware that they are avoiding a topic, it might be for some general reason such as finding it difficult to talk about emotions and feelings, or they might be suppressing a specific event. Usually, counselling will gradually (at the client's pace) encourage more openness, but for very deeply suppressed fears it may take many months. One form of avoidance is for the client to talk about everybody and everything but themselves. Often the best strategy is a good empathic statement – for example, 'You seem upset by your parents' behaviour' could bring a client back to themselves after complaining about their parents.

AVOIDANCE, BY COUNSELLORS

(*See also*: Collusion, Contract, negotiating a, Emotions, Empathy, Feelings, Paraphrasing, Questions, Self-awareness, Thoughts)

It is easy to collude with a client's wish to avoid a subject, especially if it is also a difficult subject for the counsellor. Each time the client approaches the subject the counsellor might focus on a safer topic or ask an unnecessary question, encouraging the client to continue avoiding. The question 'what are you feeling?', which is intended to help clients look deeper at themselves, is often unhelpful here, for the following reasons:

1. It is a question, which tends to make clients think. They may therefore answer in terms of thoughts only, and avoid relevant emotions, images or feelings.

2. It is asked by the counsellor in desperation as they have not managed to pick up emotions already stated or implied by the client. Thus the client's real feelings have been ignored, which reinforces avoidance.

3. It might push the client towards an emotion which is very frightening and which they are not ready to face. They then become even more likely to avoid.

In all these cases, an empathic response is likely to achieve more.

BEGINNINGS

(*See also*: Assessment, Codes of ethics, Confidentiality, Contract, negotiating a, Duration, Expectations, clients', Fees, Frequency of sessions, Information, giving, Questions, Rapport, Referral, Working alliance)

The beginning of counselling can be crucial. Some clients are optimistic and ready to work hard, others are very anxious about counselling (Pipes *et al.*, 1985). This is not surprising: they are putting themselves in the hands of a stranger at a point in their life when they feel vulnerable, and when they may have limited or inaccurate knowledge about counselling.

From the counsellor's point of view, beginning work with clients involves both content and process: helping your clients explore what is troubling them and establishing a relationship. Different counsellors and approaches to counselling place more or less emphasis on each of the following:

1. **Role induction.** This includes helping clients explore any fears, fantasies and expectations, in particular how long counselling might last and what will happen in the sessions. You may find it helpful to prepare a brief account of your own view of counselling. It is most important that you and your clients work towards and negotiate a common understanding of what is involved.

2. **Establishing rapport** (sometimes called 'the therapeutic alliance' or the 'working alliance').

3. **Information-gathering.** This is about encouraging your clients to talk openly about themselves and their problems. Other possible topics are the 'trigger' – why they came to counselling at this point – and previous experience of counselling.

4. **Assessment** (see separate entry).

5. **Practical arrangements** – for example, about times and days to meet, how to cancel or change an appointment, fees.

BEHAVIOUR

(*See also*: British Association of Behavioural and Cognitive Psychotherapies, Homework, Thoughts, Theoretical schools)

Behaviour therapy encompasses a variety of therapeutic methods that aim to change self-defeating behaviour through direct action. The behaviour may be labelled a behavioural deficit (e.g. phobic avoidance) or excess (e.g. compulsive behaviour). The main aim is to alter behaviour that detrimentally affects the quality of the client's life (Marks, 1986). Behaviour therapy is successful in its pure form for the treatment of a variety of problems, such as using graded exposure programmes to desensitise individuals to feared situations (O'Sullivan, 1996). However, in more recent years behaviour and cognitive therapy have become integrated to form cognitive–behavioural therapy. Research suggests that such integration makes for faster and more effective treatment of client problems (Scott and Dryden, 1996).

Broadly speaking, there are four steps in the process of client change:

1. Problem identification and rating.

2. Explaining the exposure principle.

3. Behavioural tasks.

4. Maintenance.

For example, a client might be frightened of travelling in lifts and on a scale of 0–8 (0 = no discomfort, 8 = panic) may produce a hierarchy of different types of lifts and associated fear responses:

1. Large enclosed lifts I cannot see out of: 4

2. Small enclosed lifts I cannot see out of: 6

3. Enclosed glass lifts on the outside of buildings: 8

The principles of an exposure programme are explained to the client. It is important that the client understands the nature of fear and the principle that avoidance of feared situations maintains and may even increase fear, whereas regular exposure to the feared situation usually eradicates it. The client may fail to complete the behavioural task because he or she does not fully understand the principles behind an exposure programme, or has not been properly prepared with coping strategies for the feelings they might experience. Failure is likely to reinforce the fear and any negative views clients may have of themselves. In severe cases the therapist may accompany the client on an exposure task: for example, someone with agoraphobia to a shopping centre.

Behavioural tasks are set with the client as homework. For example, the client might decide that they will spend 20 consecutive minutes a day for one week travelling in a large enclosed lift at their local shopping centre. When deciding on behavioural tasks it is usually helpful for the client to choose an activity in the middle of the range on their rating scale of feared activity. Attempting to tackle the most feared situation first may lead to failure, reinforcing negative evaluations of self and risking refusal to continue with the work.

Once the client's fears have become extinct it is important that the client continues to integrate the once-feared situation into her or his life. Failure to do so may lead to recurrence of the problem. Clients also need to be prepared for the possibility that in times of stress old feelings may resurface. However, they should be assured that, if old fears do start to surface, exposing themselves to the feared situation is likely to ensure that the problem does not escalate (O'Sullivan, 1996).

BELIEFS, IRRATIONAL

See: Thoughts

BEREAVEMENT

See: Loss

'BLOCKED' CLIENTS

See: Avoidance, Challenge, Referral, Reluctant clients

BOOKS, SELF-HELP

(*See also*: Research)

Counsellors sometimes recommend self-help books to their clients. Although these can work well there are also problems with them (Rosen, 1981, 1987). Some of Rosen's (1981) guidelines for evaluating the helpfulness or not of a self-help book or tape, simplified and combined with those of Webb (1981), are:

1. Does the book claim or promise too much?
2. Does the book specify its limitations?
3. Is the advice specific or vague?

4. Is there a warning about placebo effects?

5. Does the book include or cite sound evidence of effectiveness (i.e. more than opinions, anecdotes and testimonials)?

6. Are there criteria for evaluating progress?

While these suggestions seem appropriately rigorous, others – e.g. 'Is the author appropriately qualified? and 'Has the book itself (rather than the techniques) been tested for effectiveness?' – are more arguable. The first could be seen as self-interest on the part of psychologists, and irrelevant if the other criteria are met. In support of the second suggestion, Rosen cited studies showing that techniques which work with 'minimal therapist assistance' do not work, or work much less well, without it. Indeed, some self-help programmes have been shown to make a problem worse. On the other hand, when the effectiveness of self-help books, tapes and programmes is unknown, and appropriate guidelines for use are given, it seems reasonable to suggest things to try. Rosen's criteria are firmly within an empirical framework, but often in counselling and self-help the research has not yet been carried out, or is inconclusive. However, in situations where research has been done and seems sound, it would be unethical and unprofessional to ignore it.

BOREDOM

(*See also*: Challenge, Confrontation, Congruence, Immediacy, Intuition, Process, Self-awareness)

When you feel bored in a counselling session, it is usually better not to be stoical about it. One strategy is to focus on the client's non-verbal behaviour, another to 'change gear' into a free-flowing attention and see what comes to mind. A third possibility is to say in a positive and constructive way that you are bored and that you want to find out what's going on. This strategy is not itself boring.

A fourth possibility is to be more concrete. Yalom (1989, pp.95–99) discusses in detail his decision to confront Betty about boredom as the outstanding characteristic of his experience of their relationship, and how he proceeded. First, he clarified how much of the boredom was his problem, and identified two characteristics of Betty that were boring: the fact that she did not reveal anything intimate about herself and her 'forced gaiety'. Then he chose to confront her, initially about how much she revealed, and later with her being 'jolly' and 'entertaining'. A principle which Yalom (1989) draws on is that 'if something big in a relationship is not being talked about ... then nothing else of importance will be discussed either' (p.114).

BOUNDARIES

(*See also*: Abuse, Assertiveness, Burnout, Confidentiality, Contract, negotiating a,

Drama triangle, Endings, Friendship/making friends with clients, Power, Privacy, Sexual attraction, Stress, Supervision, Time boundaries)

Boundaries are a part of being clear with yourself and with clients, and being reliable and trustworthy. Relevant boundaries include those of time, space (privacy), confidentiality and the counselling contract. They offer stability, and apply the idea (and existential fact) that there are limits to relationships, including the counselling relationship. However, counsellors do sometimes become too involved and want to give more and more to clients, or to a particular client. This is counterproductive for everyone.

Walker (1992b, pp.126–129) discussed the boundary of availability, under the heading 'Ring me whenever you need to'. She acted 'with good intentions but poor judgment' with a particularly distressed client, by offering to be available between sessions. It is not that this was undesirable in itself, but it was ill-considered at the time, and reflected her own needs and anxieties. It also did not help the client.

BRAINSTORMING

(*See also*: Counselling, Freewriting, Power, Values)

Brainstorming is a standard element in generating possible goals and planning action. Once your clients are sufficiently clear about a problem, the next step is for them to decide what, if anything, to do about it, and the usual procedure is simply to write down lots of ideas in a freewheeling way, without judging or censoring them at all, and going for quantity, including what may seem absurd ideas. The next step is to try combining and grouping the ideas and, finally, to select the most appealing options and evaluate the possible methods and consequences of implementing them.

BRIEF COUNSELLING

(*See also*: Contract, negotiating a, Contraindications for brief counselling, Effectiveness of counselling, Evaluation)

Brief counselling is now understood to be anything from around six to 20 sessions (Feltham, 1997a). Dryden and Feltham (1992) cite a number of surveys of student counselling services in the UK where the average attendance was between two and five sessions, and another survey of mental health out-patient settings in the USA where nearly 70% of clients came for six or fewer visits. These findings indicate brief counselling by default rather than by design.

Some approaches seek to use the element of time in a constructive and deliberate way to motivate clients to face up to the source of their problems. An example is Mann (1973), who offered (say) 12 weekly sessions of 45 minutes. Right at the beginning he arranged each appointment and overtly consulted his calendar so that the client could see its role in setting the exact date of their last meeting. Mann suggests that a client's rate of progress may be influenced by an understanding of how long the treatment will last.

Brief counselling typically focuses on well defined problems with modest and constrained goals. However, Feltham (1997a) describes successful treatment of a variety of client problems including depression, PTSD, self-harm, low self-esteem, anorexia and personality disorders in 1–16 sessions.

Brief counselling demands a high level of counsellor skill, and is not an easier option than longer term work. Generally, short-term counselling is suitable for clients who are not severely disturbed and who, apart from the presenting problem, are functioning adequately in other areas of their lives. Clients tend to be actively involved, work between sessions to try out new behaviours and practise what they have learned, and well motivated to change. Although some approaches to brief counselling make claims to the contrary, it is doubtful whether it is suitable for all clients, for example people who have not resolved early issues concerning basic trust and who therefore find it difficult to establish a good working relationship with you (Peake *et al.*, 1988). One risk is that such people will be harmed by the experience of further loss, and that this overshadows any gain in more immediate problem management.

In addition to their training and experience levels, the individual counsellor's personality and philosophical beliefs may influence their ability as a long or short-term therapist. Feltham (1997a) discusses a set of dominant values which may influence the counsellor's predisposition towards a particular length of counselling. Thus, short-term counsellors may prefer pragmatism, emphasise the client's strengths and resources, accept that many changes occur 'after therapy', not accept the timelessness of some models of therapy and may see 'being in the world' as more important than 'being in therapy'. On the other hand, long-term counsellors may seek change in a client's basic character, believe that psychological change is unlikely in everyday life, see presenting problems as reflecting more basic pathology, want to 'be there' as the client makes significant changes and view counselling as almost always benign and useful. Many counsellors see themselves as manifesting the qualities and attitudes of both the long-term and short-term counsellor and use whichever approach fits the needs of the client (McMahon, 1998).

Brief counselling has developed largely out of economic necessity, with the pressures of increasing demands for counselling and often diminishing financial resources (Feltham, 1997a). However, valuable outcomes can be achieved over relatively short periods, so financial pressures and effectiveness are in harmony to some extent.

BRITISH ASSOCIATION OF BEHAVIOURAL AND COGNITIVE PSYCHOTHERAPIES (BABCP)

(*See also*: Accreditation, Behaviour, British Association for Counselling, British Psychological Society, Codes of ethics, Professional Development, Supervision, Theoretical Schools, Thoughts)

Established in 1972, the BABCP is the main multi-disciplinary body for people involved in the practice and theory of behavioural and cognitive psychotherapy throughout the UK. The Association offers workshops, conferences, training programmes, local branches, a journal and newsletter, a code of ethics, complaints procedures, accreditation and access to UKCP registration.

BABCP
23 Partridge Drive, Baxenden
Accrington, Lancashire
BB5 2RL, UK
Tel/Fax: 01254 875277
email: membership@babcp.org.uk

BRITISH ASSOCIATION FOR COUNSELLING (BAC)

(*See also*: Accreditation, Codes of ethics, Complaints about counsellors to BAC, Counselling)

The BAC has its roots in the Standing Conference for the Advancement of Counselling in the late 1960s and was established as a voluntary association and charity in 1977. Today it is registered as a company limited by guarantee. The rapid growth in membership reflects the increasing general interest in counselling in the UK. In 1987, the BAC had 3500 individual and 250 organisational members; by 1998 this had grown to over 15 000 individual and about 1000 organisational members. These represent diverse views and degrees of involvement in counselling: the title of the Association embodies the idea of an association *for* counselling rather than an association *of* counsellors. There is an inevitable but often creative tension among different interest groups within the Association.

The BAC's Strategic Plan 1998–2003 (stage one) seeks to promote a new emphasis on the Association's original objectives. Its vision is to lead the effort to make counselling widely recognised as a profession whose purpose and activity is understood by the general public. Its mission is to be the professional body for counselling and the automatic reference point for anyone seeking information on counselling in the UK. It wishes to be recognised as an organisation which values integrity, impartiality and respect, promotes equality of opportunity, embraces a diverse range of counselling approaches, promotes accessibility for clients to counsellors, undertakes research, is responsive to emerging trends, consults widely and is enterprising.

The BAC is already widely seen as the voice of counselling in Britain, representing its membership and client needs to government and other institutions. It has a full-time headquarters office staff including a Chief Executive and departmental heads, and an elected Management Committee which delegates specific responsibilities to the appropriate committees (e.g. Standards and Ethics, Training, Complaints). The UK Register of Counsellors Executive Committee is also accountable to the BAC Management Committee.

The special interests of the membership are served by divisions, which have their own constitutions and elected executive committees. The divisions represent different areas or settings of counselling: Association for Pastoral Care and Counselling, Association for Student Counselling, Association for Counselling at Work, Counselling in Education, Counselling in Medical Settings, Personal Sexual/Marital/Family Counselling and Race and Cultural Education in Counselling. Membership of one or more of the divisions runs concurrently with BAC membership. Throughout the country local groups of BAC members form Branch organisations and set up their own programme of activities.

Acceptance of the BAC codes of ethics and practice is a condition of membership. There are published codes for counsellors, trainers and supervisors, and for the use of counselling skills. Full individual members may apply for accreditation as counsellors. In addition, there are accreditation schemes for counsellor training courses and for supervisors of counsellors. All three procedures are peer-assessment schemes drawn up by members, approved by the annual general meeting and operated by volunteer members of the Association. BAC individual counsellor accreditation is increasingly being required for employment as a counsellor.

The BAC's Information Office provides information and advice for members and others, and produces a range of publications and directions about counselling and psychotherapy resources. The quarterly journal *Counselling* is sent free to members. Currently, the BAC has legal and financial responsibility for the management of the UK Register of Counsellors.

BAC
1 Regent Place
Rugby
Warwickshire CV21 2PJ
UK
Tel: 01788 550 899
Fax: 01788 562 189
e-mail: bac@bac.co.uk

BRITISH ASSOCIATION OF PSYCHOTHERAPY (BAP)

The BAP runs training programmes in individual psychoanalytic (Freudian) and analytical (Jungian) psychotherapy for members of the helping professions, and in child psychotherapy.

BAP
37 Mapesbury Road
London NW2 4HJ
UK
Tel: 0181-452 9823
Fax: 0181 452 5182

BRITISH PSYCHOLOGICAL SOCIETY (BPS)

(See also: Accreditation, British Association for Counselling, Codes of ethics, Professional development, Supervision)

Psychology is the major discipline underlying counselling, while counselling is a skill claimed by many of the specialist groups within psychology: occupational, clinical, educational and counselling psychologists. The BPS introduced its Register of Chartered Psychologists in 1990, primarily to protect the public and employers from unqualified 'psychologists'. Two differences between a BAC-accredited counsellor and a chartered psychologist are that a requirement of accreditation is that 'supervision' continues (the term is used differently by the two organisations) and that accreditation is for five years at a time. However, the two schemes are also very similar in some respects; for example, in elements of training and counselling practice, in requiring continuing professional development and in agreeing to abide by the respective codes of ethics.

The Division of Counselling Psychology was set up in 1994 and signified recognition within the BPS of counselling psychology as a professional area in which training and qualifications have been developed. Two distinctive features of counselling psychology are its emphasis on the role of research in counselling practice and a focus on well-being and development rather than on illness and clinical issues. Woolfe (1990) and Lane (1990) recognise the disputes between counsellors and counselling psychologists, and between counselling psychologists and occupational and clinical psychologists, but see the different groups more as complementary than in competition.

BPS
St Andrews House
48 Princess Road East
Leicester LEI 7DR
UK
Tel: 0116 254 9568
Fax: 0116 247 0787
e-mail: enquiry@bps.org.uk

BURNOUT

(See also: Difficult clients, Role conflict, Stress, Supervision, Support groups, peer)

'Burnout' is a vivid but unclear term, with deep exhaustion probably at the core of the various definitions. Other key characteristics are anger, frustration and cynicism, and a sense of futility and failure. The positive, enthusiastic practitioner is transformed by burnout (Corey and Corey, 1993; Maslach and Goldberg, 1998). Moreover, like the stress which precedes it, burnout approaches insidiously, aided by such thoughts as 'it's only one more' and 'I've coped with extra work before'.

Chronic overload and persistent conflicts with colleagues appear to be two of the main sources of burnout in the helping professions (Maslach and Goldberg, 1998). They, and other factors such as lack of a sense of control and unfair treatment, probably interact. For example, counsellors who work in an organisation which has values they respect may be able to cope with greater workloads. Generally, strategies for coping with burnout are the same as those for stress (see entry on coping with stress) and can focus on situations and organisations as well as on individuals.

BUSINESS

(*See also*: Advertising, Fees, Marketing, Private practice, Stress)

Operating a private practice requires many of the skills associated with running a small business. Most new businesses fail, 66% of them within the first two years and 80% within five years (McMahon, 1994). Many counsellors dislike the idea of setting fees and discussing them with clients. However, running a business includes financial planning, keeping accounts, budgeting and paying out and receiving money. It means having good time management skills and an effective administrative system. Successful business people have drive and ambition, are logical and creative thinkers, recognise the need for acceptable risk taking, ensure they have the relevant knowledge and skills and are able to plan and pay attention to detail (McMahon, 1994). The marketing of services including undertaking appropriate market research, networking and appropriate advertising can mean the difference between success and failure (McMahon, 1997). Feltham (1995b) discusses the economic stress that counsellors in private practice can face. A counsellor may be tempted to take on more clients than is ethical or healthy in order to be able to pay the mortgage.

'CASE' STUDY

See: Supervision, presenting clients for

CATHARSIS

See: Anger, Emotions, Journal, writing a

CHALLENGE

(*See also*: Assertiveness, Boredom, Confrontation, Counselling, Empathy, Immediacy, Information giving, Patterns, Questions, Self-disclosure by counsellors)

Challenges are invitations to change or to see what may be going on. The idea is to help clients move where they need to go rather than push them to where you (the counsellor) think they ought to be. The intended result of a challenge is a broader horizon, deeper perception, or changed point of view. Challenging is more likely to be effective if you have earned the right by being empathic and developing a trusting relationship; if you are open to being challenged yourself by your client; and if you listen hard to the impact of your challenge (which may after all be wholly or partly wrong, or at the wrong time).

Some effective challenges involve picking up what the client has (in your view) implied, but is not very aware of.

1. **Advanced empathy:** e.g. a client talks a lot about their partner and very little about themselves, to which you might say 'You've spoken with great feeling about X's behaviour. You seem to feel overwhelmed and powerless about X'. Thus the focus of attention is brought back to your client, who might move deeper into their feelings (whether your advanced empathy is accurate or not).

2. **Linking ideas (interpretation):** bringing together things your client has said and suggesting probable patterns or connections in their behaviour. For example, 'You say your boss ignores you and makes you feel unwanted. I think I heard you say the same thing last week about your mother.' Essentially, you are suggesting (very tentatively) a pattern or causal connection among various behaviours, emotions or ideas.

3. **Contrasting ideas:** e.g. 'You say you like going to the cinema with Sue, but not with Mary. I wonder what the difference is for you.'

4. **Immediacy:** e.g. 'When you stare at me like that I sometimes feel a bit intimidated and wonder what you are thinking.' This is more direct and would normally need a good deal of trust between you before saying it.

5. **Questioning:** in our view questions should be used sparingly in counselling. The risk is of working with what *you* are thinking about rather than staying in your *client's* frame of reference. Usually a good empathic statement is better. However, questions can sometimes help the client move further – for example, 'What else could you do in that situation?' or 'What else was going on for you?'

6. **Moving-on statements:** these are perhaps the simplest form of challenge, but can be very effective in helping clients move deeper into a topic. It may be necessary to repeat only one important feeling or word for your client to explore it further, e.g. 'upset'.

7. **Information giving:** see separate entry.

8. **Counsellor self-disclosure:** hearing about someone else's experience is sometimes helpful – e.g. 'What I've found helpful (but you may not) is ...'

9. **Confrontation:** a more insistent way of challenging, see separate entry.

10. **Concreteness:** see separate entry.

CHALLENGING, SOME GUIDELINES FOR

These guidelines are in two sections: aspects to consider challenging, and suggestions on how to challenge.

Aspects to consider challenging

- What is implied; thoughts and feelings on the 'edge of clients' awareness'; what seems vague or confused; underlying meanings.
- Verbal and non-verbal mixed messages; discrepancies; contradictions, distortions, evasions or 'game playing'; blind spots.
- Resistance to change or to applying learning; failure to own problems; self-defeating behaviour; under-used strengths or resources; dysfunctional interpretations or irrational thinking.
- Transferential patterns; dynamics of relationship between counsellor and client.
- Themes, patterns, connecting 'islands'.

Challenging

- Start by encouraging your clients to challenge themselves.
- Be tentative in the way you challenge.
- Be concrete; challenge specific examples of thoughts, feelings or behaviours rather than making vague inferences.
- Use 'successive approximations' rather than 'all-at-once' challenges that make heavy demands on clients in a short time.
- Give time and space for your client to respond; avoid 'hit and run' or a string of challenges, especially towards the end of a session.
- Challenge on the basis of your client's values rather than your own.
- Challenge strengths and resources rather than weaknesses or deficits.
- Elicit and explore your client's reactions to any challenge; help your clients share and work through any defensive emotions.

CHANGE

(*See also*: Common factors, Effectiveness of counselling, Metaphors and similes, Theoretical schools)

Counselling is about enabling people to make positive changes in the way they feel, think and/or behave. Learning to feel better about oneself, learning to accept that a particular situation is not going to change and recognising the need to adapt to it, learning to be more assertive, gaining a deeper understanding of a problem making a decision and feeling less confused about something, all constitute potentially beneficial changes.

Counsellors from different theoretical orientations may work primarily with emotions, cognitions or behaviours. The assumption is that if, for example, you change the way you think about something then this will result in concomitant changes in how you feel and behave towards it. However, psychologists differ in their views on the relationship between cognitions, emotions and behaviours. Some argue strongly that cognitions determine emotions, while others believe that an improved emotional state can result in more positive thinking. Another view is that emotions and cognitions are separate and partially independent systems. Overall, clinical evidence seems to suggest a circular relationship. For discussions see Fonagy and Higgitt (1984) and Cornelius (1996).

Levels of change

An alternative to working with cognitions, emotions or behaviour is to focus on different types or levels of problem. Prochaska and DiClemente (1992) identify five hierarchical and distinct yet interrelated levels at which change can take place:

1. Symptoms or problematic situations.
2. Maladaptive cognitions.
3. Current interpersonal conflicts.
4. Family systems conflicts.
5. Intrapersonal conflicts.

Historically, particular approaches have attributed problems to one or two levels. For example, cognitive counsellors would focus on maladaptive cognitions and psychodynamic counsellors on intrapsychic conflicts. The further down the hierarchy the more complex the problem and the further removed from awareness and more historically remote are the determinants of the problem likely to be. At the deeper levels, problems are more closely associated with sense of self, and a greater resistance to change is probable.

Counsellors may focus initially on symptoms or problematic situations, usually the primary reason for the person coming to counselling. Change tends to occur more quickly and easily at this level. However, the levels are interrelated (for example, symptoms or situations often involve intrapersonal conflicts), and changes at one level may produce changes at other levels. Some counsellors work with the client to agree on the level to which they attribute problems or the level that is the target for change. This joint decision is seen as a critical part of the process of change.

Mechanisms of change

Most single or pure theoretical orientations assume the importance of a particular therapeutic factor or mechanism of change. However, it seems highly likely that there are a number of therapeutic factors common to most forms of counselling. It is difficult to identify precisely the relative contribution of the various common factors, which remain for the most part opinions or assumptions, albeit derived from clinical experience and case evidence, yet which are not clearly demonstrated as empirical facts.

Garfield (1992 pp.185–192) describes what he believes are the common mechanisms of change:

1. The quality of the relationship between counsellor and client.
2. Expression of emotions or catharsis.
3. Provision of some explanation, interpretation, rationale or new perspective on the problem.
4. Reinforcement of client strengths, resources or positive client responses or behaviours.
5. Increasing levels of exposure to the problem, desensitisation by facing and confronting what is being avoided.
6. Provision of information and skills training.
7. Time to work through problems.

A more comprehensive list of common factors that describe client characteristics, therapist qualities, change processes and treatment methods that facilitate therapeutic change is provided by Grencavage and Norcross (1990).

General principles of change

Beitman (1994, pp.221–224) presents some general principles that underpin the process of change and for which, Beitman argues, research evidence seems to indicate usefulness and generalisability to all forms of counselling. These principles are adapted and summarised here.

1. Identify a focus or target of change and potential areas for intervention.
2. Assume the client is responsible for change.
3. Identify and build on client strengths and resources.
4. Explore and confront reluctance to be a client and resistance to change.
5. Recognise the social and cultural influences that impact on counselling as an activity, on the client and the origin and maintenance of the client's problem and on the social and cultural differences between counsellor and client.
6. Facilitate learning and the acquisition of new perspectives.
7. Encourage the application and generalisation of learning to the client's everyday life.

CLASSIFICATION SYSTEMS

See: Psychodiagnosis

CLIENTS WHO DON'T COME BACK

(*See also*: Beginnings, Contract, negotiating a, Difficulties in being a client. Distress at the end of a counselling session, Expectations, clients', Missed sessions, Multicultural counselling, Readiness to change)

It can be worrying when a client does not show up, especially if you know that he or she is having a lot of serious problems, or if the last session was unsatisfactory in some way. The most obvious form of positive feedback is when your clients come back, so a client not turning up can cause you to question your effectiveness as a counsellor.

Even the most experienced counsellors have clients who don't come back, or who break off the counselling relationship unexpectedly. It is important to explore your reactions in supervision, and to consider different ways in which you might contact these clients. Telephone calls, although encouraged by some agencies, can be intrusive or unwelcome. Perhaps the best way to respond is to send the client a brief, friendly, note enquiring after their welfare and inviting them to get in touch. If your client does not reply, we think you've been sufficiently caring and done enough; clients have the right not to reply and chasing after them doesn't respect that right.

If you are particularly concerned, more direct action may be needed – but again this is something to think through carefully in supervision. There may be times when a telephone call or, in the last resort, a visit, is necessary. But visiting clients at home should be considered only in extreme circumstances, and should be done only after you have explored the implications in supervision.

CODES OF ETHICS

(*See also*: British Association for Counselling, Counselling, BAC basic principles of, Ethical dilemmas)

The main purposes of codes of ethics are to help maintain standards of practice, to inform and protect clients, to provide a framework for counsellors to consult when trying to clarify an ethical dilemma and within which to operate a complaints procedure, to demonstrate the maturity of an organisation and profession and to encourage recognition and discussion of ethical issues (Bond, 1993a, p.12).

The following are available from the BAC:

- The Code of Ethics and Practice for Counsellors;
- The Code of Ethics and Practice for the Supervision of Counsellors;
- The Code of Ethics and Practice for Trainers;
- The Code of Ethics and Practice for the Use of Counselling Skills.

Codes of ethics have become longer and more complicated, and the BAC has therefore developed a set of basic principles for counselling, which are more concise and comprehensible, especially to clients and non-practitioners (see separate entry on BAC's basic principle of counselling).

COGNITIONS

See: Assertiveness, Behaviour, Challenge, Depression, Emotions, Interpersonal process recall, Self-awareness, Theoretical schools, Thoughts, Values

COLLUSION

(*See also*: Avoidance, Boundaries, Confrontation, Drama triangle)

People come to counselling with many needs, some overt and others covert. Sometimes the overt needs are in opposition to the covert ones. For example, a client might state that her friends are very important to her, so the overt need is to have friends, but underneath may be a fear of being left alone. In this case the covert need (which the client may or may not be aware of) is motivated by fear and the overt need is a desperate attempt to avoid the more painful covert one. It would be collusion if the counsellor concentrated solely on the client's issue with her friends. It is particularly easy to collude with avoidance if the subject is difficult for either the client or the counsellor.

COMMON FACTORS

(*See also*: Core conditions, Contraindications for brief counselling, Counselling, Effectiveness of counselling, Emotions, Integration and eclecticism, Working alliance)

There is fairly general agreement that the main approaches to counselling work about equally well, despite radical differences in theory and techniques. One interpretation of this finding is that they have factors in common, and that these are the crucial therapeutic ingredients; however, as yet there is no clear evidence or agreement on what these factors are (Stiles *et al.*, 1986; Grencavage and Norcross, 1990). The most obvious common factor in all forms of counselling is the quality of the relationship between the counsellor and the client. Four categories of other common factors (which may or may not be the crucial ingredients) are:

1. **Client characteristics:** for example, a willingness to become actively involved in the relationship and in counselling, readiness and motivation to change, realistic expectations and confidence in the process and in you.

2. **Counsellor qualities:** e.g. empathy and warmth, ability to encourage hope and positive expectations.

3. **Processes of change:** e.g. new perspectives, plausible explanations, interpersonal learning, opportunity for emotional expression, acquisition of new behaviours.

4. **Treatment methods:** such as use of rituals or techniques, adherence to a theory, explanation of client and counsellor roles.

Whatever approach is taken, counselling always contains opportunities for clients to disclose and work on their problems. Indeed, it is often the first time a person has experienced being listened to and taken seriously at length and this aspect of counselling may itself be helpful. What counsellors actually do with what they hear may be of only secondary importance or even irrelevant. Counselling also contains opportunities for clients to clarify or rediscover their emotions. It gives people permission to become emotional, which might be especially important to people who are otherwise denied such opportunities.

Norcross and Grencavage (1989) refer to the identification of common factors as the most important psychotherapy trend in the 1980s. In contrast, Stiles *et al.* (1993) argue that this area of research is stagnating, and that further research is necessary into such issues as:

- Can the common or non-specific factors of therapeutic change be more clearly specified?
- How do they operate within different theoretical approaches?
- Are there any parallels with other types of human interaction?
- How do the common factors interact with client characteristics?
- Is the distinction between common factors and specific interventions useful or are they interrelated in some way?

COMPLAINTS, ABOUT COUNSELLORS TO THE BAC

(*See also*: British Association for Counselling, Codes of ethics, Insurance, indemnity, Sexual attraction)

Great care is taken with complaints to the BAC. The Complaints Committee tries to be fair to both parties, and to find a balance between being dauntingly formal and too informal (British Association for Counselling, 1993a). The overall aim is to be professional, sensitive, consistent and fair, while also upholding the BAC's ethics, standards and values. Accordingly, when the Committee asks someone to take on the task of initial investigation/conciliation, they try to ensure that she or he is experienced in the particular area – training/education, private practice, etc. – sensitive to issues of difference, and not known to the people involved. The same criteria are used in choosing members of the Adjudication Panel, if the complaint reaches that stage (British Association for Counselling, 1993a).

Complaints can be seen as opportunities to create trust and goodwill (Calnan, 1991). To use complaints in this way, it is crucial to respond speedily and remember that the client is probably upset and disoriented. Calnan's suggestions include treating every complaint (however trivial it may seem) with respect, staying calm, dealing with a complaint on the day it was made (or at least reporting progress), listening until the client and the person dealing with the complaint agree about 'the heart of the matter', investigating, explaining in a straightforward way and apologising if appropriate. Calnan also recommends three steps to take in response to being accused of professional negligence or incompetence. In a different order from Calnan's they are:

1. Inform your manager and ask a colleague to take over the client's care.
2. Inform your administration.
3. Contact your professional insurers quickly. Send a brief statement and photocopies of relevant documents.

For advice and details of the complaints procedure, contact the BAC. For discussion see Bond (1993a).

CONCRETENESS

(*See also*: Counselling, Challenge, Empathy)

Concreteness is the skill of inviting clients to be more specific. The purpose is to get below the surface communication that may not fully or accurately represent the client's experience or meaning. It also helps to ensure that you don't project your own meaning on to the client. The client has an opportunity to explain their, often idiosyncratic, definition of common feelings or experiences e.g. anger, depression, anxiety. Cormier and Cormier (1991, p.46) identify three linguistic errors or common ways in which clients incompletely represent their experience: deletions, when things are left out, distortions (when things are not as they seem) and generalisations (when a total life experience or whole group of things are associated with only one feeling or event, or when conclusions are reached with no evidence).

For example, your client says 'Things are going badly.' You might respond in many ways, perhaps with a paraphrase or silence. If you chose concreteness you would say something like 'Can you give me an example?' or 'Which things'? The potential benefit is much greater clarity and therefore opportunity to empathise; the risk is sounding intrusive or like an interrogator. Concreteness therefore more often has the 'flavour' of a challenge and should be used accordingly.

CONFIDENTIALITY

(*See also*: Contract, negotiating a, Ethical dilemmas, Good counsellors,
Information giving, Record keeping, Sued, being, Suicide, Supervision, Trust)

Most people (one USA figure is 69%) believe that counsellors offer absolute confidentiality (Corey and Corey, 1993, p.319). However, counsellors and counselling organisations do not usually consider confidentiality to be an absolute. Given that you respect a client's privacy as far as you can, but that there are limits, a key question is: 'In what circumstances might I break confidentiality?' Perhaps the most problematic circumstance here is breaking confidence to protect your client's welfare or to protect another person, maybe one who is threatened by a potentially dangerous client. Are *all* threats by your clients to be reported? What if you have a hunch that a client is suicidal or dangerous, but no evidence? And what about discussing an aspect of a client anonymously with, say, a colleague? Lazarus (Dryden, 1991) and Feltham (1996) argue that it is sometimes helpful to do so. Such judgements are complicated but not uniquely so; the law rests on notions like 'reasonable care' and trusts professionals to make such judgements. On the other hand, counsellor education and training could include more on ethical analysis (Bond, 1993a) and on coping with uncertainty.

Some guidelines for practice are:

1. Inform clients early (as part of your contract with them) about limitations on confidentiality. For example, what they say may be discussed with your supervisor or supervision group (though not by name, and both discussions often focus more on the counsellor than the client and are confidential themselves).

2. Tell clients about any legal or organisational factors. Some agencies require their counsellors to inform them of incest and child abuse.

3. Consult professional colleagues when you're unsure.

4. Records should be brief and kept securely – however, see the next point.

5. If you decide to break confidentiality, whenever possible discuss your decision with your client first, perhaps encouraging him or her to inform the appropriate authority themselves. In this instance, keep detailed records in case there is a complaint against you.

CONFRONTATION

(*See also*: Challenge, Counselling)

Confrontation is a form of challenge in which a counsellor describes apparent distortions or discrepancies in the client's emotions, thoughts or actions. Like the other forms of challenge, confrontation needs to be done in a responsible and caring way with the client's well-being firmly in mind. It is an attempt to help your client see something differently, and is not directing, praising or criticising. The following situations show when confrontation can be used:

1. **Blocking and avoiding:** e.g. 'You talk about your family quite often, but I notice you never mention your daughter.'

2. **Self-defeating attitudes and beliefs:** e.g. 'I hear you frequently calling yourself silly, which sounds as though you are being hard on yourself.' You could stop talking at this point or add: 'What evidence do you have for thinking you are silly?'

3. **Discrepancies:** e.g. 'You say you are quite happy, yet I see you here looking sad and sitting hunched up which gives a different picture.'

4. **Distortions:** e.g. 'You say *everyone* dislikes you.'

CONGRUENCE

(*See also*: Boredom, Common factors, Core conditions, Counselling, Immediacy, Self-awareness, Self-disclosure by counsellors)

Congruence is a term usually associated with client-centred counselling but which has become part of the everyday language of many counselling approaches. 'Genuineness', 'sincerity' and 'authenticity' are related concepts. Many counsellors, particularly those from the Humanistic approaches, see congruence in the sense of sharing some of their feelings with their clients as part of the counselling process, though most psychodynamic counsellors would be more circumspect.

Rogers' (1959) definition of congruence includes '... when self-experiences are accurately symbolised (in awareness), and are included in the self-concept in this accurately symbolized form, then the state is one of congruence of self and experience...' (p.206). This definition is expressed in terms of the distinction between self and experience, not in terms of the behaviour of the counsellor, and is consistent with Rogers' (1957) definition where, in discussing his ideas about the six necessary and sufficient conditions for therapeutic personality change, he wrote '...the therapist should be, within the confines of this relationship, a congruent, genuine, integrated person. It means that within the relationship he is freely and deeply himself, with his actual experience accurately represented by his awareness of himself ... It should be clear that this includes being himself even in ways which are not regarded as ideal for psychotherapy. His experience may be, "I am afraid of this client", or, "My attention is so focussed on my own problems that I can scarcely listen to him". If the therapist is not denying these feelings to awareness, but is able freely to be them (as well as being other feelings), then the condition (congruence) we have stated is met' (p.97).

Ideally, the core conditions of empathy, respect and congruence (all subjective states or attitudes existing within the counsellor) would all be fully present together, but in practice it is rarely possible for a counsellor to be so consistent. The theory of client-centred counselling predicts that the extent to which the therapist experiences these attitudes determines the extent to which the relationship is likely to be effective in promoting change. Because the therapeutic attitudes are seen as existing together rather than separately, it is not usually helpful to ascribe more importance to one or other of them, but Rogers believed that therapist congruence sometimes takes priority (Rogers, 1959, p.215). In other words, at those times when counsellors are unable to experience empathic understanding, or are unable to be unconditionally accepting, then they should be aware of those experiences, attend to them and allow them accurately into awareness.

The question often arises about the degree to which it is necessary for counsellors directly to communicate their feelings and thoughts to their clients in order to be 'congruent'. Congruence does not require that a counsellor *should* communicate thoughts and feelings that arise from within their own frame of reference. 'Being real involves being thoroughly acquainted with the flow of experiencing going on within, a complex and continuing flow. It means being *willing to express* the attitudes that come *persistently* to the fore, especially perhaps the negative attitudes, inasmuch as the positive ones can rather easily be inferred from behavior and tone. If the therapist is bored with the client, it is only real to express this feeling ...' (Rogers and Sanford, 1980, p.1381, our italics).

Rogers and Sanford realised that this concept could create difficulties and was open to misinterpretation: 'It certainly does not mean that the therapist burdens the client with all her problems or feelings. It does not mean that the therapist blurts out impulsively any attitude that comes to mind. It does mean, however, that the therapist does not deny to herself the feelings being experienced and that the therapist is willing to express and to be any persistent feelings that exist in the relationship ... When the therapist is feeling neither empathic nor caring, she must discover what the flow of experiencing is and must be willing to express that flow, whether it seems embarrassing, too revealing, or whatever.' (p.1381).

Mearns and Thorne (1988) also point out that congruence is not the same as self-disclosure, and that being congruent does not imply that a counsellor has to be open about herself and her life: 'When the counsellor is being congruent she is giving her genuinely felt response to the client's experience at that time. Only rarely would this response disclose elements of the counsellor's life, and even then the focus of attention would remain on the client rather than the counsellor' (p.82).

CONTRACT, NEGOTIATING A

(*See also*: Boundaries, Brief counselling, Duration, Expectations, clients', Fees, Frequency of sessions, Information giving, Multicultural counselling, Time boundaries, Trust, Values)

A contract is an agreement negotiated between you and your client at the beginning of your work together. It commonly has two elements: a therapeutic element concerned with the purpose of counselling and your approach, and a business element concerned with practical arrangements and conditions. Some counsellors prefer an informal approach to contracting, almost to the extent that it is not an explicit process. They feel that their client's understanding of what is going on, what can be achieved and how, needs to evolve gradually through their work together. Other counsellors are more formal, in some instances making use of written contracts (these may include such details as specific goals, strategies to be followed and duration) which they invite the client to sign, thereby giving informed consent to the process. These represent extreme positions on the degree of formality of negotiating a contract.

Closely related to the issue of formality is the degree of specificity: how concrete and detailed the contract is. Some counsellors and clients agree on working towards greater self-awareness. Other contracts may be much more concrete and specify clear objectives, such as 'to eliminate or significantly reduce the frequency of panic attacks.' Such a contract may also identify some of the steps and strategies towards achieving this goal. Greater specificity can help to communicate a sense of direction and purpose, stimulate clear thinking and motivate the client to change. It can also provide a rational basis for evaluation. On the other hand, clients and counsellors don't always know where they are going until they get there. This is not to imply a lack of purpose, but it does make specific goals rather pointless.

The therapeutic contract is sometimes described as the counselling or treatment plan. It is a negotiated agreement about what you and your client want to achieve together and how you might work towards it. This element of the contract may follow from an initial assessment and typically is reviewed from time to time. Sometimes a more explicit form of agreement about what needs to be achieved and the strategies involved will be relevant only at a later or action-planning stage of counselling.

The business contract is intended to protect both counsellor and client by specifying the arrangements for counselling and the boundaries within which it will take place. Part of this element will be information giving and may be non-negotiable or negotiable only within limits, for example, time and fees. The conditions typically include the length of each session, frequency and pattern of attendance, duration of the contract, fees and time-keeping. The contract on time-keeping may involve an explicit commitment to punctuality on the part of both counsellor and client, with an additional commitment to cancel an appointment in advance rather than simply not turn up to a session. It needs to be made clear whether, if a client arrives late, any additional time will be allocated. Making these conditions explicit from the very beginning should save misunderstanding and resentment.

CONTRAINDICATIONS FOR BRIEF COUNSELLING

(*See also*: Assessment, Avoidance, Brief counselling, Common factors, First impressions, Referral, Trust, Working alliance)

Some clients may not be suitable for counselling, and counselling isn't the answer to all psychological problems. The difficulty is in judging accurately whether or not someone is likely to benefit from counselling. However, it is possible to identify various characteristics in a potential client that may serve as contraindications for brief counselling. In making such clinical judgements, it is appropriate to be cautious, for the following reasons:

- It is not always possible to identify contraindications in the first session.
- Patterns of behaviour provide a more reliable basis than single items of evidence.
- It is important to look for evidence of the client's ability to modify or change then experiences and/or behaviour.
- Contraindications are only indicators: there are no sharp boundaries or operational criteria that can be used to distinguish clearly between clients who are suitable and those who are unsuitable for brief counselling.

- Many of the contraindications will be evident at some time or other in most clients and it is their degree and persistence which is important in interpreting them as valid contraindicators.
- Identifying certain characteristics may help you adjust your expectations of what might be achieved with the person in a limited period, rather than necessarily assessing him or her as unsuitable for counselling.
- Some contraindications might actually provide an initial or continuing focus for the counselling itself.

The following characteristics raise questions about a person's suitability for brief counselling, subject to the caveats discussed above.

1. **Unrealistic expectations which persist:** some people expect counselling to give them immediate solutions to their problems, to be told what to do, to be given advice and direction. It is when such unrealistic expectations persist that they become a contraindication.

2. **No real desire to change:** clients need, at some level, to want to change if counselling is to be effective. Most clients are in some way resistant to change; despite the pain and distress, they find it hard to give up troublesome aspects of their behaviour, perhaps because of hidden 'pay offs' or because they give expression to unheard parts of themselves. Some clients, especially but not necessarily involuntary clients, may show little if any willingness to change. You might find it useful to explore how and why such clients came to counselling.

3. **No clear problem:** it is hard to discover what some people want from counselling.

4. **Long history of seeking psychological help:** some clients have seen numerous helpers over many years, and tend to have had only a few sessions with each. Typically they may also currently be seeing someone else for counselling or therapy. It may be evident that they habitually talk about their problems to everybody and anybody, but are reluctant to enter into any form of developing relationship. You may find it useful to start by exploring their views on why the other forms of helping were unsuccessful.

5. **Unresponsive clients:** counselling is based on talking and can't make much progress, certainly in the short term, with clients who have great difficulty in talking about their experiences and putting their thoughts and feelings into words. Here, as Jacobs (1988) points out, it is important to distinguish between those clients who lack social skills and those who have become withdrawn and silent through depression or some trauma, and who were until recently more able to communicate actively.

6. **Avoiding emotions:** some clients talk a lot about what they have done or are going to do, about their experiences and behaviour and, more especially, other people's experiences and behaviour. It is as if the preoccupation with the story is a way of avoiding their emotions and

feelings. One of the factors common to all forms of psychological therapy, identified by Frank (1981), is the emotional arousal of the client, particularly during assessment. Frank argued that this is essential if a client is to achieve learning and associated change. If clients sustain a cool and rational view of themselves and their problems and the counselling is devoid of emotion, it is very unlikely to result in change. On the other hand, some issues are more amenable to problem-solving techniques than others and may be satisfactorily resolved by thinking them through.

7. **Inability to relate to others:** most approaches to counselling place a high value on the need to establish an effective working relationship. You can look for evidence of a capacity to relate to others, irrespective of whether the relationship was experienced as positive or negative. It is unlikely that clients who have found it very difficult to relate either well or badly to others will find it possible to form a working relationship with you.

8. **Lack of capacity to trust:** people vary in the time it takes for them to learn to trust others. The capacity to trust is essential in order for the client to be open and revealing of very personal problems and concerns. Clients will test whether they can trust you in a variety of ways – often by asking questions – but may not be consciously aware of what they are doing or why they are doing it. While counsellors should not want to foster a dependent relationship, clients need to place some reliance on the counsellor and counselling. Fiercely independent clients won't stay long. Indications of this are the request for only occasional counselling sessions, or clients who persistently say 'yes but'. Other clients find any face-to-face relationship too intimate and threatening; they also tend to drop out of counselling.

9. **People who are too dependent:** people who depend on a high dosage of drugs to carry on with their day-to-day routine are unlikely to benefit from brief counselling. Another form of dependence is on the counsellor and counselling. Clients need to be able to tolerate painful feelings and feel secure enough to be able to cope with life between sessions.

10. **Reluctance to accept responsibility:** while many people come to counselling wanting other people or their circumstances to change, counselling can only work towards helping them change the way they themselves feel, think or behave. Some people seem unable to see the ways in which they might be contributing to their own difficulties or the ways in which they might change, and typically lack empathy with others.

11. **Out of touch with reality:** disturbing and irrational thoughts and behaviour which make it difficult for a person to manage everyday life are a further contraindication. The key criterion is the extent to which the client is actually aware of what is going on. Some people with these characteristics are quite unaware of the implications of their behaviour and the havoc caused in their lives and in the lives of those around them. Others seem

unable to tolerate their disturbing thoughts and feelings and seriously fear that they are 'going mad'. A sometimes related pattern of behaviour is the way some people flit from one subject to another (Jacobs, 1988). Daines *et al.* (1997) recommend referral to the mental health services if a client is clinically manic, confused, obsessive etc. Most counsellors do not have the experience of a general practitioner or psychiatrist.

CORE CONDITIONS

(See also: Acceptance, Common factors, Congruence, Counselling, Empathy, Power, Respect)

The term 'core conditions' is generally associated with client-centred (or person-centred) counselling. Rogers (e.g. 1957, 1980) believed that effective counselling was most likely when the counsellor was able to offer clients a relationship rich in the qualities of empathy, congruence and unconditional positive regard. However, although most forms of counselling would agree that these three counsellor qualities are necessary, only client-centred counselling regards them as both necessary and sufficient. In other words, Rogers argued that the relationship that develops between counsellor and client is the most significant agent of change, not the counsellor's repertoire of techniques.

Rogers' position remains a controversial one (e.g. Patterson, 1984). Research has tended to support the necessity rather than the sufficiency of the core conditions at best (Bergin and Garfield, 1994), but Hill and Corbett (1993, p.8) concluded that the question is unresolved: 'Researchers will need to clarify what they mean by constructs such as empathy and develop more sophisticated measures and methods.'

CORE MODEL

(See also: Counselling, Theory)

One of the guiding concepts of counsellor education and training is that it should provide substantial grounding in a 'core theoretical model' which can include integrative and systematic eclectic approaches (British Association for Counselling, 1996). The BAC argue that the core model should be reflected in the theory, skills and client work of a course and in the way it is structured, assessed, taught and administered. A core model that underpins a training programme provides coherence and internal consistency both within the training and in the counsellors' subsequent practice. Feltham (1996, 1997b) offers a contrary view, and Wheeler (1998) a reply.

Elton Wilson (1993), Inskipp (1993), Ivey *et al.* (1997) and Horton (1998). discuss aspects of developing your own model of counselling.

COST-EFFECTIVENESS, OF COUNSELLING

See: Effectiveness

COUNSELLING

(*See also*: Beginnings, Change, Core model, Core conditions, Frameworks, Integration and eclecticism, Multicultural counselling, Multiculturalism, Psychological type, Readiness to change, Referral, Theories)

One approach to defining 'counselling' is to distinguish between different kinds of counselling, for example between counselling for personal growth, with people who are functioning well in most respects, and counselling with severely distressed people. Other systems for describing counselling are based on theories or kinds of problem (e.g. Woolfe *et al.*, 1989; Dryden, 1996; Corey, 1991; Ivey *et al.*, 1997). The systems can help to clarify what counselling is and is not, both for yourself and for others – and therefore when to offer counselling to someone and when to suggest referral.

An integrative process model of counselling

The model of counselling outlined in this section is consistent with the work of Brammer *et al.* (1993), Egan (1975), Ivey *et al.* (1987, 1997), Lang *et al.* (1990) and others. It is an elaborated version of the model in Table 3. Both versions are intended to help counsellors articulate what they are doing and why they are doing it.

Table 3

An integrative model of counselling (basic version)

Stage one: *explore*
The counsellor accepts and empathises with the client and is genuine. The client explores her or his emotions, thoughts, behaviour and experiences related to a problem.
Stage two *(if necessary):* *understand*
The counsellor suggests, or helps the client to suggest, themes and patterns or other ways of looking at the problem, and decide what, if anything, the client wants to do about it.
Stage three *(if necessary):* *act*
The counsellor helps the client to decide exactly what to do, taking costs and benefits for self and others into account, and to evaluate the results afterwards.

Source: Horton and Bayne (1998, p.7)

By 'integrative process model', we mean that it provides a model of the process through which counsellor and client work together but without implying any one theory of personality or human development. Rather, it provides an organising framework for integrating concepts and techniques from other approaches.

Alternatively, it can stand alone as an approach to counselling. It requires an understanding of the counselling process, a range of communication skills and an awareness of when to use specific strategies and skills (Beitman, 1990; Ivey *et al.*, 1987, 1997; Egan, 1990; Mahalik, 1990).

Three developmental and interrelated themes – relationship, content and planning – run through each of the three broadly defined stages of the model. Each stage is characterised by the need to achieve particular 'tasks'. The model can be summarised in a matrix of themes and stages (Table 4).

The developing *relationship* between the counsellor and client is the first theme. In stage one, the task is to establish an effective working alliance. The counsellor is empathic, accepting and genuine and this is seen as therapeutic and sometimes sufficient. In stage two the quality of the relationship is maintained and the main task is to facilitate change. Stage three is concerned with ending the relationship.

The second theme is the *content* of the client's problem or problems. In stage one the counsellor helps the client explore and define the problem. In stage two the main task is to facilitate learning and change, with counsellor and client working towards a deeper understanding, exploring different ways of thinking, feeling and/or behaving, and perhaps identifying goals and ways of achieving them. In stage three the task is to work with the client to consolidate and generalise new ways of being or behaving.

The third theme running through each stage is *planning and reflection*. This is concerned with articulating goals and strategies and with reflection and evaluation, both with the client and internally, as a 'reflective practitioner' (Horton, 1993). Two kinds of goals are identified: those concerned with helping the client to discover solutions (or, more typically, specific action plans for coping with or managing immediate problems) and broader goals such as developing a stronger sense of personal identity.

Table 4

An integrative model of the counselling process (elaborated version)

Theme	Stage 1 tasks	Stage 2 tasks	Stage 3 tasks
1. Relationship	Establish	Maintain and use	End
2. Content	Assess problem and client resources	Facilitate learning and change	Consolidate and apply learning
3. Therapeutic planning and reflection	Develop therapeutic plan; negotiate client goals	Monitor and revise plans; reflect on process	Evaluate process and outcomes

Source: Horton and Bayne (1998, p.7)

The model makes a distinction between strategies and skills. Strategies are ways of achieving particular tasks, while skills are the behaviours (interventions or responses) used to actually do so. For example, the task of establishing a working alliance is achieved by communicating the 'core qualities' while the strategy is implemented by using the skills of active listening. The strategies and skills are essential tools, which provide a set of logical and practical guidelines, but they are not an end in themselves. Rather, they need to be integrated into counselling through the quality of the relationship.

The model makes explicit the tasks for each stage of counselling. Its function is to provide a sense of direction and purpose, a kind of 'cognitive map with delivery potential' (Egan, 1975) which is intended to help the counsellor and client plan, monitor and evaluate. It is not intended as a ready-to-apply mechanistic formula. Similarly, although the stages are developmental and sequential, the model does not imply a linear progression. As new needs or different aspects of the problem emerge, the actual process, especially around the content theme, will continually move backwards and forwards within the organising framework.

The model's rationale is based on assumptions in two areas – human development and the counselling process. Six key assumptions are summarised next:

1. Psychological problems are regarded as multidimensional and seldom attributable to one source, situation or factor. It is assumed that people are too complex to be explained by any one theory, and that social context plays an important part (Brammer *et al.*, 1993).

2. The client's readiness to change (Prochaska and DiClemente, 1984) and psychological type (Bayne, 1995a) may influence the way in which the counsellor works.

3. It is possible to identify common steps and stages in the counselling process, irrespective of the counsellor's theoretical orientation (Ivey *et al.*, 1987, 1997; Beitman, 1990; Lang *et al.*, 1990; Brammer *et al.*, 1993). On this basis the concept of a model of process can be used as an integrating framework. This is a form of systematic eclecticism, or what Brammer refers to as a creative synthesis approach to theory. The principles and criteria for integration are expanded by Lebow (1987), Brammer *et al.* (1993) and Horton (1998).

4. It is essential for counsellors to develop the necessary personal qualities and skills to counsel effectively. To have a map of the process is not enough; counsellors need to be able to select appropriate strategies and explanatory concepts for assessment and change, and have the skills to implement them.

5. Counselling is culture bound, class bound and monolingual. These generic characteristics may clash with the cultural values of various minority groups (see entries on multiculturalism and multicultural counselling).

6. Some styles and approaches to counselling may be more effective with some clients than others (Dryden, 1991; Provost, 1993; Bayne, 1999).

COUNSELLING, BAC BASIC PRINCIPLES OF

(*See also*: Codes of ethics, Complaints about counsellors to BAC, Counselling)

The BAC developed the set of principles shown in Table 5 mainly with clients in mind, but also as a statement representing BAC members' very diverse approaches to counselling. The principles are spelled out in more detail in the BAC codes of ethics.

Table 5

Basic principles of counselling

1. The aim of counselling is to provide an opportunity for a client to work towards living in a more satisfying and resourceful way.
2. Counselling is voluntarily and deliberately undertaken by counsellor and client. It is different from other ways of helping.
3. Before counselling starts, the counsellor clarifies with the client the basis on which counselling is to be given, including method, duration, fees and confidentiality; changes can subsequently be made only with the agreement of the client.
4. In counselling the right of the client to make his or her own decisions is respected.
5. Counsellors continually monitor their own skills, experience, resources and practice.
6. Counsellors will be properly trained for their roles and be committed to maintaining their competence.
7. Counsellors will not misrepresent their training or experience.
8. Counsellors have regular and appropriate supervision/consultative support.
9. Counsellors do not abuse their position of trust financially, emotionally or sexually.
10. All that takes place between counsellor and client is treated with respect and discretion.

Source: British Association for Counselling, 1993b

COUNTER-TRANSFERENCE

(*See also*: Emotions, First impressions, Process, Self-awareness, Supervision, Transference)

Counter-transference is a psychoanalytic term, referring to the counsellor's largely unconscious reactions towards a client, confusing her or him with someone else, and thus distorting their judgement and ability to empathise (Jacobs, 1988; Hawkins and Shohet, 1989). Hawkins and Shohet (1989, pp.65–66) identify four types of counter-transference:

1. Reactions to the client that originate from the counsellor's past – situations or relationships with other people – or which are an aspect of the counsellor projected by the counsellor onto the client.
2. The counsellor's reactions that arise out of taking on the role transferred onto the counsellor by the client – for example, if the client treats the counsellor like a parent, the counsellor may feel critical or angry with the client, in the way the client's parents did.

3. The counsellor's reaction used to counter the client's transference – e.g. the counsellor becomes overly friendly or casual about time in response to being treated as an expert or authority figure by the client.

4. The counsellor feels like an 'emotional skip', taking on projected material from the client.

Stewart (1992, pp.56–57) suggests several indicators of counter-transference, including preoccupation with a particular client in the form of daydreams or fantasies, behaving differently towards the client (more lenient, more strict), not wanting to end counselling with him or her. Whatever your theoretical orientation, and whether or not you use the term counter-transference, it is important to explore your reactions to clients in supervision and in this way to make more space to respond appropriately to clients.

CROSS-CULTURAL

See: Multiculturalism, Multicultural counselling

CRISIS, FOR THE COUNSELLOR

(*See also*: Burnout, Congruence, Core conditions, Referral, Self-disclosure by counsellors, Stress, Support groups, peer, Supervision)

Counsellors often feel that, no matter what they are going through in their personal lives, they should always be available and helpful to clients. There is an expectation that counsellors can leave their personal concerns behind when they enter the counselling room and, to a great extent, this expectation is a reasonable one. But counsellors can experience problems in their own lives, and if these are very difficult or even overwhelming they are very likely to affect the counsellor's ability to give full attention to the concerns of others. At such times, counsellors can feel uncertain about whether they should say anything about their personal troubles (perhaps in the name of 'congruence'), or the point at which it is advisable to cease counselling until their personal problems have been resolved.

Some approaches, particularly those with a psychodynamic orientation, suggest there should be very little self-disclosure or none at all. Client-centred counsellors tend to be more self-disclosing, but even so would not wish their self-disclosure to shift the focus of counselling away from the client to the counsellor. The most unhelpful thing of all would be to draw clients into your own personal life and problems so that they became distracted from their own concerns. This would also be unethical.

In times of crisis, the strength of your support network becomes crucial. If immediate colleagues are not approachable or are unavailable, your supervisor would usually be the first person to whom you turn for professional advice and support. He or she should be able to help you separate those issues that are of a personal nature and best dealt with through your own counselling (or by other means) from professional and ethical issues. The decision about whether to take a break from counselling also needs to be explored in supervision. The BAC accepts a period of up to six months away from counselling without affecting the chances of re-accreditation.

Counsellors are inevitably reminded of their own unresolved problems by clients, though often as a 'vague awareness' at first. Lambers (1993, p.71) suggests some questions for possible use in supervision, about how well (or not) the counsellor can, in the circumstances, communicate the core qualities and what the counsellor might do – e.g. 'Can I refer the client to someone else?' 'How can I do this sensitively?' and 'What help do I need?'

CRISIS COUNSELLING

(*See also*: Crying, Depression, Emotions, Empathy, Literal description, Loss, Psychological type, Referral)

The word 'crisis' is usually applied to immediately threatening and highly stressful situations that seem to demand some urgent response or action. People typically feel overwhelmed by stress, unable to cope and often angry, fearful and despairing. In a crisis, people face a situation that upsets their characteristic patterns of thought and behaviour. Their habitual ways of responding to and dealing with problems are insufficient, although Moos (1991) suggests that as people cannot remain in a state of disequilibrium a crisis is necessarily self-limiting. By definition a crisis is a turning point, and some (even temporary) resolution will be found. The resolution may be a healthy adaptation or foreshadow further problems.

Crisis counselling differs from other forms of counselling in several ways (Morley *et al.*, 1967):

1. It tends not to be based on any particular theoretical orientation or school.
2. The goal is resolution of the immediate crisis and restoring the individual's normal level of functioning.
3. There is relatively little concern with the client's past; only when it may help to understand their response to the present crisis. Problems or symptoms not directly related to the crisis are not dealt with.
4. It tends to be brief and intense, and the client may be seen more than once a week. The counsellor may take a more active and sometimes a more directive role than usual.
5. It can involve general support, direct encouragement of adaptive behaviour and practical steps taken on behalf of the client. Techniques and strategies vary, limited only by the counsellor's flexibility and creativity.
6. Crisis counselling often involves the client's family members, close friends or other social support networks.

Four major goals and three 'balancing factors' are prominent in the literature (e.g.

Worden, 1984; Moos, 1991). In crisis counselling, the counsellor aims to accomplish the goals by helping the client with the three balancing factors. The relative presence or absence of these factors seems to determine an individual's ability to deal with crisis and whether their return to equilibrium is likely to result in a healthy or a problematic adaptation. The goals are:

1. To understand the personal meaning and significance of the situation.
2. To preserve or encourage a positive self-image by confronting and accepting the reality of the situation.
3. To experience the painful emotions and re-establish a reasonable emotional balance.
4. To maintain a sense of competence by adjusting to the environment and responding to the crisis.

The related 'balancing factors' are as follows:

1. **Realistic perception of the situation.** If someone has a realistic perception of what has happened, and can recognise the relationship between the crisis and their feelings of stress, then attempts to manage the problem and reduce the level of stress are more likely to be effective.
2. **Adequate coping resources.** Throughout their lives people learn to cope with difficult situations in many different and individual ways. These skills and strategies can focus on finding meaning and coping with the practical aspects of dealing with the emotions linked to the crisis.
3. **Basic human support.** Humans are social beings and there is good evidence to suggest that the existence of a natural support network of family and friends, and the person's ability to make use of it, has a vital role in outcome (Raphael, 1984; Duck, 1998).

Crisis counselling may also involve helping the client understand the nature of the crisis. Parry (1990), Moos (1991) and others have identified several variables that help define a crisis and the nature of its impact on the individual:

- **Focus:** was the person directly involved or did the crisis happen to someone else?
- **Predictability:** was the event unexpected or was it possible to predict that it was going to happen?
- **Intensity:** how suddenly did it all happen? Was there any warning? How long did it last?
- **Choice:** did the person voluntarily enter the situation that resulted in a crisis? For example, choosing to separate from a partner may end up as a traumatic situation.
- **Pervasiveness:** does the crisis permeate many different areas of the person's life or is it contained within one area?

- **Magnitude:** how unfamiliar or different was the new situation? To what extent did it disrupt the routine pattern of living?
- **Controllability:** once the crisis happened, did the person feel they could do anything at all that might help in some way?
- **Risk:** was there any threat or danger?
- **Distress:** was there any pain, suffering or humiliation?
- **Revelation:** was anything negative revealed during or as a result of the crisis?
- **Loss:** loss is part of all crisis situations – the loss of things as they were before the crisis. 'Loss' here is a very general term – e.g. of status, independence, role or relationship, identity, valued possession or ideal, a loved person and so on. Reactions to loss vary considerably (Wortman and Silver, 1989).

In addition to these eleven factors, Moos (1991) identifies demographic, personal, physical and social environmental variables that may also affect the outcome and influence the person's appraisal of the crisis, the nature of the specific tasks and the choice of strategies.

Guidelines

The basic steps in crisis counselling are assessment, planning and intervention.

1. **Assessment.** The first clinical judgement is whether the person should receive immediate and intensive support. This decision is based on an assessment of, first, the likelihood of any imminent danger to the person or other people and second, whether the individual is able to maintain normal responsibilities and obligations or whether these should be temporarily and explicitly transferred to others.

   The assessment then moves on to examine, often in great detail, the precipitating event(s) and the effects of the resulting crisis. The purpose is to understand what has happened and assess the person's ability to cope with the situation. It is often some time before the precise nature and full extent of the crisis is recognised. It can be useful to encourage the client to talk through what has happened over the previous 48 hours or so. Assessment is basically concerned with gathering information.

2. **Planning.** This step is about identifying the central issues. Priorities and goals are decided. Alternative strategies and solutions to reduce the effects of the crisis are generated and the best options chosen. Tentative explanations are put forward to account for the individual's reaction.

3. **Intervention.** After the necessary data are collected, the focus is on the immediate situation and possible ways forward. The client needs to leave the first session with some positive guidelines for coping. These are evaluated and revised in subsequent sessions. Later sessions work on anticipatory planning and developing realistic goals for the future. The counsellor and client continue to work towards resolution of the crisis and may, at least initially, meet several times a week.

Checklist

This is a checklist of principles and strategies for crisis counselling (adapted from Worden, 1984, pp.39–48). Their effectiveness depends on a high level of trust and the quality of the relationship between the counsellor and client.

1. **Facilitating the expression of emotion.** Family, culture or personality may inhibit the expression of emotion, which can block the effective resolution of a crisis and be very destructive.

2. **Assurance of normality.** Some people need to be reassured that they are not losing their sanity. An acute sense of distraction, total preoccupation with what happened and hallucinations are examples of common and normal responses to a crisis. It is also important to allow for a very wide range of individual reactions.

3. **Recognising chronic reactions.** This is the other side of the need to reassure the person that their behaviour is quite normal. Counsellors need to remain alert for chronic or pathological reactions and the possible need for referral.

4. **Encouraging a realistic perception.** This is about helping the client establish the personal meaning and significance of what has happened. It is understanding and accepting the reality of the crisis and what it means for the future, and may involve going over the memories and circumstances many times. Literal description can be useful, and in itself can reduce distress and have therapeutic value. A realistic perception is necessary for problem management.

5. **Facilitating emotional withdrawal.** It is essential to help the client let go of the past and recognise that things are different and will never be the same again. Exploring previously relevant experiences can be helpful. This is not the same as forgetting – clients may want to hold on to memories, and painful and distressing episodes will reoccur – but it is about investing some emotional energy in the future and in new ways of living.

6. **Evaluating coping strategies.** Some coping strategies and defences are useful, at least for a limited period. However, others – e.g. excessive use of alcohol or other drugs – bring problems of their own. Clients can be encouraged to explore their coping behaviour, evaluate its effectiveness and consider alternatives.

7. **Adjusting to the new situation.** People who have been through a crisis could need help to adjust to the changed situation. They may need to work through their emotions in familiar surroundings and should be discouraged from immediately making major life decisions such as selling their home and moving. It might be helpful to encourage people to pay attention to looking after themselves, eating properly, taking exercise, discovering 'anchor points' in their day and developing a routine. Anticipating possible low points in the day or critical points in the future (e.g. anniversaries and

special days) and exploring possible ways of minimising their impact can also be useful.

8. **Allowing time to readjust.** There is a tendency for people to feel that they should get over the crisis quickly; there is often social pressure to recover from the loss and pain of the crisis and return to a normal routine. However, the process can be a gradual one, and for some it will take many months or years. Conversely, for other people distress is neither inevitable nor necessary (Wortman and Silver, 1989).

9. **Continuing social support.** Exploring possible ways of developing and maintaining an adequate social support network is an important part of crisis work.

10. **Facilitating problem solving.** This is the essence of crisis counselling. It is about helping the person to make decisions and manage problems. Egan (1990) identifies some clear steps in the process:

   • Identify and define the problem.
   • Establish priorities.
   • Specify desired goals or outcomes.
   • Generate possible action plans or strategies.
   • Mentally rehearse each alternative and the possible consequences.
   • Select one alternative.
   • Implement, step by step.
   • Evaluate and revise as appropriate.

CRYING

(*See also*: Depression, Emotions, Non-verbal communication, Touch)

When clients cry, it is tempting (but of course unhelpful) to distract them with a cup of tea or other form of comfort or sympathy, even though this is a natural response to people in distress. Counselling helps people explore the depth of their present emotions, however distressing and painful they are. More subtly, it is also unhelpful to believe that people *should* cry, and that if they don't there must be something wrong either with them or with you as a counsellor. Mills and Wooster (1987) make the useful point here that individuals vary greatly in the form their crying takes at its *peak*: from watery eyes to silent weeping to noisy sobbing and wailing.

Some counsellors feel very uncomfortable or embarrassed with clients who cry, or who begin to express very deep or powerful emotions, and some have different expectations of women and men in these respects. It can be difficult to stay with someone in very deep distress without wanting to interfere, and you can begin to feel very distressed yourself sometimes. If this does happen, you could be over-identifying with your client, or some deep emotions in yourself may be restimulated. Discussion with your supervisor, undertaking counselling for yourself, or both, are probably the best actions to take.

DEFINING COUNSELLING TO CLIENTS

See: Beginnings, Contract, negotiating a, Expectations, clients', Information giving, Multicultural counselling

DENIAL

(*See also*: Abuse, Avoidance, Challenge, Collusion, Empathy, Interpersonal process recall)

Some parts of each of us are difficult to look at or 'own' and we may therefore deny their existence or their full significance. Usually there is a fearful or upsetting experience behind the denial; particularly painful times may have been suppressed beyond easy recall. If you think a client is denying something it is better not to be persistent in trying to unearth the problem, as the client may become more defensive and put up further barriers.

Prevention is probably the best approach to conscious denial, through helping clients feel safer and less threatened, listening to the underlying sense of what is said, and reflecting back any unease. Part of the contract between you and your client can include an agreement that the client can say if there is something they don't want to talk about and that the counsellor will respect that wish. By feeling safe, clients are able to face up to and talk about the subject they at first wanted to avoid, without being pushed into a situation of denial. Some clients are helped by exploring their difficulty in talking about a topic rather than the topic itself.

Unconscious denial is perhaps more difficult to deal with, as its existence to begin with is unknown both to client and counsellor. Good empathic skills help the client to trust and feel safe, and gradually allow the memories and emotions to surface.

Sometimes a client denies a gentle challenge (e.g. 'It sounds as though you find endings difficult.' 'No I don't.'): they may be right or may be denying the loss and pain in ending. In either case it is usually best to accept what the client says. The challenge might, however, have triggered something in the client and, as they reflect, they realise that endings *are* difficult for them. The topic of difficult endings might surface again during another session and the counsellor could link the two incidents, perhaps enabling the client to explore further.

DEPRESSION

(*See also*: Books, self-help, Crying, Loss, Psychodiagnosis, Self-awareness, Suicide, Supervision, Thoughts)

Depression may mean anything from temporarily feeling 'down' to being so debilitated as to be unable to move or speak. Anxious or angry clients may also be quite depressed. Counselling usually involves trying to enable clients to express the underlying feelings they have suppressed, or to learn to counter negative unhelpful thoughts with realistic thinking. One of the traps for counsellors is to take on to themselves the feelings of despair in the client (whether overtly expressed or not) to such an extent that they too feel hopeless. Supervision may be used to help the counsellor separate her or his feelings from the client's.

Cognitive counselling is perhaps the best researched of the psychological interventions (Weishaar, 1993) and appears to be particularly helpful with depression (see Barker, 1992; Gilbert, 1992; Stern and Drummond, 1991). It involves helping clients to change their negative automatic thoughts to realistic ones and recording what gives them pleasure and what they achieve. This form of counselling may be sufficient in itself to alleviate depression. Some counsellors use cognitive counselling as a way of helping break the negative cycle of self-defeating thinking so that the underlying problems and suppressed feelings which caused the depression in the first place can be explored. Systems of psychodiagnosis such as ICD-10 or DSM-IV can be used as a way of helping both the client and the counsellor understand the severity of the depressive episode and whether or not medication may be of help (Stern and Drummond, 1991).

Gilbert's (1996) outline of the cognitive interpersonal approach to depression takes five factors into account: past relational patterns, core-self and other relational schemas, dysfunctional attitudes and rules for living, social roles, and critical events. He argues that understanding the *emotional core* of the schemas can be crucial. Thus his approach to treating depression is integrative.

Barker's (1992) book includes a self-help guide on depression using Beck's and Ellis's ideas, and has a number of unusual features: it is written in the first person, to try to encourage receptivity, the reading level is equivalent to that of a tabloid newspaper, and the publishers have waived copyright on it. The guide is also published separately (Barker, 1997). Gilbert has also designed a self-help book (Gilbert, 1997) based on cognitive–behavioural principles with exercises for the reader to engage in. Part of Gilbert's approach is that negative thoughts are 'waiting in the wings' but that with greater awareness of their presence and ways to interrupt them, these thoughts can be controlled.

Radically different views and methods of working with depression are put forward by Storr (1990) and by Bugental and Bugental (1980). Storr sees a need to help depressed people 'disinter' the active, aggressive elements of themselves, for example by discussing their feelings towards their parents, who they're likely to see as perfect. Bugental argues that a period of depression can be healing, and a valuable signal that change is needed. He helps clients 'go with' depression and rest, patiently and acceptingly, simplifying life and treating depression as important to their well-being.

Sutherland (1998) provides a vivid account of his own depression and a critique of a wide variety of treatments.

DIAGNOSIS

See: Assessment, Psychodiagnosis

DIFFERENCES BETWEEN CLIENTS AND COUNSELLORS

See: Multiculturalism, Multicultural counselling

DIFFICULT CLIENTS

(*See also*: Contraindications for brief counselling, Drama triangle, Empathy, Referral)

Difficult clients are those whom you find particularly challenging. Specific difficulties are covered elsewhere, but general strategies for coping with difficult clients include:

- Presenting your difficulties openly to your supervisor or supervision group.
- Asking yourself what, exactly, you find difficult about this client.
- Exploring the extent to which this client reminds you of people you have found difficult in the past.
- Reflecting on the quality of the relationship you are able to offer to this client.
- Making a distinction between what clients say to you, and the ways in which they express themselves. For example, you might 'switch off' to clients who swear or who repeat themselves a lot, but they are still expressing themselves, perhaps the best way they can, and you should try to focus on that, rather than on the language itself.
- Similarly, making a distinction between clients whose values are unacceptable to you and professional responsibility (Walker, 1993).
- Looking to see if the clients you find difficult have features in common or if there are recurring 'themes'. Again, these are issues that may be explored with your supervisor or in your personal counselling.
- Trying to distinguish between the person and the quality or behaviour you find difficult.

You might find it very difficult to counsel some clients, however hard you try. In such circumstances, it may be better to refer them. It is, of course, advisable to discuss how to do this in supervision, so that you do it as constructively as possible.

DIFFICULTIES IN BEING A CLIENT

(*See also*: Avoidance, Contract, negotiating a, Distress at the end of session (clients), Expectations, clients', Fees, Multicultural counselling, Respect, Trust)

Many clients come to us at times when they have difficulties in making any decision, including the decision to seek help. Some clients feel a sense of failure, that they ought to be able to take care of themselves, and this in itself may lower a client's already threatened sense of self-esteem. Your client may have had to overcome much resistance and prejudice about counselling before coming to see you, and this makes the first few minutes of your first session even more important. Treating any expression of fear or anxiety with empathy will help your client feel that you respect their doubts, and will also help to establish trust in your capacity to understand.

People from some cultural groups can find it especially difficult to talk in personal terms to complete strangers. You need to be patient and understanding here, particularly if you are not familiar with your client's cultural traditions and norms. Some clients also have to overcome strong feelings of guilt or disloyalty to members of their families before they can talk openly. Other factors that can be put forward as difficulties include time commitment and travelling distance. These may be a sign of avoidance, which you can offer to help the client explore; otherwise there is not much you can do, and the final decision about whether to continue or not will have to be left to your client.

The key question is: 'What could make counselling easier for my client?' Arranging to see clients at times when they do not have to spend time alone in dark railway stations or bus stops, or have to walk far after dark may help a lot. Similarly, people who cannot negotiate stairs or who are in a wheelchair obviously find many buildings and streets difficult. What you can do to an old building or to a private house to make access easier will be limited, but removal of obstacles from hallways and provision of a wooden ramp to help negotiate steps both make a contribution.

Once a client has decided to start counselling with you, he or she may find difficulties in continuing. Finance could have a part to play in this, and if you operate a sliding scale according to clients' ability to pay, your client might ask to renegotiate this part of the contract. How you respond to this is up to you, but decisive factors could include your own income level, a point below which you are not prepared to go, and a point at which you feel exploited.

DISTRESS AT THE END OF A COUNSELLING SESSION (CLIENTS)

(*See also*: Difficulties in being a client, Frequency of sessions, Length of sessions, Suicide, Time boundaries)

In deep personal exploration of the kind that can occur within a counselling session clients can often become aware of painful emotional material that has been buried or half-forgotten for a long time. It is often the case that such material surfaces towards the end of a session, and the counsellor may have some concerns about whether or not there is time to resolve the problems before the client has to leave. Some counsellors, if they become aware that deep material is surfacing with little time remaining, prefer gently to remind the client of the time and suggest that it might be better to take this exploration further in the next session – the risk here is that the opportunity might be lost for good and that the client may never return to the painful experience. Other counsellors view the use of time as entirely the responsibility of the client, and prefer not to direct sessions in any way – the risk here is that the client may leave the counselling room in a distressed state and be at some risk in 'the outside world', especially if they are driving, or going back to work in a dangerous environment.

Your experience with a client will help you decide what course of action to take if you think he or she is likely to be very distressed at the end of the session. For example, how does this person usually manage distressing experiences? Does he or she become disoriented and unable to make rational decisions, or does he or she have strong personal resources and coping mechanisms? Will the client be returning to a relatively safe place, among friends or family? Is there is a history of suicide threats or self-harming? You need to balance this 'risk assessment' against your respect for your client's autonomy and right to manage his or her own affairs. You are not there to make your client feel good at the end of each session, and distress is often a part of the process to which your client has committed him- or herself. An attempt to avoid painful experiences on the grounds of lack of time could be counterproductive, and might reflect your discomfort rather than any real risk to your client.

An ideal situation with a very distressed client is to have somewhere where he or she can rest and regain composure before leaving. For many counsellors this is not a possibility, however, and you may have other clients waiting to see you. Extending the time of the session is also not a possibility for many counsellors – and, in any event, you need to consider the disadvantages of running over time and make it a rare exception rather than the rule. If you think the situation warrants it, you have the option of ringing a friend or family member, the client's general practitioner (all with your client's permission) or, in *very* exceptional circumstances, taking the client to their home yourself if you can – even though this may mean postponing other appointments or keeping other clients waiting.

If you work in a team or as part of an organisation it is a good idea to establish a strategy of what to do in the event of an emergency, so that you can minimise disruption and inconvenience to other clients whilst taking proper care of someone who may be at significant risk. If you work on your own, it is useful to contact other counsellors in your area in a similar position and agree a method of mutual support and cooperation in times of difficulty. This form of networking and mutual support could also be useful in other ways.

DISTRESS AT THE END OF A SESSION (COUNSELLORS)

(See also: Counter-transference, Crisis, for the counsellor, Stress)

Counselling can be a risky activity for counsellors if emotional material brought up by clients is particularly distressing or touches on areas of personal pain for the counsellor. Counsellors can feel a range of emotions at the end of a session, from exhilaration to sadness, depression and, occasionally, distress. Clients sometimes have very upsetting stories to tell, and different counsellors are vulnerable to different levels of distress. Some counsellors are particularly open to feelings of personal distress if their clients are exploring issues of child abuse or violence, others find issues to do with (for example) isolation, loneliness or suicide particularly difficult.

You should remember that it is not a sign of personal or professional weakness to be touched, or even deeply moved, by clients exploring painful or distressing emotions. Your approach to counselling will guide you as to the degree of openness you can allow yourself during a counselling session, and you can explore in supervision situations that you find particularly moving or personally upsetting.

You might encounter problems if, at the end of a session, you feel more deeply distressed than can be accounted for simply by feelings of sympathy or compassion for your client. Something in the client's material may be touching you in an area where you have unresolved or strong feelings. Again, this is not necessarily a matter for alarm, but it could be a sign that you have some work to do on this material for yourself.

If you are feeling deeply distressed it may be ethical and professional to postpone other appointments until you have regained your equilibrium. It is also sensible to organise your counselling appointments to give you a break between clients: even ten minutes can be enough to clear your mind in readiness for your next client. Some counsellors find relaxation and breathing exercises useful, others recommend a short walk or finding something to do that marks the temporary end of your contact with a client – writing, telephoning a friend or even making a cup of tea.

There are two longer term strategies to consider. First, you need to talk over the situation with your supervisor or with a trusted colleague, focusing on your reaction to your client rather than on the client personally. Your discussion might lead to the second strategy, which is to consider going into personal counselling yourself or, if you are already in counselling, to bring up the distressing experience at your next session.

If your feelings of distress happen more often with particular clients, or are connected with particular issues, you have some indication of a pattern that needs to be explored in some way. You should view this as an opportunity for personal growth in yourself rather than as a 'problem' to be overcome. The worst thing to do is stoically 'grin and bear it': this is not only unhelpful, and perhaps damaging, to you but also unhelpful to your client, and may miss an opportunity for both you and your client to move on.

DNA (DID NOT ATTEND)

See: Clients who don't come back, Missed sessions

DRAMA TRIANGLE

(*See also*: Assertiveness, Collusion, Immediacy, Patterns, Self-awareness)

The 'Drama Triangle' (Karpman, 1968) is a model which some counsellors and clients find useful in explaining certain patterns in behaviour, especially between two people. It suggests three complementary roles: Victim, Rescuer and Persecutor. Examples of the roles as brief, normal responses are: seeing pictures on the television of starving children (victims) and immediately writing out a cheque to help their cause (rescuer), or being ill (victim), which may bring someone to look after us (rescuer) and lead to a colleague being angry with us (persecutor) because they have to do our work. These examples show normal behaviour; the people concerned don't carry on and on in the same roles and therefore don't become caught in the drama triangle.

Problems occur when people are stuck, either in one of the roles or going round and round the triangle, drawing in others. A classic Victim role is taken by someone who feels, or actually is, hard done by and seems constantly being put upon. Some people get angry with them (Persecutor), others might try to help (Rescuer), but nothing seems to change matters. The original Victim might then alternate to Persecutor, blaming the others, who could then become Victims.

People who get caught in the triangle, in whatever role, tend to have low self-esteem and see themselves as having little control over their lives. Others may view them differently and perceive them as being very powerful or frustrating as they stay firmly in their role in the triangle. Counsellors can try to help them increase their self-esteem, become more self-sufficient and escape from the trap. However, the more deeply the client is stuck in their role in the triangle the easier it is for the counsellor to become trapped too. Some clients make it very difficult for the counsellor to resist telling them what to do or doing things for them (rescuing), while others leave the counsellor feeling angry (persecuting). If the counsellor is unaware of this and gets caught in the triangle, the client is again pushed into the victim role, the place that is so familiar to them. So the triangle continues, even within the counselling relationship.

DRAWINGS

See: Journal, writing a, Life space diagram, Paper and pencil exercises

DRINKS/REFRESHMENTS

(*See also*: Non-verbal communication)

The way you establish or fail to establish a concentrated and 'focused' mood may affect the counselling process significantly. Offering drinks and other refreshments to clients can cause problems in this respect. If you work in a place with a waiting room and/or receptionist, it is possible to supply refreshments in a way that is unobtrusive and does not interfere with the counselling process. However, if you work on your own, and your refreshment facilities are in your counselling room, it can be quite distracting for clients if their counsellor spends time filling kettles, washing cups, etc. There is also the problem of what to say while this process is going on. Do you start 'counselling' while making drinks, or engage in 'small talk'?

A further problem is that on the one hand a drink can help clients to relax, but on the other it can become something to hold and 'hide behind', with clients feeling exposed when they put the cup down.

However, if you can prepare a drink with the minimum of fuss, there seems to be no real reason why you should not offer one to your client, especially on a very cold or hot day or when the client has had a long journey. Having drinking water readily available is a helpful idea, especially as increases in adrenaline levels can make the throat very dry.

DROPOUT

See: Clients who don't come back

DRUNK AND/OR DRUGGED CLIENTS

(*See also*: Anger, Boundaries, Emotions, Violence and its prevention)

If you work for an agency that specialises in treating people who misuse alcohol or other drugs, you will have a clear procedure for dealing with a drunk client or one who has obviously recently taken a drug other than alcohol. A problem for the generic counsellor is to be confronted with a client who is drunk or drugged when this is not a familiar state to you. The behaviour of a drunk person or a person under the influence of other drugs can be unpredictable, threatening and frightening. If your client does become aggressive or threatening or behaves unpredictably, get help if necessary, as calmly and quietly as you can.

All drugs affect a person's behaviour and perceptions to some degree (see Daines *et al.*, 1997 for a discussion of the effects of commonly used drugs). Some prescribed drugs may, for some people, reduce their anxiety sufficiently to allow counselling to take place. On the other hand, an obviously drunk or drugged client is unlikely to be in a suitable frame of mind for counselling. If you have reason to believe a client is affected by drugs you can try to explain to them that counselling is unlikely to be effective under such circumstances, and that it is better to postpone the session rather than continue. If your client is not receptive to this advice, you may decide to try to continue, even though any counselling is likely to be a waste of effort. You can discuss the issue later with your client when he or she is not influenced by drugs. It is probably advisable to be clear at this point that you will not attempt to continue with counselling whenever the client is using any drugs, including alcohol. A further consideration is that you may be open to prosecution if you knowingly allow your premises to be used for taking controlled drugs.

DURATION

(*See also*: Brief counselling, Contract, negotiating a, Endings)

Counselling was originally conceived as a process that 'takes a long time' but in recent years, against a background of economic constraints and concerns about the allocation of resources, there has been growing pressure for short-term counselling. Moreover, although there are conflicting views, there is no current research to strongly support the principle that the longer counselling goes on the better or more effective it is. Indeed, some research seems rather to support the value of short-term counselling (e.g. Barkham, 1990, 1993a). Time-limited and brief approaches have therefore emerged within various theoretical positions in an attempt to make counselling less expensive and more available, and the typical length of time people actually remain in counselling is between six and eight sessions (Feltham, 1997a).

The term 'brief counselling' is usually taken to describe anything up to 20 sessions. 'Time-limited' counselling is a variation; it specifies the actual number of sessions at the start of counselling – such as once a week for, say, 12 sessions. There are of course different patterns of counselling contract: 15 sessions, for example, would normally be held in consecutive weeks but could be spread over a year. The duration of counselling may be influenced by several factors including your own preference, experience and training, agency policy restricting the length of time for each client, the nature of the presenting problem, the desired goals and outcomes and the extent to which it is possible to identify limited aims and focus on specific issues.

ECLECTICISM

See: Integration and eclecticism

EFFECTIVENESS OF COUNSELLING

(*See also*: Common factors, Counselling, Evaluation, Journal, writing a, Research)

It is now firmly established that counselling is effective (Stiles *et al.*, 1986; Barkham, 1990, 1993b; Bergin and Garfield, 1994), though this statement needs qualification. First, the degree of effectiveness is generally seen by researchers – perhaps unfairly – as modest, in tune with Freud's remark about transforming 'neurotic misery' into 'common unhappiness'. The unfairness lies in expecting radical change, as if counselling was like reprogramming a computer or washing out a test-tube. Second, there are problems with defining 'success' in counselling: some changes in behaviour are relatively easy to measure (e.g. smoking less); others, such as deeper self-awareness, are more difficult.

A number of researchers have argued that the effectiveness of counselling only *appears* to be modest. It depends what you compare it with. For example, Rosenthal (1990) discussed an acclaimed study of the effects of aspirin on reducing heart attacks. The reduction in number of heart attacks was 4%: four people in a hundred, on average, would improve (avoid suffering a heart attack) by taking aspirin. He then points out that the average effect size for counselling is about 10% and that this is, by these standards, considerably better than 'modest'.

Gallo (1978) described two hypothetical situations that have the same effect size as counselling (about 10%). In the first, assume that the average life-expectancy of someone who is now 40 years old is 70, and that a treatment lasting as long as, and costing the same as, counselling raises the life expectancy by 10%. Seven extra years of life (assuming equal quality of life) would be highly cost-effective! The second situation is a device fitted to a car for the same cost as counselling and improving mileage by 10%: at 15 000 miles per year and American prices, it would take 22 years for the device to pay for itself. The same effect size is therefore enormously important or completely trivial, depending on the context.

The question of whether counselling is worth the effort and expense needs three pieces of information (Gallo, 1978):

1. Its cost.

2. The benefits it brings.

3. The benefits of alternative courses of action.

A fourth factor could also be included: the risk of deterioration.

Several studies in organisations seem to have shown substantial benefits – for example, in the UK Post Office study (Allinson *et al.*, 1989) an average of three interviews reduced absence from work by more than 50%. Even if the benefits seem small – months rather than weeks between periods of depression, two weeks more at work per year – economically and personally they can be very worthwhile.

Two recent sources show conflicting results in some respects, but both agree that counselling is effective. First, Seligman discussed a national survey by *Consumer Reports*, the American equivalent of *Which?* There were 22 000 participants, about 4000 of whom had experienced some form of psychotherapy. The study reported a very positive experience: 'Most respondents got a lot better' (Seligman, 1995, p.968). Among the other results were that longer-term treatment was considerably more effective than short-term treatment, that psychologists, psychiatrists and social workers were equally effective, that Alcoholics Anonymous did particularly well, and that no one particular kind of counselling did any better than any other for any problem. Seligman argued that the methodology of this survey is valid and complements the standard experimental approach; others (e.g. Brock *et al.*, 1998) disagree with him.

Second, the experimental research has recently been reviewed by Lambert and Cattani-Thompson (1996), who conclude, in apparent contrast to Seligman (1995), that the effects of counselling can be achieved quite quickly (five to ten sessions) with at least 50% of clients. Those with whom brief therapy is least likely to work tend to be hostile or passive. A second contrast with Seligman (1995) is that 'some specific techniques seem to be especially helpful with particular symptoms and disorders' (Lambert and Cattani-Thompson, 1996, p.606). Among Lambert and Cattani-Thompson's other conclusions are that some clients get worse during counselling (this is not necessarily because of counselling) and that 'the best predictors (and possible causes) of success outside of client variables are counselor–client relationship factors' (p.606).

Little is known about *why* counselling is effective. Radically different techniques seem to be equally successful. One explanation is in terms of common or non-specific factors such as support ('warm involvement') and challenge ('communicating a new perspective on client or situation') (Stiles *et al.*, 1986). Another possibility is that different approaches 'fit' different clients.

A final, major, point about effectiveness is that it is very easy to believe that a particular method 'works' when it is actually irrelevant. This is partly because what we see and remember are open to bias but also because many people (perhaps 40%) improve, or report they have improved, without counselling. If they had been in counselling they would probably have improved anyway, and they might well have inferred that the counsellor or technique was effective. This does not detract from the general conclusion that counselling helps people change more quickly and perhaps more substantially than no counselling.

For arguments against the effectiveness of most approaches to counselling, see Eysenck (1992). You might also like to examine a reanalysis of the data in his original and stimulating attack (Eysenck, 1952): McNeilly and Howard (1991) found a very substantial improvement rate of 50% after about 15 sessions, compared with 2% in people not counselled, using the same data that Eysenck sees as demonstrating the ineffectiveness of counselling.

Mellor-Clark and Barkham (1996) provide practical guidelines for counsellors who wish to evaluate their own counselling and perhaps to make out a case for more resources.

E-MAIL COUNSELLING

(*See also*: Confidentiality, Core conditions, Journal, writing a)

The growing use of computers as a means of communication in recent years, and the development of electronic mail (e-mail) systems, has provided opportunities to explore how e-mail could be used in counselling. Lago (1996) for example, has pointed out that in his university setting (Sheffield) students live dispersed around the city and often cannot afford the time or expense of travelling to the counselling centre but, because computers are widely available in universities and more generally, it might be possible for e-mail to supplement (or in some cases replace) face-to-face contact.

E-mail counselling is in its infancy, and the advantages and disadvantages associated with it are not yet well documented. Lago (1996) has pointed out that, since most counselling depends on the existence of a relationship between counsellor and client, a relationship in which neither party is present in the same space brings particular problems. Telephone counselling at least has the advantage that each person can hear the other, and the tones of voice, inflections and emphases that form part of the non-verbal relationship are still available. E-mail counselling, on the other hand, can take place in what Lago refers to as 'asynchronous time' – you send me a message today, and I reply tomorrow. This point is considered by King *et al.* (1998) an advantage in a family therapy context because it becomes possible for each family member to participate in their own time. Further advantages of e-mail counselling include the fact that all parties involved can keep a complete transcript of all communications, and e-mail can be a great help to the housebound or those in very remote locations.

An example of computer use in counselling is the Internet-based service Therapy Online (http://www.therapyonline.ca) (Murphy and Mitchell, 1998). Here, clients are supplied, by e-mail, with a 'Virtually Solve It' (VSI) worksheet – a kind of questionnaire designed to help clients express their problems. The completed VSI provides the therapist with the information required to 'provide a caring, professional therapeutic response, again via e-mail' (Murphy and Mitchell, 1998, p.22). In this system the lack of human contact may be somewhat ameliorated by the process of 'emotional bracketing' (p.24), where appropriate emotional material is included in the therapist's e-mail message in brackets. For example, 'It's been several weeks since I heard from you John (concern, worry) and I would very much appreciate it if you could at least acknowledge this e-mail (feeling pushy, demanding).'

Sanders and Rosenfield (1998) distinguish between computer-assisted counselling (e.g. in a careers guidance process), computer-simulated methods (where a computer is programmed to give therapy-style responses) and computer-mediated methods (where computers are used as an aid to remote therapeutic relationships). Taking their cue from Lago's (1996) question 'Do the existing theories of psychotherapy continue to apply, or do we need a new theory of e-mail therapy?', Sanders and Rosenfield question whether the core conditions of counselling can be effectively met through the use of computer technology. They point to the lack of any real research in the area of technology-mediated communication of those conditions and suggest that it is unlikely that Lago's question can presently be answered.

Apart from the obvious problems with counselling at a distance, e-mail counselling also raises some unusual ethical considerations: for example, there are particular concerns with confidentiality. E-mail systems are vulnerable to 'hackers' (people able to break into communication systems and read messages without either party being aware of it). There are also possibilities for the unscrupulous to offer remote counselling without any real training or knowledge and with little possibility of being held responsible. Bloom (1998) reports eight areas of ethical concern:

1. Confidentiality.
2. Validity of data delivered via computer networks.
3. Inadequate counsellor intervention.
4. Misuse of computer applications.
5. Lack of counsellor awareness of location-specific factors (concerning events and other cultural issues that affect clients but of which the counsellor may not be aware).
6. Equality of access to Internet resources (concerning the fact that for many people computer technology is not a financial possibility).
7. Concerns about privacy.
8. Credentialing (the possible absence of traditional credentials regarded as necessary for practice).

Finally, Lago (1996) offers a number of themes to consider when contemplating establishing some form of e-mail counselling service:

- The ability to establish contact through computers.
- The ability to establish relationships.
- The ability to communicate accurately with minimal distortion.
- The ability to demonstrate understanding and frame empathic responses.
- The capacity and resources to provide appropriate information.

EMERGENCY

See: Difficulties in being a client, Distress at the end of a counselling session, Drunk and/or drugged clients, Violence and its prevention

EMOTIONS

(*See also*: Collusion, Emotions, naming, Emotions, talking about versus experiencing, Empathy, Feelings, Paraphrasing, Process, Self-awareness, Thoughts)

The advantage of our emotions is that they lead us astray. Oscar Wilde.

Most counselling and psychotherapy is based on the idea that we need to be aware of our emotions and feelings, and how they affect us. The difficult part is in identifying and owning them. One obstacle is that emotions are often confused with thoughts. As a rule of thumb, emotions usually come directly after a verb, e.g. 'I am happy'; 'I feel sad'. Exceptions include 'I feel thirsty' (a sensation) and 'I feel cheated' (an experience about which people feel a variety of emotions). However, when the word 'that' can be inserted after the verb, it is a thought, e.g. 'I feel all is lost', and 'I feel that all is lost'. The real emotion here remains unstated: it could be fear, anxiety or another emotion; we don't know. It is at this point that the counsellor may need to help clients become aware of the emotions underlying their statements and of the difference between thoughts and emotions.

Sometimes clients have great difficulty in expressing emotions, and counsellors may be unaware of this or even collude with it, because they also don't want to talk about the subject. One way of picking up unspoken emotion is by becoming aware of your own emotions. If there is a strong emotion or feeling around, checking it out with the client may increase their awareness of these feelings. An example of this is a trainee counsellor who in supervision complained of feeling hopeless and useless as the client had said very little. She was encouraged to check these emotions out with the client in the next session, who confirmed this was just how she (the client) felt. On the other hand, the much-used question 'how do you feel about that?' is often unhelpful, because the client is unsure. It also tends to make clients think, which takes them away from emotions and feelings. Instead, an empathic statement like 'you sound worried' may help clients' awareness of their emotions.

Some counsellors find Greenberg's and Safran's (1990) distinction between primary, secondary and instrumental emotions useful. Greenberg and Safran argue that it is only working with primary emotions that leads to change. Primary emotions are typically referred to as 'authentic' or 'real', while secondary emotions are a response to them or to thoughts, and ways of coping with rather than experiencing primary emotions. An example is being angry (secondary emotion in this case) as a reaction to feeling afraid (primary emotion here). To focus on your client's secondary emotion would in their view simply reinforce it, and not lead to change. In Greenberg and Safran's terms, instrumental emotions have been learned, and are used to influence or manipulate others. Generally, counsellors therefore need to challenge them (or help clients self-challenge). For example, some people have learned that if they get angry others tend to give way to them.

Physiologically, emotions originate in the limbic system, an older part of the brain in evolutionary terms, and can be suppressed by activity in the cortex, or new brain. This means that by thinking we can suppress emotions and that, conversely, by reducing cortical activity (e.g. by deep relaxation) we can allow emotions to rise (Mueller, 1983; Lancaster, 1991). Thus an understanding of physiology helps to clarify what is happening when, for example, a Gestalt counsellor asks a client to express emotions or a cognitive therapist suggests that a change in thinking will change emotions. Both are accessing the emotional system through speech, but have differing rationales about what will help the client and why. For a recent discussion of research on emotion, in a more personal style than most psychology texts, see Cornelius (1996).

EMOTIONS, NAMING

(*See also*: Anger, Emotions, Empathy, Feelings, Literal description, Paraphrasing)

Table 6 provides one way of helping clients find the right or most accurate words for their emotions by choosing the general category or categories first, then narrowing the search down. Another way is to assign ten 'units', with a miscellaneous option, as in 'I'm three parts happy, five parts confused and two miscellaneous' (Green, 1964). A third option, which some clients find particularly helpful, is to try to 'ground' an emotion, sensation or thought in the person's body e.g. 'Where do you feel empty?' 'Can you describe your sense of empty?' Repetition by the client and repeating at a slower pace can also help clients to clarify.

Table 6

Four categories* of emotion, with examples

Category	High	Medium
Angry	Disgusted Furious Bitter Seething	Angry Exasperated Frustrated Miffed Provoked Sore Annoyed Fed-up
Sad	Depressed Defeated Devastated Empty Worthless Hopeless Crushed Battered	Discouraged Unhappy Low Bruised Disappointed Hurt Ashamed Upset Guilty Gloomy Fed-up
Afraid	Petrified Terrified Deeply shocked Horrified Panicky Frozen	Anxious Insecure Nervous Shaky Cautious Unsure Muddled Confused Lost Apprehensive Threatened Vulnerable Scared

Category	High	Medium
Glad	Ecstatic	Pleased
	Elated	Happy
	High	Cheerful
	Delighted	Confident
	Strong	Contented
	Enchanted	Calm
	Powerful	Affectionate
	Dynamic	Trusting
	Loving	Friendly
	Devoted	Peaceful
	Enthusiastic	Hopeful
	Proud	Relieved
	Inspired	Interested
		Alert
		Determined
		Excited

*The subcategories of high and medium intensity are very rough guides; what matters is that the client (or counsellor) finds the right word or words, modified perhaps by 'very' or 'a bit'. A word like 'jealous' might be (1) helpful in its own right but also (2) a combination of, say, 'angry' and 'sad', so that sometimes words from these categories will be clearer still. Mad, sad, bad and glad are the terms used by Yalom (1989). As a group they have the advantage of resonance and therefore memorability, but two of them can be easily misinterpreted.

The four-category system assumes that there are basic emotions and that these four terms describe them. Both assumptions are disputed by researchers: Ortony and Turner (1990, p.315), for example, argue that 'there is little agreement about how many emotions are basic, which emotions are basic, and why they are basic.' However, nearly all the theorists agree on anger, sadness, fear and happiness. For a reply to Ortony and Turner, see work by Ekman (1992, 1993), who is particularly interested in those emotions that can be observed from facial expression, and in the high level of agreement across cultures in selecting emotion words that fit facial expressions. Ekman also mentions the familiar idea to counsellors that people differ in their habitual 'affect-about-affect' (e.g. some people are afraid of their anger, others disappointed in themselves for being angry, others disgusted, and so on; Ekman, 1993). There is great similarity across different cultures about the categories of emotion (Russell, 1991, 1995). However, there are emotion words in some languages with no English equivalent – such as *Schadenfreude* (the German word for 'pleasure derived from someone else's displeasure'), and *itoshii* (the Japanese word for 'longing for an absent loved one', though the English word 'pining' may come close) (Russell, 1991).

EMOTIONS, TALKING ABOUT VERSUS EXPERIENCING

(*See also*: Empathy, Experiments by clients, Immediacy, Interpersonal process recall, Paraphrasing, Self-awareness)

Emotions can be talked about in a distant unemotional way. In counselling, particularly, this is often not helpful and counsellors have many approaches for encouraging clients to make greater contact with their emotions and experience them more clearly and deeply. These approaches include asking the client to go through their reactions to an event more slowly, to repeat a word or a gesture, to use the word 'I', to say something louder or in an exaggerated way, to exaggerate it yourself, to ask where and how something feels, immediacy, and using the two-chair technique. It seems to be particularly helpful (in clarifying thoughts and wants as well as emotions, and making more sense of things) to experience emotions as they feel at that moment.

EMPATHY

(*See also*: Core conditions, Counselling, Frame of reference, Intuition, Metaphors and similes, Paraphrasing)

In the everyday sense, empathy means the ability to understand how another person is feeling and experiencing the world from their point of view. In client-centred counselling, empathy is seen as one of the most important concepts, and the communication of empathic understanding as one of the core conditions without which personal change in counselling is unlikely to happen. Barrett-Lennard (1993) describes empathy as having an 'aroused, active, reaching out nature'. To Rogers, empathy meant: '... entering into the private perceptual world of the other and becoming thoroughly at home with it. It involves being sensitive, moment by moment, to the changing felt meanings which flow in this other person, to the fear or rage or tenderness or confusion or whatever that he or she is experiencing ... It includes communicating your sensings of the person's world as you look with fresh and unfrightened eyes at elements of which he or she is fearful ... You are a confident companion to the person in his or her inner world' (Rogers, 1980, p.142). Rogers' concern with his clients' inner, subjective, experiencing meant that it was most important for him to achieve as complete an understanding of a client's personal world as possible.

The place of empathic understanding is not restricted to client-centred counselling or even to the various Humanistic approaches. In psychodynamic counselling, for example, in particular that based on the 'self-psychology' of Kohut, empathy is regarded as an important 'ingredient' of counselling. 'It seems to me it is the essence of the science of psychoanalysis to have harnessed empathy to the slow and careful approach of science. We are not empathic in sudden intuitive flashes' (Kohut, 1987, p.275). Kohut viewed empathy as a means of information gathering to enable him to make more accurate interpretations, but he also stressed the value of empathy as a means of letting his clients know he was doing his best to understand them.

Kahn, in attempting an integration of the approaches of Rogers, Kohut, Gill and Freud, remarked 'Thus our job is not to give advice, opinions, or answers, but continually to do our best to *understand* the client: To understand what clients are experiencing and what they are feeling at this moment. To understand the gradually unfolding coherence of the themes of their lives ... What therapists need to learn is less a technique or a group of techniques than ways of opening themselves, first to their clients' experiences and then to their own spontaneity. That spontaneity will reveal their own special, idiosyncratic way of communicating empathy at that moment' (Kahn, 1991, p.168); see also Kahn (1997).

Almost without exception, counsellors from any school of thought would agree that empathy is an important characteristic of effective counselling. However, Rogers went further by noticing the therapeutic benefits of listening and understanding, and concluding that this form of listening, when communicated to the client as empathic understanding, was helpful in its own right, not as a preparation for other counselling techniques 'To my mind, empathy is in itself a healing agent. It is one of the most potent aspects of therapy, because it releases, it confirms, it brings even the most frightened client into the human race. If a person is understood, he or she belongs' (Rogers, 1986, p.129).

Empathy is not sympathy or identification. Counsellors should guard against their responses being sympathetic at the expense of being empathic. Identification – where you feel a client's situation is familiar to you – can lead you to respond from your own experience rather than from your client's frame of reference. Your client may find this either helpful or distracting, but it is not empathic.

Empathy involves a process of being with another person; that is, attempting to 'step into the other person's shoes' and 'see the world through the other person's eyes', laying aside your own perceptions, values, meanings and perspectives as far as possible. However, two other aspects of empathy deserve to be emphasised here. The first is the *as if* quality of empathic understanding. This refers to the idea that one can enter the frame of reference of another person to the extent that events, feelings etc. can be experienced, to some extent, *as if* those events were one's own – but without losing the *as if* quality. In other words, empathically understanding someone does not imply 'getting lost' in their world. The empathic counsellor maintains his or her separate identity, and does not become overwhelmed by what may be strong or frightening feelings.

The second aspect for emphasis is that empathy needs to be communicated if the other person is to become aware of being understood. This communication is usually, though not exclusively, verbal – holding someone's hand, or even crying along with someone, may be equally as empathic as anything said. An empathic response would capture the content of the client's words but, more importantly, it would also capture some, at least, of the emotion that lies behind those words. Responding empathically is a way of showing your clients that you understand something of their inner or subjective worlds and what it means to be them.

For example, a client says, 'I don't know what I feel towards my father. There are so many layers of feeling, some really deep, but one minute I seem to hate him, and the next to love him. I wish I could sort out what my real feelings are.'

If the counsellor responds 'You just don't know what you feel', this would be accurate in part, but not very empathic.

If the counsellor responds 'There are so many mixed feelings, you get really confused. But you would like to get clear what are the real and deep feelings you know are there somewhere,' this would be more empathic because it responds both to the other person's confusion, and to their desire for clarity.

Barrett-Lennard (1993) suggests several 'channels' for empathy: sensitive restatement, metaphor and imagery (both as reflections and when they form spontaneously and intuitively in the counsellor), some actions, and sometimes a question 'pops forward', which 'could not be asked – would not occur – without an empathic awareness of the others' experiencing' (p.8). (See also Mearns and Thorne, 1988; Merry and Lusty, 1993; Merry, 1995.)

Truax and Carkhuff (1967) developed an eight-point scale to estimate the level of empathy present in an interaction between client and counsellor, and Mearns and Thorne (1988) offer a simplified four-point scale:

Level 0: responses show no understanding of feelings being expressed by the client. Responses may also be irrelevant, hurtful, judgemental, etc.

Level 1: responses show some limited understanding of feelings most clearly expressed or closest to the surface. Sometimes called 'subtractive empathy' because the responses miss or lose something of the feelings as expressed.

Level 2: responses show understanding and acceptance of feelings and thoughts: sometimes called 'accurate empathy'.

Level 3: responses show understanding of deeper feelings just beyond those of which the client is immediately aware.

What becomes clear from most of the writing on empathy is that it is best not regarded as a skill or technique. Being able to paraphrase accurately, for example, is not the same thing as experiencing empathic understanding, though it is a useful skill in communicating the empathy you experience. Rogers in particular was keen that empathic understanding be regarded as a valued 'way of being' with clients (and others) rather than as a technique.

Levenson and Ruef (1992) discuss definitions and measures of empathy, emphasising the inadequacies of self-report measures and discussing their provocative finding of a relationship between 'shared physiology' (i.e. autonomic response) in two people and accurate judgement of 'negative' emotions in one of them by the other. Duan and Hill's (1996) review of research on empathy concludes that the 'lack of specification and organization of different views of empathy has led to theoretical confusion, methodological difficulties, inconsistent findings, and neglected areas of research' (p.269). One of the major problems has been adequate measurement (see Marangoni *et al.*, 1995 for an incisive review).

Empathy: a second example

The client says: 'When I took my new boyfriend home for the first time, it was quite a big risk for me. I thought about it for ages, but I thought I'd give my Mum the benefit of the doubt, but she went absolutely spare. I was so embarrassed, and I thought, why is she doing this? This is a big mistake. She doesn't trust me to know my own mind at all. I was furious.'

Response 1: 'mmhmm'

Response 2: 'I guess you felt hurt and discounted after plucking up the courage to do this. It sounds like you gave it a chance, but got really badly let down, and you're just so very angry with her.'

Response 3: 'How did your father take it?'

Response 4: 'Has your mother always been like this with you?'

Response 5: 'You thought about it for a bit, but you took him home anyway. Your Mum was upset about it, and this annoyed you.'

Response 6: 'Is this the same kind of thing as before? Like when you were telling me that your mother always disapproved of your friends at school?'

Response 1 has been wrongly described as 'empathic, showing understanding, and that I was with my client and listening'. It is *not* empathic.

Responses like 2 are by far the most empathic.

Responses like 3 have been described as 'an open question or probe inviting my client to explore the situation further', but are not empathic.

Responses like 4 have been described as 'trying to look for patterns', and are not empathic.

Responses like 5 (which has some content accuracy, but little empathy) have been described as 'empathic', with no awareness that the emotions have been diluted from 'absolutely spare' to 'upset' and from 'furious' to 'annoyed'.

Responses like 6 have been described as 'making links with things from the client's past which she has already mentioned', and again are not empathic.

ENDINGS

(*See also*: Contract, negotiating a, Duration)

Ending counselling with each client can be by default, as frequently happens, with the client failing to turn up or leaving a message about not wanting to continue, or, more satisfying from the counsellor's point of view, by design. You may negotiate at the start how long counselling will last and even specify the ending date. More usually, however, the idea of ending will be put forward by you or your client when it feels appropriate and negotiated at that time.

Peake *et al.* (1988) suggest that counsellors may find it helpful to reflect on three questions about ending, concerned with explicitness, flexibility and the client's needs.

1. **How explicit is the issue of ending?** Should you make use of the fact that counselling will end or give way to the temptation to let it pass without any mention, inwardly promising to deal with it when it happens? Knowing that 'the end is near' can enhance motivation; it helps some clients to concentrate their efforts on making the best use of the time available. Similarly, it can work against the procrastination and resistance to change that can

accompany a sense of counselling as open-ended and everlasting. The loss, whether it is real or symbolic, embodied in ending the counselling relationship can be a very potent force for positive change.

If you use ending to try to stimulate change the next question is when to raise it. At the beginning, many counsellors will have discussed client expectations of how long it may take and there may be at least some implicit understanding that it will be a matter of so many sessions or so many weeks, months or years. After that, unless there is an explicit time-limited contract, it would probably be premature to raise the issue until counselling is firmly under way and some real sense of progress has been achieved. In brief counselling some counsellors find it useful to remind clients during each session how many sessions have gone and how many remain.

2. **How rigid is the decision about ending?** There are several related questions here. Should counselling finish on the agreed date, or can it be allowed to continue if the client wants it to do so? How flexible should a counsellor be about ending and what are the ramifications? What circumstances justify an extension? The answers to these questions depend on the nature of the counselling goals and of your philosophy and theoretical model.

Some counsellors favour a staggered ending, increasing the time between sessions towards the end of a contract. This seems an especially useful way to work towards ending with a client you have seen for a long time Another option is to offer a follow-up session some three to six months after the counselling has ended. This can help to consolidate progress made.

3. **What are the needs of your client around ending?** Many clients experience little if any difficulty, seeing the end of counselling as an inevitable and natural event. This may be most likely when the counselling is relatively short term, where there isn't a strong attachment, or where the focus is on problem management. However, other clients find ending very difficult. They feel they won't be able to cope without the counsellor, and ending may stimulate earlier painful experiences of loss and separation. You may need to help these clients cope with ending by talking through their existential or developmental needs, acknowledging their achievements and resources, and deciding on particular strategies.

Some practical suggestions for endings

The aims of spending some time on ending are to help clients to sustain any changes they have made and to look forward to a new beginning. The following questions provide a flexible framework:

1. **How does the client feel about ending?** You might need to encourage clients to talk about ending. Sometimes it is helpful to reassure clients that ending can produce feelings of loss and that this is a normal and natural part of the process.

2. **What has been achieved?** The intention here is to consolidate learning by

examining the initial goals and the changes that have occurred. Further changes may be anticipated and it may be appropriate to review and celebrate the client's strengths and achievements.

3. **How has it been achieved?** This question is concerned with helping your clients identify the ways in which they have contributed to or are responsible for, what has been achieved and the positive aspects of their relationship with you. The client's account of what has happened is the best predictor of whether changes will last; if clients attribute responsibility for any gains to the counsellor they might find it difficult to sustain and build on any useful changes beyond the ending (Peake *et al.*, 1988, p.227).

4. **What still needs to be achieved?** This question is about identifying unmet goals, relative weaknesses and aspects clients feel they still want to develop. Many counsellors believe that a lot of learning and change goes on not only between counselling sessions but after counselling has ended. It is useful here to examine your client's available resources and support network and other options for maintaining and developing the gains achieved in counselling.

5. **What might happen in the future?** You may wish to help your clients look positively towards the future, while not ignoring the possibility that problems or symptoms could return. It may also be appropriate to anticipate stresses and 'rough spots', and ways of coping, or trying to cope, with them. Here it can be helpful to identify indications of the need to start counselling again. Typically people go in and out of counselling rather than having only one continuous period. A good ending makes it more likely that clients have positive feelings about this prospect rather than feeling like a failure or seeing counselling as a waste of time.

6. **What has this counselling relationship been like?** The intention here is to help clients evaluate helpful and difficult aspects. It may also provide you with valuable feedback on your approach.

The framework outlined above focuses on the client. You may also wish to reflect on your own experience, to review what has been achieved and how, and to work through your own reactions to an ending.

ETHICAL DILEMMAS

(*See also*: Boundaries, Codes of ethics)

Bond (1993a), as part of his review of ethical issues in counselling, suggests a six-step process for resolving, or at least clarifying, dilemmas:

1. Describe the ethical problem or dilemma briefly.

2. Ask whose dilemma it is. Consider in what way it is a problem for the client, counsellor or for other people.

3. Consider all available ethical principles and guidelines. Use codes of ethics,

consider general ethical principles such as respect for autonomy, non-maleficence (the principle of causing least harm), beneficence (achieving greatest good) and justice, and possibly seek legal advice.

4. Identify all possible courses of action and their probable consequences.

5. Select the best course of action. Negotiate with the client if there is joint responsibility.

6. Evaluate the outcome.

For useful examples and discussion, see Bond (1993a, pp.190–201; 1996).

ETHNIC ORIGIN

See: Multiculturalism, Multicultural counselling

EUROPEAN ASSOCIATION FOR COUNSELLING (EAC)

(*See also*: British Association for Counselling)

The European Association for Counselling (EAC) was registered in June 1993. Its aim is 'to develop an interactive view of counselling which approaches in a holistic way the special cultural, economic and emotional issues facing inhabitants in Europe.' Since the formation of EAC, other European countries have started to form national associations for counselling which, like the BAC, support the EAC.

The BAC has a European Working Party to represent the interests of BAC members in European events. The European Association for Psychotherapy, based in Vienna, and founded in 1991, is working with EAC. For more information, see van Deurzen Smith (1992).

The EAC can be contacted though The British Association for Counselling.

EVALUATION

(*See also*: Effectiveness of brief counselling, Feedback from clients to counsellor)

Evaluation can be either formal or informal. A counsellor may arrange an informal verbal review with a client to evaluate progress and discuss whether the counsellor is meeting the needs of the client. For example, a series of simple questions such as 'Where did you feel you were when you started counselling?', 'Where are you now?' and 'Where would you like to be in terms of the work still outstanding?' may be enough to stimulate a useful evaluation.

Within the growing field of workplace counselling many Employee Assistance Programmes insist on a system for evaluating and auditing the counselling service (Megranahan, 1997). There is increasing pressure for services to evaluate practice (Mellor-Clark and Barkham, 1996). Evaluation differs from research in that its

CLIENT SATISFACTION QUESTIONNAIRE

Your views are very important in helping monitor the quality of the counselling work offered. Please return this questionnaire in the s.a.e. provided. As with your counselling work, any information you provide will be treated as confidential.

Using a scale of 0–8 (0 = very poor, 8 = excellent) please rate the following.

Pre-counselling contact:

1. How well was your initial enquiry dealt with?
   0   1   2   3   4   5   6   7   8

2. How useful did you find the client information sent to you?
   0   1   2   3   4   5   6   7   8

The counselling environment:

1. How would you rate the counselling facilities offered?
   0   1   2   3   4   5   6   7   8

The counsellor:

1. How helpful did you find your counsellor?
   0   1   2   3   4   5   6   7   8

2 What did you like most about your counsellor?

_____

_____

_____

3. Was there anything your counsellor could have done differently that would have been helpful?

_____

_____

_____

Your progress:

Using the rating scale 0–8 (0 = 'feeling really awful', 8 = 'feeling really good') please rate the following.

1. At the beginning of your counselling how would you have rated yourself?
   0   1   2   3   4   5   6   7   8

2. After the counselling how would you rate yourself?
   0   1   2   3   4   5   6   7   8

3. What did you find most helpful about the counselling offered to you?

_____

_____

_____

Thank you for taking the time to complete this questionnaire.

Figure 1

Example client evaluation form

primary purpose is to assist decision making and is usually written up for local consumption. In addition, evaluation may prove a useful tool for helping counsellors consider further their individual training needs and meet existing ethical requirements for continued professional development as outlined by professional bodies such as the BPS, BAC and BABCP.

An agency may require a client to complete a diagnostic questionnaire such as the Beck Depression Inventory (Beck and Freeman, 1990) before and after counselling, comparing results as a way of measuring outcome. With the advent of National Vocational Qualifications (NVQs) it is likely to become more important that counsellors seeking validation through this scheme provide written evidence of client evaluation perhaps by using a simple evaluation form for the client to complete at the termination of counselling. An example of an evaluation form is shown in Figure 1.

EXERCISE

See: Physical activity

EXERCISES/ACTIVITIES

See: Experiments, by clients

EXPECTATIONS, CLIENTS'

(*See also*: Effectiveness, Common factors, Contract, negotiating a, Information giving)

Clients do not usually enter counselling in complete ignorance of what to expect, or of how counselling might help them. Some clients, however, have unreasonable or mistaken ideas about counselling. For example, they expect to be given helpful advice or to be told how to overcome their problems. Others expect to *have* to talk about childhood memories, or to lie on a couch and be 'analysed' (see McLeod, 1990, for a review of research on clients' experience of counselling and their expectations). If you do an assessment interview or contract-setting interview you will be able to explore these expectations, and be clear with your clients what is expected of them, and what they can reasonably expect of you. Launching straight into counselling without exploring expectations can store up problems for later, particularly when clients feel disappointed or let down because they had unrealistic expectations to start with.

Reasonable (and common) expectations of clients include: confidentiality, the chance to be listened to, the possibility that painful memories or feelings may be stirred up, the probability that counselling will have a positive effect on their lives, that they will feel differently after counselling than they did before it, and that they will gain fresh insights and perspectives on themselves and their lives.

Unrealistic expectations include: instant 'results', the solving of financial or social problems such as bad housing or unemployment, that they can change other people's behaviour, that the past can somehow be changed or that they will supply the problems and you will supply the solutions. People whose expectations are low or non-existent very rarely enter counselling voluntarily, and if they do they tend to leave early. Clients with very high expectations may be disappointed when changes don't happen overnight, and may also leave counselling early. Other clients need time to adjust their expectations gradually; for them the process of induction is partly about learning what is realistic.

The degree of faith or belief the client has in the effectiveness of counselling is likely to influence how effective the counselling will actually be. The fact that counselling exists at all suggests that people do believe that change is both possible and desirable, and that it can be accomplished through a relationship with a skilled and trained counsellor. This expectation is supported by research (see entry on effectiveness), and therefore it is a matter of being optimistic about the possibilities without exaggerating them.

EXPERIMENTS, BY CLIENTS

(*See also*: Challenge, Counselling, Homework, Information giving, Non-verbal communication)

The idea of inviting clients to try an experiment is a common strategy in co-counselling, Gestalt and some forms of behavioural counselling. For example, the Gestalt two-chair technique, which can seem a very strange thing to offer to clients, can be introduced in this way. 'There seem to be two parts of you arguing here, and going round and round, so that you feel exhausted and helpless ... I'd like to suggest a kind of experiment to try and clarify the two sides. It means you sitting in this chair when you're arguing one way and in this chair for the other side. Would that be OK?'

If an experiment is approached in this way – as an invitation to try something and see what happens – clients can reject the idea more easily. If they do, it may be useful to talk about what it is that they find difficult. The word 'experiment' has the drawback of sounding cold to some people, but it also suggests trying something out. 'Exercise' is sometimes accepted more readily.

Experiments can take place during counselling as well as between sessions – for instance, you might invite the client to pay attention to the way their arms are folded across their stomach, and to stay in that position, then perhaps to pull their arms in tighter and talk about how that feels. Alternatively, you might invite them to put their arms down by their sides and to talk about the difference. As an experiment outside the counselling session, you might invite your client to try to count to ten before saying anything the next time a particular situation occurs and to discuss whether the client was able to do it, and what it felt like, in the next session. The beauty of an experiment is that it is just that – an experiment. If it is introduced sensitively it can't go wrong, and it can help to change a client's familiar and distressing pattern of behaviour.

However, inviting a client to try an experiment is very different from a counsellor experimenting on a client. We regard this as unethical and potentially harmful. As a general rule, we strongly advise that you offer to clients only those experiments that have a clear purpose, and that you have experienced as a client or at least tried out in controlled training situations with colleagues.

FEEDBACK FROM CLIENTS TO COUNSELLOR

(*See also*: Challenge, Clients who don't come back, Drama triangle, Endings, Evaluation, Immediacy)

It is important that you remain open to feedback from your clients, to help you check the extent to which you are enabling them to move towards more fulfilling or effective ways of living. In counselling sessions you will get feedback from your clients concerning the extent to which they feel understood and valued, both indirectly through comments like 'Yes, that is how things feel at the moment', and directly – what clients actually tell you about their experience of you. Some counsellors invite feedback as part of regular review sessions and in the final evaluation session.

Whether or not the client continues to attend counselling with you is a form of feedback. It is possible, however, for clients to continue with counselling even though they don't seem to be deriving any benefit from it, or for clients to drop out for their own reasons, quite separate from the counselling or you. If you have a client who is often late, or often wishes to leave early, or who misses sessions regularly he or she could be making an indirect statement about the counselling itself. It is usually helpful (and clear) to find a way of bringing this indirect form of communication out into the open, perhaps by sharing your feelings of concern about it.

The things clients say about their lives in general may contain important indirect feedback for you as a counsellor. For instance, someone who reports having a wider circle of friends and acquaintances than before may be providing some positive feedback. Likewise, someone who reports more isolation from others may be providing useful feedback. Related forms of feedback are, for example, how far your clients are able to speak about themselves and their feelings more directly than before, how far your clients seem to be less dependent on other people for their sense of self-esteem and how far your clients are becoming more proactive and 'in charge' of their lives. It is helpful to become sensitive to these kinds of 'clues' about how your client is making use of counselling and, where appropriate, to incorporate them into the relationship you have with your client. However, it is important to interpret these clues cautiously; they may say more about the client or the client's need for a particular response from you than about you.

FEELINGS

(*See also*: Emotions, Psychological type, Self-awareness, Support groups, peer, Values)

Nichols and Jenkinson (1991) suggest that a feeling is more complicated than experiencing emotion. They define feeling as 'the current physiological and psychological stance of the person' and the general 'atmosphere' of your body – relaxed or fidgety, calm or restless (p.45). 'Feeling' may also refer to a way of making decisions, one which is based on values. Rogers' term 'organismic valuing process' has a similar meaning. Unfortunately, in practice, the terms 'feeling' and 'emotion' will probably continue to be used by different people in different ways, as will 'think', 'intuition', 'sense', and 'experience'.

FEES

(*See also*: Boundaries, Business, Contract, negotiating a, Information giving)

Apart from inviting clients to pay a donation – common practice in some agencies – there are three main ways of setting fees: (1) a fixed fee per session, (2) negotiating a lower fee in certain circumstances, (3) a sliding scale, negotiating with each client an agreed point on that scale (for example a 50-minute counselling session for 1/40 of the client's income per week). In addition, some counsellors offer the initial interview free of charge, and part of this interview is concerned with agreeing fees. An underlying principle which may appeal is that neither you nor your client feels exploited.

Options for payment are at the beginning or end of each session, in advance for a fixed number of sessions, or by invoice every month or so. If you choose the first option, you are likely to lose the fee for a missed session. If you choose the second option you need to discuss with your clients the consequences of missing sessions. A good way forward is to establish with your clients a minimum period of notice for missing sessions, after which the fee will not be refunded or carried over. Some counsellors ask for a set reduced fee for cancelled sessions. The same period of notice – typically not less than 24 hours – can apply to the counsellor postponing a session. As a general guide, fees in 1998 ranged from £10–40 per session, with an average fee of £20–25. Not many counsellors in private practice can afford to have more than one or two clients at the lower end of this scale. Bartering (of services or goods) may be an attractive possibility, though maintaining boundaries is the primary consideration. Moreover, if your 'income' in this form is regular and can be defined by the Inland Revenue as coming from a business, then you may still be liable to tax on the monetary equivalent.

The Inland Revenue require accurate records of all payments made to you, and of all expenses incurred as a result of your practice. You may wish to consult an accountant about what expenditure can be offset against tax.

FINDING CLIENTS

See: Advertising, Marketing

FIRST IMPRESSIONS

(*See also*: Furniture, Intuition, Non-verbal communication, Self-awareness, Transference)

First impressions can have a disproportionate power. We tend to form them very quickly and almost automatically, then interpret later information in terms of these impressions – i.e. to treat our first impression as accurate and any later information that conflicts with it as untypical. This is likely to lead to bias; accurate judgements are more likely if equal weight is given to equally important pieces of information, whether they come first or later. Good counsellors do this anyway: treating impressions (which are probably inevitable) as hypotheses but being ready to revise them. Intuitions and first impressions are thus neither ignored nor believed, but checked.

Useful strategies for being more accurate (Bayne, 1995a) are:

- Look for patterns, over time and across situations.
- Therefore, treat first impressions as hypotheses.
- Look for evidence against your first impression, as well as for it.
- Take situation into account (some situations, such as selection interviews or first dates, tend to constrain behaviour much more than others).

Compelling first impressions are particularly likely to be wrong, because there hasn't been time to gather enough evidence and because their strength must come from something in you. Co-counselling refers to 'restimulations' and suggests a procedure for dealing with them. A version of this is given below:

1. Ask yourself 'Who does this client remind me of?' (It could be an actual person or a stereotype, e.g. a teacher.)
2. In what ways? (Be as specific as possible and persistent: repeat the question until all the possibilities seem exhausted.)
3. What do I want to say to this person? (What haven't I said that I want to?)
4. In what ways is this client *not* like this other person? (Again, repeat the question as often as necessary and be persistent.)

Sometimes, of course, a client may be restimulated by you, and you can ask them the set of questions above.

Similarity is the strongest general source of bias in first (and later) impressions. We tend to like people who are like ourselves. Physical attractiveness is also potent: we tend to believe that 'what is beautiful is good'. For discussions of research on forming impressions, see Aronson (1999) and Bayne (1995a).

FIRST SESSION

See: Assessment, Beginnings, Clients who don't come back, Contract, negotiating a, Contraindications for brief counselling, Defining counselling to clients, Contract, negotiating a, Difficulties in being a client, Expectations, clients', Fees, First impressions, Furniture, History taking, Information giving, Multicultural counselling, Referral, Smoking

FOCUS

See: Counselling, Summaries and 'moving interviews forward'

FORCE-FIELD ANALYSIS

(*See also*: Counselling, Journal, writing a)

Force-field analysis is a generic technique for helping clients clarify a problem or decision (e.g. Egan, 1990). Part of its value lies in actually writing things out, externalising them instead of churning them around in your head. Each arrow in Figure 2 represents either an obstacle or a positive force. Your client first explores each one and then, if appropriate, chooses some form of action. Suppose the problem is whether to get married or not, and one of the obstacles is your client's concept of marriage; in particular an underlying irrational belief about marriage. The action could be for him or her to replace the belief or to negotiate with the intended partner, or both – or the obstacle may just become unimportant as your client explores it.

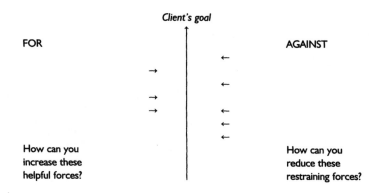

Figure 2

Force-field analysis

In more detail, the procedure is to work through the following steps:

1. First state the goal – what the client wants to achieve, avoiding either/or goals.

2. Generate a list of obstacles or forces against achieving the goal and a list of forces that contribute towards achieving it. The reasons for the client wanting to achieve the goal may not always be a positive force. Be aware of the impact of each force. Not every positive force will have a corresponding negative force. It is important not to censor at this stage, but record all ideas as they come.

3. Analyse the forces. Perhaps circle significant forces – those that are real and not assumed. Inadequate information could make this difficult and more information may be needed. The forces on each side could be graded.

4. Identify ways to maximise the positive forces and minimise the forces against achieving the goal. Focus on the most significant forces. Again, be specific and relate action to particular forces. Make a note of significant forces for which no action is possible.

5. Assess the feasibility of the stated goal. Does the action substantially offset the obstacles? Overall, do the positive forces outweigh the obstacles? If so, go ahead. If not:

6. Forget or adapt the goal. The goal might be too general and not reflect the real problem. It may also contain more than one goal; if so, try to break it down further.

In force-field analysis there is a 'battle' between restraining forces, which might include guilt, irrational beliefs and practical problems on one 'side' and positive forces, say a strong desire, a sense that things could be much better, some opportunities, on the other. Each force should be explored and could lead to workable action to either increase the positive forces or decrease the restraining ones.

FRAME OF REFERENCE

(*See also*: Empathy)

'Frame of reference' is another way of expressing the idea of empathy. To stay within the client's frame of reference is to be empathic in a sustained way. An accurate paraphrase is, by definition, in the client's frame of reference. Conversely, in your own frame of reference, you see the client from your own viewpoint – e.g. 'It doesn't look that bad to me', or 'I don't think you're overweight.'

FRAMEWORKS

(*See also*: Counselling, Theories)

Frameworks are working maps, designed to help counsellors make sense of, or offer plausible explanations for, aspects of clients, counselling and themselves.

They therefore have a similar purpose to theories and models, and indeed the three terms often seem to be used interchangeably. Some people seem to be drawn to very simple frameworks, which they may then complicate when trying to understand a person or a process; others seem to be drawn to initial complexity, from which they then select to clarify or 'get hold of' particular instances. An example of a simple framework is 'support and challenge'. You can ask during a counselling session (or later) 'At this point am I supporting or challenging, and which do I want to be doing? And why?' A simple framework can quickly lead to quite complex considerations.

FREEWRITING

(*See also*: Assertiveness, Journal, writing a, Self-awareness, Stress, Writing)

Freewriting (Elbow, 1973, 1997) is a way of exploring inner experience. It is also a technique for tackling writer's 'block'. There are three steps in the following variation:

1. Write *without stopping* for several minutes (e.g. 10) either on a particular subject or on anything that comes to mind. If you are stuck, write something about that – e.g. 'I'm stuck' or 'I'm fed up with this. It's stupid' – again and again if that's what comes to mind. Write anything, but keep writing.
2. Underline significant/useful bits.
3. Freewrite about them.

Freewriting thus replaces 'Think clearly and then write' with 'Write to find out what you mean, feel and want.' Essentially, writing and editing are separated by lots of writing and lots of discarding.

If you use a word processor, Elbow (1997) suggests turning the screen down so that you cannot see your words. For some people the effect is to focus on their thoughts rather than on the sometimes off-putting words. Elbow calls this 'invisible writing'.

Freewriting can also be a group activity. In one kind of group, members write for themselves about their reaction to something for five minutes, then discuss their reactions in pairs, or in the whole group, revealing as much or as little of their freewriting as they choose (Murray, 1997, 1998). This method is rated as particularly enjoyable, and could easily be used in personal development and supervision groups.

FREQUENCY OF SESSIONS

(*See also*: Contract, negotiating a, Contraindications for brief counselling, Duration, Length of sessions)

In psychoanalysis, it is not unusual to see the same client three times a week or more, but most counsellors see clients only once a week. Once a week seems to be acceptable to most people (it is convenient and not too costly) but there is no real reason why it should be a 'golden rule'. For example, if a client is in a deeply anxious or very vulnerable state, it can help to meet more often than once a week, though most counsellors would see such a contract as temporary. It is probably better to have more frequent meetings in the early stages, and then to settle on once-weekly meetings later on, rather than the other way round.

After a while, some clients prefer to meet once a fortnight if they feel they have made a lot of progress and only need support now to consolidate the changes they feel they have made. Once a month may be too infrequent, and if a client asks for this we advise you to check out the reasons, and perhaps question whether they should leave counselling entirely. Monthly meetings may tend to become reports on what has happened since you last met, which is unlikely to be useful. A compromise is to have a batch of weekly meetings, then a break of two or three months, followed by weekly meetings if necessary.

FRIENDSHIP/MAKING FRIENDS WITH CLIENTS

(*See also*: Boundaries, Sexual attraction)

Counselling is a formal relationship and its boundaries and limitations need to be respected and maintained. This is helpful and reassuring to both counsellors and clients. Sometimes clients do ask for a relationship outside counselling, but it is not ethical to allow this whilst counselling is continuing. You can explain that it is not possible within your professional code of ethics and practice and that you can be of more help if the counselling relationship remains protected and uncomplicated by outside situations. The BAC advise that any changes in the relationship must be discussed in supervision and take into account whether or not the issues and power dynamics present during counselling have been resolved (British Association for Counselling, 1998, B.5.3.)

Once the counselling relationship is over there are still problems with becoming socially involved with clients, at least until some time has elapsed. This does not have to be seen by your client as rejection, but rather as a way of ensuring that you are available to help in the future, which might be impossible if you have become close. If you do become friends with an ex-client, and this does sometimes happen, you are no longer available as that person's counsellor. Some organisations and codes of ethics prohibit social contact with all former clients.

FURNITURE

(*See also*: Drinks/refreshments, Non-verbal communication, Power, Tape-recording)

Your furniture contributes to your clients' initial impression of you. If the impression is a negative one, you must be correspondingly more effective to compensate. In part, your choice of furniture depends on your approach to counselling (e.g. couch or not, cushions or not), but there are some general guidelines. If you take the view that the disparity in power between counsellor and client should be reduced as much as possible then chairs and seating positions should be equal. Across the corner of a desk is the position sometimes used, though this is not equal: the counsellor, seated in front of the desk, can write on it more easily. Most counsellors prefer no desk.

Perhaps the most practical suggestions are to role-play being a client in your own room, and to seek the views of colleagues and perhaps clients (near or at the end of their time with you). Some personal things in the room and an intermediate degree of tidiness seem to be interpreted by most people as welcoming, but some counsellors prefer a plain room with no distracting objects. The balance sought may best be seen as one between deterring or inhibiting clients – for example, family photos may discourage some clients – and being consistent with yourself and therefore more at ease.

GENDER ISSUES

See: Multiculturalism

GENUINENESS

See: Congruence

GOOD COUNSELLORS

(See also: Congruence, Empathy, NVQs, Psychological type, Respect)

Ideas about 'good counsellors' are usually expressed in terms of the personal qualities of the counsellor, although, from the client's point of view, a good counsellor is one they like and feel comfortable with. Perhaps the most likely characteristics of good counsellors are the 'core qualities' emphasised in client or person-centred counselling: empathy, acceptance and genuineness. Brenner (1982) suggested five qualities: empathy, composure, readiness to discuss everything ('Open, precise communication about each topic that the client introduces – directly or indirectly – is the heart and soul of successful psychotherapy and counselling' (p.7)), encouragement, or belief in the client's potential to function more fully, and purposefulness. Reddy (1987) also recognises the core qualities and suggests others but adds, tartly, that 'Taken together these qualities seem more like a preparation for sainthood than for a job' (p. 43) and that a particularly necessary quality is 'freedom from the need for perfection' (p.44). On assessing counsellors' competence, see Wheeler (1996) and McLeod (1996a).

GROUP COUNSELLING

(*See also*: Assertiveness, Referral, Self-awareness, Teams, multidisciplinary)

This is a very broad term, covering all types of counselling for more than two people. There are many different ways of running groups, but the idea with most of them is that the members listen to, support and challenge each other. Members thus learn to be assertive and to experience how other people see them. The leader of the group may facilitate in a variety of ways: some make process comments, others facilitate interactions between the members. Some clients find it useful to move from individual to group counselling. Corey and Corey (1992), Whitaker (1985) and Yalom (1986) have written major texts on group counselling.

HIDDEN AGENDAS

(*See also*: Collusion, Empathy, Immediacy, Manipulation)

'Hidden agenda' is the term used when somebody has a concealed purpose, of which they may or may not be aware. For example, someone might come for counselling with a hidden agenda of just completing a required number of sessions without really looking at themselves, or someone in a group might be there because they are attracted to someone else in the group and are not interested in the group's overt agenda.

Hidden agendas can be quite disruptive, as it usually soon becomes apparent that things are not as they seem. Something is not right, but the reason can be hard to discover. Empathy or immediacy may be the best ways of sorting out the impasse.

HISTORY TAKING

(*See also*: Assessment, Working alliance)

A client's history is a systematic collection of facts about the client's past and current life. Some counsellors do not take any form of client history as they feel not only that much of the information will be irrelevant but also that it may simulate the medical model in which clients, after responding to requests for information, may expect a diagnosis and a solution to their problem. Perhaps a more important objection is that the whole process of history taking can set up a relationship pattern which interferes with establishing an effective working alliance with the client. Attitudes vary with theoretical approach. For example, Adlerian counsellors may conduct a fairly long (i.e. over more than one or two sessions) lifestyle assessment inventory that is used for evaluation and diagnostic purposes (Dinkmeyer, 1985). This information, however, is gathered after an initial rapport has been established.

When an intake interview, sometimes called an initial assessment interview, is carried out, it is viewed as primarily informational rather than therapeutic. For this reason, and/or because it is sometimes thought that an experienced or more senior person should be responsible for initial assessment and subsequent allocation to the most appropriate counsellor, the intake interview can be conducted by someone other than the counsellor who will work with the client.

The purpose of a client history is to gather information about the client's background, especially as it may relate to current problems. A clinical history is not sought as an end in itself or because the counsellor will use it to structure the counselling or explore and focus on the client's history. Rather, it is used as part of the overall assessment process that may help the counsellor to understand the client's presenting problem. The assumption is that current problems are precipitated and maintained by events and experiences in the client's history.

Some counsellors prefer to collect some or all of the information in a brief questionnaire that is completed by the client. Others ask clients to write autobiographies, keep personal journals, write poetry or draw lifeline diagrams (time graphs in which key life points are marked along a time continuum), all of which can be used to supplement interview data.

Possible content and sequence

(*See also:* Core conditions, Non-verbal communication, Psychodiagnosis, Referral, Working alliance)

Various kinds of information can be obtained during a more formal history taking (Cormier and Cormier, 1991):

1. **Identification:** name, address, telephone numbers, age, sex, ethnic origin/ culture, marital status, occupation.

2. **General appearance.**

3. **Presenting problem(s):** first occurrence, frequency, concurrent events, associated thoughts, feelings and behaviours, precipitating events, situations or people, previous ways of dealing with the problem, why counselling at present time.

4. **Previous counselling/psychiatric help:** type, length, place of treatment, outcomes or reason for termination, hospitalisation and/or drugs for psychological problems.

5. **Education/work:** academic progress/attainment, relationships with peers/ staff, types and lengths of jobs, reasons for termination or change, further training, relationships with colleagues, most/least stressful and enjoyable aspects, current level of job satisfaction.

6. **Health:** childhood diseases, illnesses, treatment received, current health-related problems, allergies, family health problems, sleep, eating and exercise patterns, typical diet, current medications.

7. **Social/developmental:** current lifestyle, economic situation, contact with people, leisure interests, religious affiliation, values, priorities and beliefs, earliest recollections, significant chronological events during main developmental stages.

8. **Family, marital and sexual:**
   - Details of mother, father and siblings, quality of relationships, joint activities, parental rewards and punishments, family psychiatric history.
   - Dating, engagement/marital/partnership history – reasons for termination.
   - Current relationship and sources of satisfaction/stress, number and age of children.
   - Previous and first sexual experience, sexual orientation, present sexual activity, frequency of intercourse, masturbation, current concerns/ issues about sex.
9. **Communication style:** verbal and non-verbal behaviour (voice, eye contact, body movements, personal space).
10. **Diagnostic classification:** DSM-IV summary.

The last two categories are usually completed by the counsellor after the initial assessment or intake interview.

The sequence in which this information is obtained in the interview is important. Generally, the interviewer begins with the least threatening topics and leaves the more sensitive areas until nearer the end of the session when there is likely to be a greater degree of rapport. The nature of the presenting problem will determine the extent and depth to which each area is covered with each client.

HOLIDAYS

We suggest giving your clients as much notice of your holidays as you reasonably can, being clear about how long you will be away, and what arrangements need to be made for 're-entry' into counselling when you get back. If you will be away for long, your clients may like you to arrange for them to see a colleague meanwhile. A phone number where they can contact someone else is also helpful.

HOMEWORK

(*See also*: Books, self-help, Brainstorming, Experiments by clients, Imagery, Journal, writing a, Life space diagram, Psychological type, Thoughts)

The term homework refers to specific activities clients undertake to complete between counselling sessions. Some counsellors prefer to call these activities tasks, assignments, practice or work between sessions (Dryden and Feltham, 1992). Homework is an integral feature of cognitive behavioural approaches to counselling and in particular the brief therapies. It is not, however, exclusive to these approaches, and can encourage clients to recognise their own ability to initiate change and to make connections between counselling and the rest of their lives. Trying out new behaviours may also consolidate learning and reinforce commitment to change. The various types of homework are listed below:

- **Reading:** the client may be invited to read about some aspect of counselling theory or about someone else's experience and ways of dealing with their problem.
- **Writing:** this may be anything, from a very simple account of what the client wants from counselling, or a journal-style description of a particular situation or experience, to a full life story. Writing may also take the form of lists: of things to do, of issues or problems, of things the client is afraid of or anxious about. Making lists may also be a way of generating ideas or brainstorming ways of coping more effectively with a problem. Another form of writing is a letter to or from a real or imagined person. A letter to a real person is not usually sent to that person, but used as a vehicle for exploration or catharsis. Other forms of writing can be found in Rainer (1978).
- **Diagrams:** clients might prepare life space diagrams or genograms.
- **Questionnaires:** these might include self-descriptive checklists, evaluation questionnaires, or inventories designed to elicit specific information, e.g. psychological type, anxiety or depression inventories.
- **Recording:** this is a written form of monitoring the occurrence of particular situations, feelings or behaviours. It may be done by keeping a diary or daily log.
- **Practical exercises:** these may involve the client trying out a new or different activity or behaviour, such as some kind of physical exercise, being more assertive in a particular way, initiating a dialogue with a particular person or implementing a rehearsed action to interrupt negative self-talk or obsessive behaviour. It may also involve the use of relaxation exercises.
- **Creative exercises:** these may involve writing short poems, drawing or painting pictures or collages of special significance to the client. They are brought to a session and explored with the counsellor. Some clients may be able to use guided imagery and visualisation rehearsed during the session.

Guidelines

The following guidelines are adapted from Dryden and Feltham (1992, pp.114–34):

- Explain the rationale behind any task.
- Avoid appearing to 'set homework': negotiate, and encourage the client to offer alternative ideas and modifications.
- Make sure that the task relates directly to the client's problem.
- Listen for and challenge any ambivalence and encourage commitment.
- Take the client's ability and circumstances into account.
- Discuss when, where and how the client will attempt the task.

- Establish with the client the criteria for evaluating the outcome.
- Explore any possible obstacles.
- Help clients to prepare by mentally rehearsing what they are going to do.
- Emphasise that whether clients feel they do it well or badly or don't actually do it at all, something valuable is likely to be gained from discussing their experience.
- Before the end of the session check that clients really do understand what to do and why they are doing it.

At the next session:

- It is essential to follow-up the task.
- Discuss what has happened.
- Discuss any reasons for not attempting the task.
- Explore what happened if the task was attempted, but not completed.
- Invite clients to take increasing responsibility for setting their own tasks.

Dryden and Feltham also advise that counsellors might well learn how to help clients with homework assignments by first setting some for themselves!

HOOKED

(*See also*: Drama triangle, Emotions, Patterns, Process, Transference)

This rather jargonistic term is used in an interactive sense when the 'process' of one person catches – or hooks into – the 'process' of another person. This is most clearly seen in the drama triangle, or in very emotional interactions when the emotion aroused seems out of proportion to the incident. It is also sustained in a compulsive way. For example, if someone is in a victim role others try to do too much for them or get angry with them, thus getting 'hooked' into their process. If you avoid being hooked, you can encourage the other person to develop their own sense of worth and self-esteem, and to free themselves, at least to some extent, from their self-defeating pattern.

HOSPITALISATION

See: Contraindications for brief counselling, Referral

HUMOUR

(*See also*: Challenge, Empathy, Immediacy)

Clients who use a lot of humour, who try to 'entertain' you, who laugh too much at difficult situations or make too many jokes about themselves and their experiences, may be communicating an inability or reluctance to face difficult circumstances openly. We suggest treating excessive displays of humour, or hostile humour, with caution. You may need to confront or challenge your clients with such behaviour, and explore what it might mean for them. This does not, of course, mean that every joke or laugh need be treated as a 'cover up'.

Using humour as a counsellor can be useful to offer a new perspective: seeing the absurd aspect of something and thereby gaining some control over it. However, too much or inappropriate humour can of course deflect the client from exploring difficult or painful experiences.

HUNCHES

See: Challenge, Intuition

ILLNESS/DISABILITY

See: Multiculturalism

IMAGERY

Visualisation and the use of imagery have been used for centuries as ways of increasing well being (Bry, 1978; Gawain, 1978). Many different schools of counselling use imagery in some form or another. For example, in Rational Emotive Behaviour Therapy (REBT) imagery can be used as a way of encouraging the client to experience negative emotions such as anxiety, and then, once the feeling has been evoked, the client works at changing the feeling by disputing the underlying irrational beliefs (Dryden and Yankura, 1995). As imagery is pictorial, a client whose response to a crowded room is to have a panic attack may be encouraged to visualise herself or himself being able to cope in just such a situation. The use of imagery is also very popular in relaxation training (Palmer and Dryden, 1995).

Lazarus (1989) outlines six ways in which imagery can be used:

1. Anti-future shock imagery (preparing oneself for a feared future event).

2. Associated imagery (using imagery to track unpleasant feelings).

3. Aversive imagery (using an unpleasant image to help counter an unwanted behaviour).

4. Goal rehearsal or coping imagery (using images of being able to reach a goal or manage a situation).

5. Positive imagery (using pleasant images for relaxation purposes).

6. The step-up technique (exaggerating a feared situation and using imagery to cope with it).

Whitmore (1991) discusses the ways in which psychosynthesis counselling uses imagery to integrate subpersonalities and heal past traumas. Hypnotherapy uses imagery as a way of augmenting suggestions (Heap and Dryden, 1991). van Deurzen Smith (1988) outlines the way that imagination can be used to help a client deal with his or her inner world within an existential counselling framework.

The following exercise is one which uses the client's imagination to create a state of relaxation.

> Counsellor: *I would like you to sit as comfortably as possible and close your eyes ... imagine yourself in a beautiful walled garden at the time of the year you like the most ... as you are walking around you notice a door in one of the walls of the garden and as you walk closer towards it you see it is a rather splendid arch-shaped wooden door with a large black wrought iron handle ... you decide to open the door and, as you go through the door, you arrive in a wonderful special place ... somewhere safe ... that only you know about ... your own very special place...*

The counsellor says nothing for a few minutes, leaving the client to gain the benefits of the exercise.

> *you now slowly begin to say goodbye to your special place and in your own time make your way back to the door ... once there you go back into the garden and close the door firmly behind you, knowing that your special place is always there for you whenever you want to return to it ... in your own time walk slowly around the garden and open your eyes.*

IMMEDIACY

(*See also*: Assertiveness, Challenge, Self-awareness)

Immediacy can be defined as 'direct, mutual talk'; for example, 'I see us as going round in circles and I'm confused. I wonder if you feel the same way.' The following checklist defines immediacy in more detail and can be used for feedback. It is a set of guidelines rather than a prescription.

In your use of immediacy, did you:

- Give some indication that you wanted to talk about the relationship between you?
- Describe (rather than evaluate)?
- 'Own' it by using personal pronouns (I, my)?
- Use the present tense, emphasise the 'here and now' (e.g. 'At this moment I feel...')?
- Say something about (1) how you felt, (2) how you sensed the other person was feeling, (3) what you thought was happening between you, (4) how you thought it was affecting what you were trying to achieve together?

- Have a sufficiently strong relationship with your client?
- Ask for your client's view?

For a discussion on immediacy, see Cormier and Cormier (1991).

INFORMATION GIVING

(*See also*: Advice, Challenge, Jargon, Process)

There is some confusion about the difference between giving information and giving advice. We suggest that *information* is intended to help the client decide for themselves, whereas *advice* tells the client the best thing to do. There is also disagreement among counsellors as to whether giving information is appropriate. On the one hand, some counsellors give information because they believe it helps clients to understand themselves better and make decisions. On the other hand there is the view that counsellors should never give information, usually on the grounds that clients will tend to construe it as advice because the counsellor is in a position of power. Clients may also blame the counsellor for any wrong decisions they take. Other counsellors think that giving information interferes with clients doing things for themselves.

Some types of information-giving (in the sense defined above) are:

1. **Challenge:** e.g. 'I have heard you call yourself silly on three different occasions.'
2. **Reply to a request for feedback:** e.g. when the client asks 'Do other people behave like me?' Sometimes it is appropriate to ask clients to check out for themselves whether this is so, or to ask *them* to try to answer the question. At other times it may be appropriate to say 'Yes, they do and there are many different ways of behaving.'
3. **Enlarging the field of knowledge:** e.g. informing a bereaved client about the different stages of loss, and the wide variability in experiencing them or not.
4. **Helping clients to obtain information:** e.g. letting them know of a relevant book to read, or of an organisation that could help them.

Guidelines

Ley's (1988, p.179) recommendations include the following:

- Find out what the person wants to know.
- Check for jargon.
- Use short words and sentences.
- Be specific.
- Categorise.
- Summarise.
- Check understanding.

INSURANCE, INDEMNITY

(*See also*: Sued, being)

The BAC Code of Ethics and Practice for Counsellors states that 'Counsellors must consider the need for professional indemnity insurance and when appropriate take out and maintain adequate cover' (British Association for Counsellors, 1998, B 6.16). This entry takes first the current 'official' view, as implied in this quotation, and then summarises Mearns' (1993) opposing views.

Indemnity insurance policies offer indemnity for liability at law for damages – claimant's costs and expenses in respect of claims for breach of professional duties made against a counsellor as a result of alleged neglect, error or omission in the provision of counselling services. Some policies also provide cover for potential liabilities incurred outside the counsellor–client relationship, including approved research projects, teaching or seminars and written reports.

However, most policies list exclusions from legal liability which it is advisable to read through carefully. Murray (1992, R.4) suggests that there is always a discrepancy between what a practitioner thinks is covered and the problems that an insurance company is willing to accept as valid claims under the policy. The level of indemnity may vary from £1000 to £500 000 and is determined by the premium you pay. Murray (1992, R.3) suggests that you need to consider the probability that during the next 12 months you will need to pay legal fees and expenses for problems covered by the policy. It would also be helpful to know the average amount of payments made. Murray acknowledges that insurance companies may be reluctant to give such information as it may reduce their sales!

With reference to the PPS Economy Scheme which he runs, Murray anticipated that claims and damages not exceeding £10 000 could be expected to occur with a frequency of around one in 10 000 practitioners a year. Counsellors who work within the NHS or in schools or colleges may find it useful to check whether they have indemnity cover from their authority or organisation. This may depend upon whether they have 'counselling' specifically mentioned in their contract of employment. It usually isn't.

The case against

Mearns (1993) first points out that so far there have been no significant claims in the UK against professional malpractice, negligence, errors or omissions. The key concept (see entry on being sued) is 'reasonable behaviour'. However, he has other, less obvious reasons for regarding indemnity insurance 'with considerable derision':

1. If insurance exists, claims are more likely.

2. As a consequence of (1), insurers tend to advise not saying you are insured or admitting responsibility, which is dishonest.

3. Indemnity insurance assumes that counsellors are *responsible for* their clients (as a medical practitioner is for a patient), rather than responsible *to* their clients.

INTEGRATION AND ECLECTICISM

(See also: Common factors, Counselling)

'Integration' and 'eclecticism' are both defined in several different ways (Dryden and Norcross, 1990). In very broad terms, eclectic counsellors borrow the 'best' techniques and ideas from a variety of sources, and may do so haphazardly or systematically, while integrative counsellors try to form a coherent, harmonious whole from two or more theories or parts of theories.

As with the multicultural approach, it seems likely that it is desirable for counsellors to reflect on the various possibilities, find one or more that fits, and to reconsider from time to time. There is plenty of material to reflect on: Norcross and Grencavage (1989), in their introduction to a symposium on integration etc., identified 50 books 'on synthesizing various counselling concepts and theories', and there are many different, or apparently different, approaches to counselling (over 400 at the last count).

INTERPERSONAL PROCESS RECALL (IPR)

(See also: Assertiveness, Process, Self-awareness, Supervision)

Interpersonal process recall (IPR) involves playing back a video or audio tape recording of an interaction, for example between you and a client. The purpose is to help participants recall what was happening in the original interaction: thoughts, emotions, feelings, images, body sensations, perceptions and expectations. The aim is self-exploration and the development of interpersonal skills. IPR has been used in research, counsellor skills training, clinical supervision, especially reciprocal peer supervision, and the development of consultation skills.

IPR is primarily concerned with covert processes and what may be on the edge of the participant's awareness. Kagan (1984) argues that people perceive much more about each other's communications and behaviour than they acknowledge to themselves or to the other person. Barker (1985, p.155) encapsulates the underlying assumption when he states that 'accompanying even apparently trivial dialogue there seems to be an enormous breadth and depth of thoughts, feeling and fantasies – often of a surprisingly primitive nature – that are often quickly forgotten or suppressed.' For the counsellor, IPR is a way of what Barker describes as 'recapturing this internal stream of consciousness'. It is this potential wealth of information that counsellors may fail to acknowledge or, alternatively, use productively in the session with a client.

Kagan (1984) tells the story that in 1982 his university was at that time one of the few with professional video recording equipment. It was used to record eminent speakers to preserve their lectures for future use. The visitors were often curious and after their presentation asked to see and hear themselves in action. They were amazed at the detail and extent to which the recordings were able to stimulate their recall of the experience. They frequently remarked on discrepancies between how they remembered feeling at the time and how they appeared to feel, and what they actually said and did at a particular moment. Kagan explained that as they were eminent speakers he felt able only to make respectful inquiries and encourage them to elaborate rather than offer any feedback or evaluation as he might have done with students. This became a crucial feature of IPR.

IPR was developed by Kagan within a primarily humanistic orientation but it seems compatible with any orientation that accepts the value of reflecting on inner experience. Furthermore, the specified questions or leads used in the Inquirer role (see below) are very useful additions to a counsellor's repertoire of skills.

IPR and the Inquirer role

The process of recall is facilitated by a neutral third party, someone who was not involved in the original interaction. This person is known as the Inquirer. While listening to the playback the Inquirer waits until the person reviewing decides to stop the tape then, by using a series of probing but non-interpretative, neutral questions, she or he invites them to recall, clarify and explore their experience more deeply. A central feature of IPR is that the control over when and where to stop the tape, and over how far the exploration should go, lies entirely with the recaller. In this way people review their own tape, retain the power within the recall situation and are responsible for their own self-discovery and learning.

The Inquirer role is easier to conceptualise than to actually perform. It requires non-judgemental but assertive probing and consists entirely of asking brief, open-ended exploratory questions. The Inquirer assumes that participants are the best authority on their own inner self-awareness and will choose to respond to or reject any of the questions offered. She or he also recognises that the participant may not be able, or might not want, to take up some of the questions. That is fine. The task is to facilitate the participant's own self-discovery and not to be drawn into counselling, 'active listening', giving information or even sharing observations.

Participants are helped to explore three dimensions of the interaction recorded on tape: what was going on within the participant, what was going on within the other person and what was going on between them. The focus is on the participant's reaction 'then', at the point at which the tape was stopped, rather than the 'now' within the recall session. The questions seek to help the participant recall 'inside' thoughts etc. rather than specific behaviours. Some of the indicative questions from Kagan's checklist of 'often used Inquirer Leads', include:

- What were you thinking at that moment?
- What were you feeling?
- What pictures or memories went through your mind?
- What did you think the other person was feeling?
- What did you want the other person to think or feel?
- Was there anything you wanted to say but couldn't find appropriate words for?
- Did you have any physical sensations then? Where in your body did you most feel the impact?

- What had you hoped would happen next?
- Had you any goals or intentions at this point?

Other leads invite the recaller to take their initial response more deeply, exploring mutual perceptions and whether there was any special meaning or possible associations:

- What prevented you from saying what you really wanted to say?
- What effect did that perception have on you?
- How do you think the other person was feeling/thinking about you?
- Do you think he or she was aware of your feelings?
- What do you think she or he wanted you to think, feel or do?
- Do you think your description of the interaction would be the same as the other person's?
- Does that feeling have any special meaning for you? Is it familiar?
- Does she/he remind you of anyone else in your life?

Before returning to the tape playback, the Inquirer typically checks out if there were any other thoughts or feelings around at that point. At the end of a recall session Inquirer leads might include the following questions:

- Did the setting affect you?
- How did you feel about your own behaviour?
- If you had it to do over again, what (if anything) would you do differently?
- What things have you learnt from this recall?

IPR can uncover important aspects of an experience, helping counsellors to become conscious of messages they denied or ignored, of previously unverbalised fears and imagined vulnerabilities or of when the client says something that makes them feel uncomfortable and that touches their own problems or defences. IPR can help counsellors develop their own internal supervisor and become more aware of the ways in which their covert experience within the interaction with their clients may have influenced or determined their behaviour – what they did or didn't say or do.

IPR involving the client

The most obvious application of IPR within counsellor training or supervision is for counsellors to use an audio or video recording to recall their experience of working with a client, as soon as possible after the session. It can also be valuable if *clients* are invited to recall their experience. With the permission of the client or person in the client's role, this recall session is recorded and then used by the counsellor to learn about the client's perceptions and experience of the counsellor's behaviour and interventions. Alternatively, the Inquirer could report back to the counsellor.

A further variation is mutual recall, in which both the counsellor and the client participate in the same recall session with an Inquirer. They are both asked to share their recalled thoughts and feelings, paying attention to how they perceived each other and what meanings they attribute to each other's behaviour. This is the most difficult form of IPR. Like the skill of immediacy, it requires self-awareness, empathy, sensitivity to the other person and the courage or assertiveness to share experiences and reactions to the other person. In counsellor and client recall, participants develop the ability to talk openly and non-defensively about the ongoing process between counsellor and client. Counsellors learn by experience about their interpersonal impact, how they come across to others and the ways in which a client's concern may actually involve them. In mutual recall they learn to verbalise these processes in the relationship and to deal directly and explicitly with the relationship itself.

INTERPRETATION

See: Challenge

INTUITION

(*See also*: Boredom, Challenge, Empathy, First impressions, Self-awareness)

Counsellors often talk of working by intuition, while trainers may encourage students to develop and follow (or at least take note of) their intuition. Some writers have gone as far as concluding that counselling and psychotherapy are as much a question of intuition as science, while others say that intuition does not really exist and it is merely a matter of subliminal, unconscious, or highly experienced reaction. To mystics the intuitive is the level above the physical, emotional and mental. In the psychodynamic approach, 'free flowing attention' is letting your mind wander with the client's words in an open, wondering 'frame of mind'; in most approaches there is scope for sometimes tentatively expressing some of the images, thoughts or feelings (all intuitions) which then appear.

Whatever intuition is, there seems to be some agreement that it is enhanced when one is forced to act quickly without thinking, and that it occurs more when a person is relaxed, or thinking about something different. Conversely, when you are problem-solving, thinking, or feeling anxious, intuition is reduced; emotionality and subjective involvement also interferes with it (Lancaster, 1991). All this implies that we are dealing with a process that is different from thinking. As counsellors are encouraged to be relaxed, empathic and to stay with the client's frame of reference rather than their own, this would seem to be a good state for developing intuition. Sometimes the best strategy is 'daring to wait and to drift' (Claxton, 1998, p.219).

Intuition has been shown to be superior in some situations to conscious, rational problem-solving (Claxton, 1997,1998). However, both logic and intuition are also fallible. We see it as important that counsellors who describe their approach as 'intuitive' are able to analyse what they do and why, though not necessarily at the time.

JARGON

(*See also*: Information giving)

Jargon can be defined either as 'gibberish' or as 'language peculiar, and often useful to, a particular profession or group'. To an outsider, in this case someone unfamiliar with counselling language, these two things are indistinguishable. Avoid the use of jargon during your sessions with your clients. Using words like 'resistance', 'transference', 'empathy' and 'congruence' can be mystifying and alienating. In a similar vein, you might wish to avoid using clichés or 'counsellor speak' when counselling. Phrases such as 'What I hear you saying is ...', or 'It sounds to me like ...' can become intensely irritating if used too often. If you regularly tape-record some of your sessions, you can look out for words or phrases that sound clichéd or repetitive.

JOURNAL, WRITING A

(*See also*: Counselling, Freewriting, Self-awareness, Stress)

Rainer (1978) sees a journal as 'a practical psychological tool that enables you to express feelings without inhibition, recognize and alter self-defeating habits of mind, and come to know and accept that self which is you' (p.18). It can help you discover genuine interests, nourish you, clarify goals, free intuition, and record insights. This kind of journal is therefore very like good counselling in its purpose and its methods.

There are many approaches to writing a journal, including 'games you can play with your inner consciousness to get to know it better' (Rainer, 1978, p.26). Here are some examples from Rainer (1978) and Adams (1990):

1. Lists, e.g. of desires, things you feel uneasy about, things you're happy about, beliefs you've discarded, loves.

2. 'Portraits', e.g. describe a friend.

3. Describe a day.

4. At the end of a day, write one adjective to describe it and another to describe how you'd like the next day to be.

5. Freewriting: writing quickly and without stopping or editing.

6. Sitting quietly for a few moments before writing (to allow the most important incidents and feelings to begin to surface).

7. Writing with your other hand (the idea is to improve contact with emotions).

8. Writing about yourself in the third person.

9. Writing dialogues – with someone else, between part of you and another part of you.

A series of studies by Pennebaker and others (e.g. Pennebaker *et al.*, 1990; Pennebaker, 1993) provides strong evidence for the value to the writer of writing about troubling experiences. In one study, first-year students wrote continuously for 15–20 minutes on three consecutive days on their 'deepest feelings and thoughts' about coming to college. A control group wrote about what they'd done that morning, and were asked to be 'objective' – not to mention emotions, feelings, or opinions. In line with previous findings showing improved functioning of the immune system, the first group visited the health centre less often in the following months than the control group. Interview data supported an insight rather than a catharsis view of the more effective coping which seemed to come from personal writing (Pennebaker *et al.*, 1990). Alternatively, both processes might be at work but in different ways (Pennebaker, 1993).

In a pilot study summarised by Pennebaker (1993), participants were asked to write about their deepest feelings and thoughts each day for two weeks. On two of the days, they were given some words to include, such as 'negative' emotions, insight words like 'realise' and causation words like 'because'. They reported that these days were the least personal, most difficult to do, but also the most meaningful. In another study, without provided words, it was found that the participants who benefited most were those who used low rates of cognitive words on their first day of writing compared with their last (Pennebaker, 1993); that is, they explored emotions first, before insights and ideas.

Pennebaker *et al.* (1990) argue (1) that not talking (or writing) about upsetting experiences is stressful because there is a basic need to talk about them which is actively inhibited, and (2) that translating them into language helps the person clarify and think them through. Writing is of course much cheaper than counselling, more private, and more under the person's control, and it has a long history (Freud and Horney both wrote about self-analysis). However, this is not to say that self-analysis makes counselling redundant.

A general mode of counselling is clear in both Pennebaker's and Rainer's discussions: first, express and feel the problem fully; second, analyse and think it through. Like counselling, writing a journal aims to reduce confusion, clarify emotions, feelings, wishes, values and thoughts, and therefore to free us to act more in the present.

An example of a journal entry (from Bayne, 1998a)

Step one

Choose an experience that matters to you, e.g. part of a conversation, interview or counselling session, or something you have seen, done or read.

Step two

Describe the experience in a sentence or two, or list key words. See if you can 'go into' and, to some extent, re-live the experience.

Longer run than usual on Monday. In the night pain in my knee woke me up, and yesterday it was stiff and I hobbled.

(End of steps 1 and 2).

Step three

Write as freely as you can about your experience – not analysing, not concerned with literary merit, and for yourself only.

Felt despairing and angry: I'll have to stop running. Also annoyed that I'd just bought new running shoes, and disturbed by the strength of my reaction. I was flat and ill most of the day at work, and abrupt with some of my colleagues. During the day my knee eased. This morning it's near normal. Feel much more buoyant and constructive. I'm not crippled!

(End of step 3 – reflection – at least on this occasion).

Step four

Analyse your reactions and perhaps challenge them.

- Be specific.
- What is the evidence for any assertions, beliefs?
- Is there a familiar feeling or pattern there?
- What assumptions are you making?
- Do your reactions tell you anything else about yourself, for example suggest important values?
- How realistic are you being?
- What other ways (however unlikely) are there of looking at what happened?

I'm left wondering about my reaction to injury (and illness).
1) I believe it's awful and catastrophic not to be able to run.
2) It's a recurring pattern. It may be related to lots of illness as a child, especially being scared I'd stop breathing.
3) Everyone is ill or injured sometimes (especially good athletes!). It's normal.

(End of Step 4 – a more considered analysis. It is meant to contrast with Step 3 which is written more freely, indeed as freely as possible).

Step five

Consider action.

- Is there any action you want to take now?
- Is there anything which you might do differently next time?

Possible actions:
1) Look up knee injuries. Preventive measures?
2) Ask Dave's advice.

3) *Make a special effort re 'flatness' next time: perhaps explain to other people, 'go into' my feelings, treat it like loss. Do 1 and 2 today.*

(End of step 5 – possible actions).

Comment on the example

The steps overlap but give some shape and sense of direction. Analysis is relatively neglected. The actions are feasible, but could be expressed more specifically.

JOURNALS, ACADEMIC AND APPLIED

(*See also*: Research)

The leading UK journals for counsellors are *The British Journal of Guidance and Counselling* and *Counselling*. There are also good articles, occasionally, in several psychology journals. For examples of our choices see the references at the end of this book. The addresses of some of the major counselling journals are listed below.

British Journal of Guidance and Counselling
  Carfax Publishing Company, PO Box 25, Abingdon, Oxfordshire OX14 3UE, UK.
British Journal of Psychotherapy
  Artesian Books Ltd, 18 Artesian Road, London W2 5AR, UK.
Counselling
  BAC, 1 Regent Place, Rugby, Warwickshire CV21 J, UK.
Counselling Psychologist
  Sage Publications, 6 Bonhill Street, London EC2A 4PU, UK.
  2455 Teller Road, Newbury Park, CA 91320, USA
Counselling Psychology Quarterly
  Carfax Publishing Company, PO Box 25, Abingdon, Oxfordshire, OX14 3UE, UK.
Journal of Counseling & Development
  American Counseling Association, 5999 Stevenson, Alexandria, VA 22304-3300, USA.
Journal of Psychotherapy Integration
  Plenum Publishing Corporation, 233 Spring Street, New York, NY 10013 USA.
  British Institute of Integrative Psychotherapy, c/o 21 Priory Terrace, London, NW6 4DG.
Journal of Counseling Psychology
  American Psychological Association, 750 First Street NE, Washington DC 2000-24242, USA.

KISSING

(See also: Boundaries, Non-verbal communication, Touch)

Counsellors often find issues to do with physical contact with clients problematic. In some forms of counselling, any physical contact, even shaking hands, is thought ill advised. In humanistic counselling a more relaxed attitude is taken, and touching and hugging do sometimes occur in counselling sessions or as a greeting or farewell.

In some cultures, including some European ones, kissing as a greeting or as a farewell is a ritual that need not have any special (i.e. sexual) significance, but even so, this form of physical contact usually happens only when people have known each other for some time. Our culture is not a homogeneous one, and different cultural groups have very different attitudes to kissing. Some find it very offensive; for others it is a normal ritual. Amongst some Europeans, kissing only *appears* to happen; there is no actual physical contact. And even if their culture expects or accepts 'ritual kissing', your client might not.

The real danger here is that a kiss can be misinterpreted, or invested with more significance than it really has. Even when you feel you know your client very well, and have enjoyed a long relationship, it is best to be very careful about how much physical contact, even of a ritualised kind, you allow. If problems do arise they can, of course, be talked through, and if you or your client has made a mistake this can be accepted and explored just like any other incident in counselling.

LETTERS

See: Administration, Clients who don't come back, Referral

LENGTH OF SESSIONS

(See also: Boundaries, Contract, negotiating a, Duration, Time boundaries)

Traditionally, sessions are 50 minutes long, and most counsellors have sessions of 50 minutes or an hour. The '50-minute hour' gives you a 10-minute break between clients if you have a full day of counselling, but most counsellors don't have practices that are as tightly organised as this, and some humanistic forms of counselling, particularly those involving a lot of body work, tend to work best in sessions of one and a half to three hours, or even all day. Mearns and a client hired a cottage for a week (Mearns, 1992, p.75). Most counsellors and their clients seem to find 50-minute or one-hour sessions about right.

It is important to be clear with your clients very early on (probably in your initial interview) about the length of sessions, and to stick to your agreement – neither letting sessions drift past the agreed time nor finishing early. If clients are late for sessions, they shouldn't expect to be able to carry on past their allotted time other than in very exceptional circumstances. The way you use time is part of the way you protect boundaries in your counselling practice, and learning to use time effectively is part of what some clients need from their counselling.

LIABILITY AND THE LAW

See: Insurance, indemnity, Sued, being

LIFE SPACE DIAGRAM

(*See also*: Emotions, Experiments by clients, Life space exercise, using stones, Questions)

The life space diagram is a method of helping someone explore and clarify their relationships with others. One advantage is its immediate visual impact, another its flexibility. Several steps are suggested:

1. Briefly describe the purpose of the exercise and invite the client to try it as a kind of experiment.

2. On a large piece of paper, although A4 would be adequate, make a list of all the people who in one way or another have real significance in the client's life. Some clients feel uncomfortable about writing while someone is watching: if so, it is a good idea for you to offer to do the writing, following the client's instructions, checking whether or not you are doing it correctly. Another practical point is that some clients equate significance with positive or friendly, or people with whom they have frequent contact. It may be necessary to explain that people they dislike, who they hardly ever see or who are dead can still be significant for them, and therefore can be included in the diagram.

3. Print the word ME, which represents the client, in a small circle in the centre of the page.

4. Consider each person from the list in turn, placing them as near to (even actually touching) or as far from the ME as the client wants. Each has their own circle. The relative distance of each person from ME may represent the importance, closeness or intensity of feelings the client has towards them. The client decides what the distance or space means. The visual impact can be heightened by joining the other circles to the ME with a broken or continuous line of varying thickness. This may add some meaning for the client. A thick heavy line may represent a particularly strong attachment, whereas a broken line may represent someone who is no longer alive, yet the client still feels close to them. It is important that the client decides the order and who to include or leave out. This in itself may be worth exploring with the client.

As each person is added to the diagram, you can encourage the client to talk about the relationship they have with that person – for example, by asking:

- What do you think or feel about this person?
- What do you want or expect from them?
- What do you imagine they think or feel about you?
- What do you imagine they want or expect from you?

In a diagram which doesn't involve many people, a summary of the main thoughts or feelings could be written next to the appropriate circle.

As the life space diagram nears completion you could stimulate further exploration and discussion with a series of prompts, appropriate for the client and presenting problem. For example:

- As you added new people did you want to move others nearer or further away from you?
- Is your relationship with anyone changing? Are they moving closer or further away from you? What is happening between you at the present time?
- What might the diagram have looked like a month, a year or several years ago? What has caused any changes? What do you think it might look like in the future?
- How exact have you been in placing family and friends? Are they, or should they be, together in groups or more spread out, when you look at it carefully?
- Do you rely on certain kinds of relationships, e.g. friendship or work relationships? Does authority or power play a part in any of the relationships? What effect does this have?
- How do you feel about the way you are surrounded by your relationships? Is it a comfortable picture? How far is it a self-portrait? How would you like it to be different? What would you like to change? Can you see how you might take a step towards achieving any of those changes?

Some clients feel really good about what their life space diagram represents for them. They may have many people touching the ME and have difficulty getting everybody they wanted close enough to them. However, for other clients the exercise causes great pain and distress. When they look at their diagram they see in concrete visual form what at some level they know, but have not wanted or been able to admit. The diagram may include very few people with none touching ME and all spaced together around the edge of the paper. The empty space around the ME is seen and felt. It is important to be sensitive to the client's feelings and not to underestimate the power of this exercise.

LIFE SPACE EXERCISE, USING STONES

(*See also*: Counselling, Emotions, Life space diagram, Questions)

An alternative form of the life space diagram uses small stones. The next time you go to the beach make a collection of pebbles of different shapes, sizes, textures and colours. You might like to have them in your counselling room in a large shallow wooden bowl. (It makes an attractive decoration too!)

The exercise is approached in much the same way as the life space diagram, except that instead of drawing names on a sheet of paper, pebbles are used to represent the people. You start by inviting the client to select a pebble to represent him/herself. The pebble is placed in the centre of a piece of white paper or cloth and then other stones are positioned around the client's own stone to represent his or her life space. Each stone is carefully selected so that in some way it represents the particular person. The size, shape or colour of the pebble may be given a particular symbolic meaning by the client. You can encourage the client to talk about why they chose each stone: the colourful and attractive personality, the big and strong personality, the small and dull personality, the beautifully rounded yet flawed personality.

The advantage of using stones or pebbles is that they can be held; their smoothness, roughness, size and shape, provides a potent kinetic experience. They can also be moved about to change or adjust their position in relationship with others as new 'people' are added. Although the purpose and approach to the exercise is very similar to those of drawing a life space diagram, the experience for the client can be very different. There are obviously many variations of this exercise, e.g. using different objects. What is most important is that you recognise the potential impact of the exercise and allow plenty of time for it. The exercise is complete when the client wants to stop or has little to say. Although the exercise is usually part of the first phase of counselling, it can be safely done only when you have established a good relationship.

LIMITS, SETTING

See: Boundaries

LINE MANAGERS AS SUPERVISORS

See: Role conflict, Supervision

LITERAL DESCRIPTION

(*See also*: Anger, Experiments by clients, Interpersonal process recall)

When clients talk about or 'talk through' painful and difficult experiences, they are naturally drawn into telling their story in the past tense. They also usually avoid aspects of the experience, search for reasons, explanations or justifications for their emotions or behaviour, and are sometimes circular and repetitive, with a sense of getting nowhere. In these circumstances it can be helpful to encourage a client to intensify and expand their account, through literal description.

The client is invited to describe the past experience in the present tense, to try to relive it in as much detail as possible, recalling colours, sounds, smells, position of objects, people, movements and so on. Clients typically drift back into the past tense, often interpreting or evaluating what had happened and you need to remind them to describe it as if it's happening now, or invite them to say it again in the present tense. For example, if the client says 'then I shouted at him' you might ask him or her to say 'I'm shouting at him.'

Literal description is potentially a very powerful intervention and should be used with great care and sensitivity by counsellors who have experienced it themselves. It is best approached by asking clients if they would like to try something – a kind of experiment – to see if it would help them to get in touch with their feelings about what happened and to break through or disengage the story-telling pattern. Evison and Horobin (1983) provide an excellent source for this and similar strategies and techniques for facilitating catharsis and re-experiencing emotions (and subsequent insight). Murgatroyd and Woolfe (1982) recommend the possible use of literal description in helping clients in crisis.

LITIGATION

See: Insurance, indemnity, Sued, being

LOSS

(See also: Emotions, Crisis counselling, Crying, Stress, Suicide)

Loss is a commonly presented counselling theme. When most people think of loss they usually think of bereavement. Bereavement and reactions to it are affected by a number of factors. For example, our reaction to the death of an elderly parent is likely to be very different from our reaction to the unexpected death of a child; death by suicide and death after a long and painful illness may engender different feelings (Humphrey and Zimpfer, 1996).

About 50% of people do not experience intense anxiety, depression or grief after a serious loss, and continue to be psychologically well adjusted (Wortman and Silver, 1989). Wortman and Silver discuss several related myths about coping with loss, e.g. that distress and working through are necessary, and that recovery or resolution are inevitable. They stress the great variability of people's reaction to loss; on Wortman and Silver's review of the evidence, about 30% of people feel depressed and distressed after a serious loss, 18% are 'chronic grievers' and 2% appear well adjusted at first but are distressed a year later.

There are many factors which influence an individual's experience and ability to cope with loss. These include:

• Demographic and personal factors – age, gender, ethnic background, socioeconomic status, ego strength, emotional maturity, religious affiliation and previous experience of loss and coping.

- Social and contextual factors – support networks and the availability of helping agencies.
- Characteristics of the event – its predictability, intensity, how suddenly it happened, magnitude, whether you can do anything about it.

Loss takes many forms – for example, loss of youth, of children leaving home, of a job or status, of faith, of lifestyle, friendship, property, a part of the body. In existential counselling loss is one of the main themes that a counsellor looks for in a client's story (van Deurzen Smith, 1988). Loss can affect more than one individual, as with major disasters such as Hillsborough where families, friends and whole communities were affected (Scott and Stradling, 1992). Some people attempt to deal with loss on a 'least said soonest mended' basis (Charles-Edwards, 1992); however, this approach is more likely to cause problems at a later stage.

Positive transitions (e.g. when a client stops engaging in self-defeating behaviour) can also involve loss. Moreover, moving away and breaking off old friendships may be the only way the client can maintain their progress. The client then experiences a period of loss as they adapt to their new situation and come to terms with ending friendships which may have begun in childhood. This type of loss is well documented in the substance misuse field (Velleman, 1992). See Drennan and Rumbold (1998) on infertility and Griffiths (1998) on rehabilitation for discussions of two other forms of loss.

Adams *et al.* (1976) developed a general model of transition, which suggests that, despite significant individual differences and the fact that the phases overlap and repeat themselves, there is a generally recognisable sequence of responses accompanying a wide range of transitions. The phases implying passage of time and variations in mood are: immobilisation, minimisation, depression, accepting reality, testing, search for meaning and integration. The first three phases are concerned with attachment to the past, before a 'letting go' phase, which is followed by gradual adaptation to the new situation. There are many other similar models relating to specific situations. For example, Kubler-Ross (1981) describes five phases of bereavement: denial, anger, bargaining, depression and acceptance. See also Parkes (1986), Bowlby (1973) and Worden (1984).

LOVE, ADULT ROMANTIC

(*See also*: Challenge, Empathy, Emotions, Frameworks, Sexual attraction)

I do not like to work with patients who are in love – Yalom (1989, p.15)

Within psychology there are four main approaches to understanding love: the social psychological, psychodynamic, cognitive–behavioural and humanistic. In very broad terms, social psychology has studied first attractions and, more recently, questions about maintaining love; the psychodynamic approach recognises love's passion and drama more, but in a 'dark' way with concepts like 'dovetailing pathology'; cognitive–behavioural theorists focus on learning, rewards and costs, and behaviour, beliefs, needs and expectations, and changing them; humanistic psychologists generally add a more positive emphasis.

Lee's eclectic approach (e.g. 1988) has some unusual strengths. For example, he distinguishes several kinds or styles of love (see Table 7 for brief definitions) and, in contrast to other typologies of love, sees all the styles as equally 'true'. This can be a severe test of acceptance and empathy (and a stimulating workshop). His theory is flexible as well as pluralistic: most people have a preferred style but each of us can love different partners in different styles, or the same partner in different styles at different times.

Table 7

Some key words for each style of loving (Lee, 1988)

Eros:	ideal beauty, immediate physical attraction, delight
Ludus:	playful, free of commitment, avoid intensity
Mania:	feverish, obsessive, jealous
Storge:	friendly, companionable, affectionate
Pragma:	practical, realistic, compatible
Storgic eros:	friendly intensity
Ludic eros:	playful intensity
Storgic ludus:	friendly and playful

Another strength of Lee's theory is that it suggests answers to questions like 'Does real love appear suddenly or gradually?' 'Do I love her more than she loves me?', and 'Do you really love me?' It can thus encourage greater clarity and tolerance. Lasswell and Lobsenz (1980) discuss applications of Lee's theory in couples counselling. For reviews of research on love see Sternberg and Barnes (1988), Shaver and Hazan (1988) and Duck (1998). Shaver and Hazan's preferred approach is to relate Bowlby's attachment theory (e.g. Bowlby (1973, 1988)) to adult romantic love, recognising the possibility that thinking about and working through unpleasant childhood experiences of relationships helps people change their mental models of relationships.

MANIPULATION

(*See also*: Drama triangle, Hidden agendas, Hooked)

Manipulation is a defensive process in which overt or covert pressure is put on another person. In Transactional Analysis these are called 'games'. When somebody is playing a game with you, your interaction with them isn't quite what it seems and you can end up feeling trapped and resentful. For example, if somebody acts as if they are hard done by they may manipulate someone into helping them.

In another case someone may act as though they think they are wonderful, but underneath they are fearful of being rejected. The front is put on as self-protection and with the hope that others will be attracted and not see the frightened person underneath. This type of manipulation often fails: either it attracts the wrong type of person or the front is so transparent as to be useless or cause irritation (Stewart, 1989).

MARKETING

(*See also*: Administration, Advertising, Business, Private practice, Values)

Marketing is about matching the resources being offered by the individual counsellor or counselling agency to those being sought by the client. The first part of any successful marketing strategy is to undertake market research – the process of finding out what people want. This information helps to define the type of services offered (the product range), how best to communicate information about such services (advertising and publicity), how to present such services (professional image) and what fees to charge (McMahon, 1994). The key to successful marketing is understanding the marketplace (Lenson, 1994). One of the biggest challenges for counsellors in private practice is ensuring a regular 'supply' of clients.

Regardless of whether a counsellor works in private practice or for a voluntary sector organisation, marketing is essential. As funding becomes more difficult to secure no organisation can neglect its marketing strategies. Aspects such as what influences people and how to use these influences to best advantage are essential considerations within the marketing framework (Falloon, 1992). Marketing within the counselling world has to take into consideration the ethical requirements of professional bodies such as the BAC, BPS and UKCP as the most effective marketing strategy might not be the most ethical (McMahon, 1994).

Another way of expressing this, based on Townsend (1984), is:

- What are you selling? (What is *different* about it or you?)
- Who might want to buy it?
- How do you make contact with them?
- Fee.

Feltham (1993, 1995b) gives a sobering analysis of the difficulties many counsellors find in making their living from counselling. He discusses such aspects as the costs (training, supervision, etc.), competition for work, and the problems of juggling a variety of activities. It is a vivid and unglamorous picture, made more difficult for those counsellors (probably many) who find the idea of selling themselves unattractive, and consider the view that we all sell ourselves in one way or another all the time (Lord, 1989) too cynical. McMahon (1994) takes a positive stance about making a living from counselling, focusing on personal qualities such as drive, persistence, organisation and marketing skills.

MENTAL ILLNESS

See: Assessment, Contraindications for brief counselling, Referral

METAPHORS AND SIMILES

(See also: Change, Emotions, Empathy)

Metaphors can be used to describe general approaches to counselling and as a way of communicating empathy. Taking the first of these, which (if any) of the metaphors below are closest to your approach to counselling, and which are definitely not relevant to you?

- Magician
- Game-player
- Technician
- Adventurer
- Healer
- Warrior
- Surgeon
- Archaeologist
- Detective
- Philosopher
- Salesperson
- Guru
- Consultant
- Guide
- Companion
- Terrier
- Scientist
- Midwife
- Teacher
- Artist

The following metaphors are a variation of the list above, adapted here for counsellors from Inskipp's (1996b, pp.87–88) list of metaphors and questions for counsellor trainers.

- **Guru.** Does a guru always disempower?
- **Clown.** Do you keep a clown hidden as not appropriate for counselling? Might it be useful sometimes?

- **Earth mother.** Are you a safe harbour? Do you support more than challenge?
- **Patriarch.** Do you enjoy power and creating order without being oppressive?
- **Whore.** Do you use seduction to encourage clients to take risks, to empower or disempower?
- **Warrior.** Do you enjoy conflict and challenge? Can you find the warrior when needed?
- **Magician.** The counselling is so beautifully done, clients are entranced, but are they empowered?

There are distinct views on the value of metaphors and similes in 'capturing' emotions. One is that, when used by client or counsellor, they sometimes express emotions better than more straightforward terms. If a client says 'I feel like a coiled spring' then this may be clearer than 'angry' and 'longing to do something'. Lakoff and Johnson (1980) argue that our conceptual system is fundamentally metaphorical; metaphors structure what we perceive and how we relate to others. A second view is that metaphors are a step towards finding the emotion words that fit. A compromise is that both views are true at various times. In either situation, counsellors can offer their clients the chance to explore a metaphor.

There is some research supporting the significance of metaphors. For example, McMullen and Conway (1996) found that metaphors for self-change, especially those for the whole self, were associated with positive change in counselling. And successful therapy has been related to use by counsellor and client of a few core metaphors (Angus, 1996).

MISSED SESSIONS

(*See also*: Administration, Clients who don't come back, Contract, negotiating a, Expectations, clients', Fees, Referral)

Occasionally a client does not turn up for an appointment, and you may be left wondering why and what to do. To some extent this can be avoided by stating clearly in the contract what notice is expected and what payment is required if a client misses a session. The most straightforward situation is when a client has a regular time, pays in advance and knows that if they miss a session they still pay. Other counsellors work with clients who come at varying times, who pay at the end of each session, or who may not be required to pay at all. The contract in these cases needs to be particularly clear. Whether or not to contact a client who has missed a session and how this is to be done can be discussed in supervision. Some counsellors phone the client after 15 minutes if they have not turned up, to see if they are all right, or have just forgotten the session, although phoning can be intrusive or put the client 'on the spot'. Others write a letter suggesting another date. Occasionally a counsellor states in the contract that a session missed without notice, or without a very good reason, indicates the end of the contract.

MISTAKES

See: Assertiveness

MODELS

See: Frameworks, Theories

MULTICULTURALISM

(*See also*: Difficulties in being a client, Multicultural counselling, Psychological type)

Multiculturalism emphasises a need for counsellors to be much more aware of differences in ethnic origin, gender, social class, disability, age and other factors (d'Ardenne, 1993; Eleftheriadou, 1997; Ivey *et al.*, 1997). For example, d'Ardenne's view is that counsellors who 'are curious about their clients' cultural backgrounds and are not afraid to acknowledge their ignorance, who can ask about their clients' experiences of alienation within and beyond therapy, are half-way to dealing with the issues' (d'Ardenne, 1993, p.6). Segal (1995) refers to this attitude and skill as counsellors learning to 'use their own ignorance' (p.66), and gives the example of saying to client with a disability 'I don't know whether (you want me) to offer help or not' rather than trying to guess. She adds: 'The decision never to pretend to a client, however disabled they are, brings its own stresses, but in the long run strengthens the counselling process and the counsellor's confidence' (p.66).

The multicultural approach contrasts with the traditional focus on individuals and on personality, which emphasises the possibility of change and development for everyone, regardless of multicultural factors, and in which counselling qualities, skills and strategies are seen as generally applicable. In Bimrose's (1993) framework, the traditional position is termed **Individualistic**. She contrasts it with two others: the **Integrationist**, in which the counsellor is more ready to adapt to clients (e.g. by being active and directive or acknowledging the central role of oppression in a client's life) and the **Structuralist**, which focuses on social conditions as the major causes of individual distress. The framework can help counsellors locate and consider their own positions.

The meaning of multiculturalism, its current stage of development and possible future directions are discussed by Bimrose (1996) and Ivey *et al.* (1997). For practical discussions of developing multicultural competence, see Weinrach and Thomas (1996) and Bimrose (1998). Two key points in multicultural counselling, elaborated in the next entry, are (1) that it is vital for counsellors to be aware of their own cultural identities, their assumptions about clients and the wide range of multicultural factors which may affect a particular client, and (2) to try to avoid either diluting or exaggerating the relevance of those factors.

MULTICULTURAL COUNSELLING

(*See also*: Counselling, Frameworks, Frameworks, Multiculturalism)

There are two broad views of multicultural counselling among those who see it as an important aspect of their work. One is presented as a multicultural model of counselling, separate and distinct from other theoretical orientations. The other view assumes a set of beliefs and attitudes, knowledge and skills relevant to counselling culturally different clients that needs to permeate the counsellor's existing theoretical orientation and practice.

Three elements of multicultural counselling competence have been suggested (Ponterotto *et al.*, 1995):

1. Counsellor awareness of her or his own cultural heritage and world view and the related assumptions about human behaviour, preconceived notions, values, biases and personal limitations.

2. Understanding the world views of culturally different clients.

3. Knowledge, skills and strategies for working with culturally different clients.

Cultural and ethnic differences impact on counselling at three levels (Horton, 1995):

1. **Human development (of the client).** There are two broad theoretical positions. The first is that explanations of the origin and perpetuation of psychological problems are located within the individual. This position assumes that cultural issues are largely irrelevant and that one approach is equally applicable to all clients. The second position assumes that explanations for problems are located in the interaction between the client and his or her environment. From this position it is argued that counsellors need to develop a working knowledge of the nature and impact of a client's cultural background and identity. This is especially relevant to culturally sensitive assessment, therapeutic planning and goal setting.

2. **Relationship between counsellor and client.** Cultural similarities and differences between the counsellor and client affect the quality and development of the therapeutic alliance and are sometimes manifested in resistance, blocks, collusion and defensive cultural dynamics. However, research support for the commonly held view that ethnic similarity between counsellor and client enhances the effectiveness of counselling is limited, and divided on whether ethnic match effects outcome. In contrast, cultural and ethnic awareness and sensitivity are clearly associated with successful counselling outcomes (Beutler *et al.*, 1994).

3. **Counselling.** Counselling as a way of helping people with psychological problems is a product of the majority culture in the UK. It reflects the values, beliefs, attitudes and language of Western, White middle-class (and, arguably, male) society. It raises the issue of whether counselling can be seen as part of the solution or as part of the problem in the sense that it can be

seen and used as an agent of social control, attempting to make clients fit into the dominant culture.

Counsellors might find it useful to address cultural issues at one or all of these levels.

Principles of multicultural counselling

Bernard and Goodyear (1991) support the idea that all people carry within themselves an individual identity (or sense in which they are unique and different from everyone else), a group identity (in which they share common values or characteristics with a group or groups of other people) and a universal identity or sense of connectedness with humanity. They argue that the delicate task in counselling is to integrate all three views, especially when working with clients whose cultural group membership is especially important to them.

Ridley (1995 p.88) identifies twelve therapeutic actions; these are adapted here as possible basic principles of multicultural counselling. The assumptions and conditions for each principle are summarised.

1: Develop awareness of your own culture

Counsellors identify themselves as multicultural beings. They recognise that such things as their own personal history, family background, language, gender, ethnicity, spirituality, age and socioeconomic status affect their counselling. Counsellors are aware of their own cultural biases, values, expectations and personal agenda/issues, and that they risk projecting them onto their clients or are likely to ignore or distort their understanding of their clients' world views and experiences.

2: Avoid imposing your own values

This principle assumes that counsellor neutrality is a myth (Strong, 1968; Katz 1985). If counsellors are aware of how their own personal values are different from those of their clients they should be less likely to unknowingly impose their values on their clients.

3: Recognise the limits of your multicultural competence and expertise

Ridley (1995) recommends that counsellors 'maintain a naive position and proceed cautiously with each client' (p.91). Eleftheriadou (1997) sees the counsellor's role as, in part, 'to remain open during such delicate exploration' (p.74), but *not* with a blank mind or from a (claimed) position of cultural neutrality.

4: Communicate cultural empathy

Counsellors should communicate that they understand the client's experience from her or his unique frame of reference. They must be aware of how their own cultural bias could hinder their ability to listen. Ridley (1995, p.91) suggests three guidelines:

1. Do not pretend to understand clients and do not hesitate to ask for clarification.

2. Use language that the client is likely to understand and establish early in the relationship that it is helpful if clients ask you for clarification.

3. Ask clients for examples to illustrate their cultural experience.

5: Explore a client's cultural group identity and the cultural dynamics of the relationship

While it is essential for counsellors to understand a client's unique world view and experience there is a risk of the counsellor assuming that the client's culture is irrelevant. Cultural information can help the counsellor to understand their client's needs and concerns and should inform assessment, therapeutic goals and interventions at each stage of the counselling process. Counsellors should openly explore and confront any problematic cultural dynamics early in the relationship with their clients. White 'majority group' counsellors may be seen as a symbol of oppression and counsellors from minority cultural groups may be seen as unable to relate to minority experience. Deep-rooted fear or hostility may underlie these feelings. However, while it is important to address these feelings it is also important to remember that they are not an issue for all clients.

6: Do not stereotype clients

Cultural group characteristics do not always fit a particular client, who may be different from other members of the group. Information about particular cultural groups is useful, but clients need to be understood from their individual frame of reference. Counsellors need to be aware of their own stereotypical views of other cultural groups.

7: Remember that people have many different roles and identities

Clients may have more than one cultural or racial identity and many social and occupational roles. Counsellors should be careful not to assume, for example, that a client's religion is more or less important than her or his racial identity or role within the family. Counsellors need to work towards understanding how a client's multiple roles contribute to her or his unique experience.

8: Monitor your cultural defences in assessing client problems

Assessment and clinical formulations should be reviewed regularly and presented in supervision for feedback, preferably from someone with multicultural expertise. Counsellors should not assume a benign society. Both intrapsychic and environmental factors should be considered in making assessments of the origin and maintenance of psychological problems. Counsellors must be alert to their own cultural counter-transference.

9: Remain flexible in therapeutic planning and selecting interventions

Ridley (1995) argues that 'focusing on the individual should not be constrained by a single or favourite therapeutic orientation' (p.96). Therapeutic plans and interventions should suit the problems and needs of the individual client.

Multiculturally skilled counsellors develop a flexible and wide range of explanatory frameworks and therapeutic interventions which might need to involve a client's existing support systems (Ponterroto *et al.*, 1995).

In contrast, some counsellors believe that their skills and model of counselling are suitable for all clients, regardless of the client's cultural background. Bernard and Goodyear (1991) criticise this attitude as the 'myth of sameness'.

10: Examine your espoused theory for cultural bias

This is discussed under the heading 'Majority culture assumptions'.

11: Utilise client strengths and resources

Beitman (1994) argues that one of the basic principles of change is the need to build on a client's strengths and resources and to find ways of using existing ways of coping. This may involve exploring the positive side of behaviour that was otherwise seen as problematic, past achievements and coping strategies, and can be a useful starting point in counselling.

12: Do not protect clients from emotional pain

Ridley (1995) argues that 'some counsellors, sensitive to the pain and oppression experienced by clients from some cultures, may either consciously or unconsciously seek to protect their clients from the emotional pain associated with confronting difficult aspects of their lives' (p.100). He reminds us that the need to express painful feelings is sometimes a necessary part of healing and change.

A detailed analysis of multicultural counselling attitudes and beliefs, knowledge and skills is provided by Ponterotto *et al.* (1995).

Working with clients of minority cultures

When working with clients from minority cultural groups, counsellors should pay particular attention to the following:

1. How to spell and pronounce the client's name correctly. Do not hesitate to ask the client to help you, repeatedly if necessary. This will at least convey that it matters to you to get it right. You should become familiar with the naming convention of the client's culture.

2. How the client wishes to be addressed. If in doubt, adopt initially a formal manner of address and become more familiar later. Counsellors are often seen as powerful people; clients may feel overwhelmed at first and unlikely to correct the counsellor.

3. How you introduce yourself and how you explain the purpose of counselling, the role of the counsellor and the role of the client. The idea of counselling as an approach to 'problem solving' is culture bound. Clients from other cultures are more likely to need time to absorb this and it may be helpful to allow questions about the process and self-disclosure.

4. If you are culturally close to the client, he or she might fear loss of confidentiality. The counsellor may need to reassure the client that confidence will be respected and that counselling is not compatible with socialising.

5. How you contract. Counselling often lacks structure and is intentionally ambiguous. Counsellors respond empathically to encourage clients to talk more. Some minority clients will find the lack of structure confusing or frustrating and might prefer a more clear-cut structure and direct approach. In particular, clear contracting may be important for the following issues:

- practical aspects to do with fees, cancellation and missed appointments
- counsellor and client roles, the need for honesty, commitment and effort, directive or reflective style
- expectations and possible outcomes, the need to be realistic
- goals, what you are trying to achieve together, whether the focus is on the past, present or future
- time boundaries.

6. How you establish a working alliance. Counsellors need to be alert to concealment of feelings and suspicious clients. Minority clients (like all clients) often test for trust with questions about such things as the counsellor's personal life or qualifications etc. (see entry on trust).

7. Types of goals. Counselling goals are culture bound – for example, the emphasis on 'the self', self-development, self-awareness and self-actualisation are all very Western-style talk. (see 'Majority culture assumptions', p.118–120). A client of a minority group might not understand counselling jargon and could experience it as culturally insensitive or oppressive.

8. Whether it is important to refrain from making assumptions and assessments for as long as possible.

Non-traditional interventions

When working with clients from minority groups it might be useful to consider the use of the following types of interventions which are not usually accepted as 'good' counselling practice but which might be appropriate with some clients.

1. If a client is struggling, perhaps send them a note of encouragement between sessions (Ridley, 1995).

2. Show strong affirmation when a client makes a therapeutic gain (Ridley, 1995).

3. Exercise institutional interventions on behalf of your client. Help to determine whether a 'problem' stems from racism, prejudice or institutional oppression so that clients do not inappropriately personalise problems (Ponterotto et al., 1995).

4. Follow up when counselling is over. Ridley's (1995, p.149) suggestions are listed here:
   - write a letter to the client, demonstrating interest in their progress
   - phone the client, showing interest in their progress
   - send self-help materials to the client
   - invite the client to relevant workshops or seminars
   - inform the client of alternative counselling services that might be beneficial.

5. Employ a fairly active and directive problem-solving approach with some clients (Locke, 1992, p.59).

6. Maintain the option of involving the client's family in the counselling process.

7. Offer to visit the client at home and/or be available at irregular hours.

8. Consult traditional healers and religious and spiritual leaders and practitioners in helping culturally different clients (Locke, 1992).

9. Offer telephone counselling sessions.

10. Engage your client in social talk before starting counselling proper.

11. Follow the client's lead in regard to non-verbal behaviour. 'Some clients tend not to be "word dependent", but very proficient in nonverbal communication' (Locke, 1992, p.27).

12. Sometimes it is appropriate to give advice and offer environmental and practical help.

13. Recognise that some clients 'make a direct link between the natural and the supernatural through possession and spiritual control' (Locke, 1992, p.23).

14. Monitor carefully any tendency to pathologise (interpret as a sign of mental illness) client behaviour, thinking or experiences that may be accounted for by cultural differences in child-rearing practices, religion, language, values and attitudes, sociopolitical factors, family structures and dynamics, history of oppression and/or level of acculturation.

It may be important to learn something about the client's culture and to question the conventions and traditions of counselling practice that might not be appropriate for use with clients across all cultures.

Culturally sensitive goals

Goal setting increases the chances that counselling will be successful (Ridley,1995). Realistic and worthwhile goals are tailored to the needs of the individual client, help to give direction to the counselling process and enable both counsellor and client to negotiate what can and cannot be accomplished.

Three process goals are particularly important when working with minority clients (Ridley, 1995):

1. Establishing an effective working relationship.
2. Exploring cultural differences and racial dynamics between the counsellor and the client.
3. Negotiating explicit business and therapeutic contracts.

The basic tasks or process goals of counselling underpin the development of culturally sensitive process goals and can be summarised as follows (Bernard and Goodyear, 1991, p.203):

1. Identifying and understanding the client's problems.
2. Communicating respect and acceptance of the client.
3. Achieving a status that will allow the counsellor to help the client.
4. Finding appropriate alternatives for managing the problems more effectively.
5. Helping the client to implement the most acceptable alternative.
6. Ending counselling in such a way that it will be considered a viable option for the client in the future.

Ridley (1995, pp.112–119) also identifies three outcome goals that may be relevant to counselling some minority clients:

1. Resolution of racial victimisation experienced by the client.
2. Bicultural competence – enabling minority group clients to face the conflicting values and demands of their own culture and that of the dominant majority culture.
3. Antiracism assertion – helping minority group clients to use assertive rather than aggressive behaviour to protect their own rights without interfering with the rights of others.

Majority culture assumptions

Most theories of counselling are products of Western culture and as such may not be universally applicable (Usher, 1989). Pedersen (1987) identified ten common assumptions that reflect a Western bias in counselling theories. He argued that in cross-cultural counselling these sources of bias may reinforce 'institutional racism, ageism, sexism and other forms of cultural bias' irrespective of the particular theoretical orientation being used. The assumptions are adapted and summarised below:

1: Definitions of normality

What constitutes 'normal' behaviour is not the same to people of different social, economic, political and cultural backgrounds. Use of a culture-bound definition of what is normal/abnormal with clients from other cultures risks assessment errors.

2: Emphasis on individualism

Many approaches to counselling emphasise individual self-awareness insight or self-actualisation. Empathic understanding may be offensive in some cultures (Usher, 1989). The tendency to focus on individual change serves to devalue the cultural norms that emphasise obligation and duty to family over individual interests that are so central to some cultural value systems. It also disregards the effects of individual change on the groups to which the client belongs.

3: Limited perspectives

Client problems tend to be assessed only from the limited perspectives of counselling or psychology. Academic disciplines such as sociology, anthropology, theology and medicine are often neglected (Feltham, 1995a).

4: Use of jargon

Most theories of counselling rely heavily on abstraction or jargon. Counsellors may falsely assume that their clients will understand this terminology when it is used outside the culture in which the theory was developed.

5: Overemphasis on independence

The high value often placed by counsellors on autonomy, self-direction and independence may devalue and neglect the functions of the healthy (and sometimes necessary) dependencies on family, community, church etc. inculcated by some cultures.

6: Neglect of client support systems

The role of significant others in the client's life is often ignored and there is a tendency not to incorporate the client's natural support system into a therapeutic plan. In some cultures talking to family or friends is more acceptable than disclosing intimate personal information to a stranger (Pedersen, 1987).

7: Emphasis on cause and effect

Many approaches to counselling depend on linear thinking that seeks to determine the cause of a problem. However, some cultures do not separate cause and effect; they think in terms of the interconnectedness of seemingly separate events (Bernard and Goodyear, 1991).

8: Focus on individual change

Counsellors sometimes fail to acknowledge the often very real constraints that are placed on some clients' potential choices and actions, assuming a benign society. The assumption is that the locus of control and responsibility for change should always be on the individual client rather than the family, community or society.

9: Neglect of history

A focus on the 'here-and-now' and on the present behaviour or problem can neglect the relevance of the client's personal and cultural history, which in some cultures is seen as essential to fully understanding current problems. Counsellors from the majority culture also tend to disregard their own history. This disregard is magnified when they work with clients from different cultures (Bernard and Goodyear, 1991).

10: Lack of awareness of assumptions

Particularly harmful attitudes of counsellors are to think that they are aware of all their assumptions and to glibly accept the idea of equality and multiculturalism, without having given it serious thought (Pedersen, 1987; Eleftheriadou, 1997).

Using Pedersen's ten assumptions, Usher (1989) evaluated person-centred theory for its cultural relevance. She found that six assumptions underpinning the theory are culturally biased. Ridley (1995) argues that 'if cultural bias can be found in Rogers' strong idiographic position, the relevance of other theories to cultural minority clients can certainly be questioned' (p.99). See Ridley *et al.* (1994) for a useful approach to examining theories for cultural relevance through identifying key issues and assumptions.

Defensive cultural dynamics

The quality of the therapeutic alliance or working relationship is the most important variable associated with positive outcomes (Bergin and Garfield, 1994). A strong working relationship enables clients to self-disclose, to explore intrapsychic, relationship and environmental conflicts and issues and to take risks and begin to work through problems.

Obstacles to developing an effective working relationship are unconscious distortions of reality, automatic and habitual responses or defences that protect against or reduce perceived psychological pain. Ridley (1995) describes eight culturally related defences that may occur to varying degrees when working with minority clients. The terms used to describe the defensive reactions are quoted directly from Ridley, and the defences are summarised below each item.

1: Colour blindness

This is the illusion that clients from minority groups are no different from those of the majority culture and that cultural background is irrelevant.

2: Colour consciousness

This is the opposite of colour blindness and assumes that all the problems a minority client encounters stem from their cultural background.

3: Cultural transference

A client's (positive or negative) emotional reactions are transferred from parents or significant others, or from previous experience of someone of the same culture as the counsellor, and projected onto the counsellor.

4: Cultural counter-transference

The emotional reactions of the counsellor are projected onto clients of a different culture.

5: Cultural ambivalence

Ridley suggests that, in order to be absolved from real or imagined guilt for being part of the potentially oppressive dominant culture, some majority group counsellors try too hard to gain a minority client's approval or respect. But some counsellors have ambivalent motives and enjoy the sense of power and control over their clients. They need to be seen as the expert helper and want clients to accept their approach to counselling, unconsciously becoming paternalistic or condescending and further reinforcing a client's learned helplessness.

6: Pseudotransference

This occurs when majority group counsellors ignore the possibility that a cultural minority client's critical behaviour or apparent defensiveness is grounded in reality and labels the behaviour as pathological, problematic or simply as cultural transference.

7: Overidentification

Counsellors from ethnic minorities sometimes overidentify with clients of the same cultural group. They may collude with the client, express support or admiration for the client or even exhibit behaviour similar to that of the client, thereby gaining a sense of prestige, recognition or acceptance by the client. Although counsellors of the same culture as the client might find it easier to rapidly establish rapport and feel more deeply empathic, they risk getting caught up in the client's negative experiences, defining the client's problem too narrowly and unwittingly encouraging excessive or inappropriate exploration of cultural issues.

8: Majority identification

This occurs when minority counsellors deny their group identity, identifying more closely with the majority group culture as a way of dealing with the underlying resentment and psychological difficulties associated with racism and oppression.

Supervision provides the opportunity for counsellors to explore any cultural dynamics and what may be going on between them and their clients, and not minimise or exaggerate their psychological significance and potential impact on the therapeutic relationship (Ridley, 1995, pp. 66–78).

MUSTS

See: Thoughts

NERVOUS CLIENTS

(*See also*: Anxiety, Beginnings, Contract, negotiating a, Difficulties in being a client, Quiet clients, Non-verbal communication, Respect, Silence, Warmth)

There is no sure way of knowing whether a client is nervous or not. Rapid speech, silence, shaking hands, difficulty in speaking may all indicate nervousness but could indicate something else. Being calm, establishing the client's needs, answering questions and empathising all usually help nervous clients to feel more relaxed. It may be useful to remember that for many people being a client is difficult.

NON-VERBAL COMMUNICATION

(*See also*: Challenge, Crying, Drinks/refreshments, Emotions, Empathy, Experiments by clients, Furniture, Journal, writing a, Kissing, Life space diagram, Paper and pencil exercises, Paraphrasing, Privacy, Silence, Smoking, Touch)

Non-verbal behaviours communicate information about emotions and attitudes particularly. Table 8 outlines one framework for thinking about and observing them.

Table 8

Non-verbal behaviours

Space – e.g. distance from another person, touch
Movements, gestures and facial expressions
Aspects of speech other than words – e.g. mmhs, volume, speed
'Other' – e.g. clothes, furniture, physical attractiveness

To interpret non-verbal communications (NVCs) we suggest the following three steps:

1. Separate cues from interpretations – for example, you might decide that a person is anxious (interpretation) from their restlessness (cue) or twisting hands (more concrete cue).

2. Ask 'what other interpretations are there of this cue?' In this step, bear in mind that NVCs are ambiguous and can be faked, and that *changes* can be of most significance – e.g. a person's face 'lights up'.

3. Choose from the following options:
   - remember the NVC(s) for possible later use
   - state your observation but not your interpretation – e.g. 'I notice that you smiled when you said...'
   - ask your client to repeat an NVC, exaggerate it, or stop it. (These are powerful Gestalt/co-counselling techniques and must be used with care)
   - offer your interpretation.

For general discussion of NVCs see Hall and Hall (1988) and Duck (1998)

'NO SHOW' CLIENTS

See: Beginnings, Clients who don't come back, Contract, negotiating a, Difficulties in being a client, Expectations, clients', Information giving, Missed sessions, Multicultural counselling

NOTE TAKING

(See also: Assertiveness, Confidentiality, Contract, negotiating a, History taking, Immediacy, Record keeping, Self-awareness)

Although some counsellors take full notes during sessions, most take none at all. Perhaps the question to ask is 'What do I need these notes for?' If they are to help you build up a picture of your client's concerns and progress, it might be better to write them up immediately after the session. The same goes if you are taking notes to help you make a presentation, or write a case study. The problem with taking notes during sessions is that they distract your attention from listening and responding sensitively to your client and could have the same effect on your client. Taking notes during sessions could make your client feel more like a 'case' than a person, although you can of course discuss this. However, if your approach to counselling involves asking a lot of questions about family history, early relationships etc. you might need to make a lot of notes, at least early on.

Dalton (1992, pp.16–18) discussed what happened when she agreed that a client could see her notes, written in a style she describes as 'telegrammatic' and 'unvarnished'. The client was furious with their 'coldness', a reaction which they later agreed was to do with the client's anxieties about being genuinely liked and about ending counselling. Dalton also discussed her motives for agreeing quickly to show the client her notes, and what she is likely to do in the future: slow down, discuss the client's reason for wanting to see her notes and explain her style of note-taking.

NUISANCE TELEPHONE CALLS

(See also: Answerphone, Assertiveness)

'Nuisance' means different things to different people and there is no definitive way of categorising these calls. There does not seem to be any research on calls to counsellors in particular and there is no evidence that counsellors are treated differently from other people. Four kinds of nuisance calls can be defined:

1. Calls at antisocial times.
2. Frequent calling.
3. Threatening calls.
4. Obscene calls.

The first two categories are potentially less serious than the others. Some counsellors print the times they can be called at home on their notepaper; this appears to reduce the number of calls at other times. Giving the client gentle reminders, or information as to what is acceptable by you, may also help in the first two categories. If this fails, giving the client a chance to talk through their need to call may help. If none of these methods work, the calls enter the threatening category.

Threatening and obscene calls have been experienced by much of the general population, both male and female (Sheffield, 1989; McKinney, 1990), with a large variation in the amount of harassment perceived and received. It is very rare that these calls lead to face-to-face confrontation with the caller. Crisis centres receive a high number of obscene calls and also calls from people who make such calls and want to stop. British Telecom offer a leaflet (call 150), recorded advice (0800 666 777), and investigation (0800 661 441).

One method that has been found to be effective for dealing with threatening calls is to avoid the usual reaction of fear, anger or upset (which is what the caller probably hopes for) and to remain calm and say in a caring voice something like 'Listen to me, you obviously have a problem. I feel very sorry for you and suggest you go for treatment before you get into trouble.'

There is some evidence that a sizeable proportion of the male population have made an obscene call at some time or other (Matek, 1988; Templeman and Sinnett, 1991). Most are young, not dangerous and only mildly disturbed. They can probably be helped by the normal counselling methods. If the counsellor does not feel happy with this it is probably best to refer the client to a centre dealing with sexual problems.

Nurturing, the counsellor's need for

See: Anger, in counsellors, Assertiveness, Beliefs, irrational, Burnout, Crisis, for the counsellor, Drama triangle, Distress, at the end of a counselling session, Journal, writing a, Loss, Personal growth for the counsellor, Psychological type, Self awareness, Stress, Supervision, Values

NVQs

(*See also*: Good counsellors)

CAMPAG is the standards setting body responsible for developing national occupational standards and N/SVQs (National/Scottish Vocational Qualification) in the areas of counselling, advice, mediation, psychotherapy, advocacy and guidance (hence the acronym). CAMPAG is funded by the Department of Education and Employment and the Qualifications and Curriculum Authority (QCA). The project is designed to develop a functional map of the areas of therapeutic counselling, couples counselling and psychotherapy, and to identify commonalities and differences. It may help the establish national occupational standards and, if accredited, N/SVQs in these areas. For information on N/SVQs contact QCA, Tel: 0171 509 5555.

Views on the value of NVQs for counsellors differ radically. On the one hand they are seen as having a profound positive impact through challenging the power of various 'gatekeepers' to control who does which jobs – allowing people to develop their skills and change work roles more flexibly and with greater equality of opportunity (e.g. Russell and Dexter, 1993). On the other hand, the emphasis on what people can actually do is seen as undervaluing the subtle qualities and attitudes at the heart of counselling (e.g. Frankland, 1996).

OPENNESS

See: Congruence, Self-disclosure by counsellors

OFFICE

See: Furniture

OUTCOME OF RESEARCH (ON COUNSELLING)

See: Effectiveness

PANIC ATTACKS

(*See also*: Anxiety, Behaviour, Post-traumatic stress disorder, Thoughts)

Most recent studies estimate that 1–2 % of people in the UK present themselves to doctors each month with panic attacks (Griest and Jefferson, 1993). About 10% of the general population experience at least one panic attack in their lifetime and about two-thirds of sufferers are female (Silove and Manicavasagar, 1997). The symptoms of a panic attack include:

- palpitations, pounding heart or accelerated heart rate
- sweating
- trembling or shaking
- sensations of shortness of breath or smothering, feeling of choking
- chest pain
- nausea or abdominal distress
- feeling dizzy

- fear of losing control
- fear of dying
- hot flushes or chills.

Panic attacks can vary in frequency and intensity. One person may get a panic attack once in their lifetime and another will have up to 15 a day (Trickett, 1992). For some people, panic attacks start after an obvious traumatic event; for others they begin without any obvious trigger. It is quite common for doctors to prescribe drugs such as beta-blockers or paroxetine to clients experiencing panic attacks.

Helping a client deal with panic attacks could involve anything from providing general counselling to relieve the emotional pressure of a stressful existence to helping the client through a structured self-help programme based on cognitive–behavioural principles. About 1% of clients never recover from panic attacks (Griest and Jefferson, 1993) and counselling may help these clients come to terms with the reality of managing their panic attacks in the same way that someone with diabetes learns to manage their condition.

A self-help programme would include the following:

1. Recognition and identification of triggers (e.g. when and where the panic attacks occur).
2. Consideration of lifestyle factors (e.g. caffeine intake).
3. Understanding the physiology of panic (e.g. the role of adrenaline).
4. Changing unhelpful cognitions (e.g. 'everyone will laugh at me').
5. Developing coping strategies (e.g. relaxation, breathing).

In addition, clients may benefit from taking advantage of self-help literature, such as *Overcoming Panic* (Silove and Manicavasagar, 1997) and *Coping Successfully with Panic Attacks* (Trickett, 1992).

PARALLEL PROCESS

(*See also*: Challenging, some guidelines for, Process, Supervision)

Parallel process is a term for someone's experience in one situation being repeated in another situation. The idea has its roots in the concepts of transference and counter-transference and relates primarily to supervision. Parallel process can be both a trap for unwary counsellors and a possible way of understanding your relationship with your client. For example, the supervisee might say 'I really don't know how to begin' and the supervisor would work with this difficulty on the assumption that it was also a difficulty for the client. Or the supervisor says 'I feel blamed by you', and then works with this as a feeling that the supervisee may have had during counselling. Some supervisors work most with the 'here and now' on the grounds that it will mirror the 'there and then' of the counselling session itself.

PARAPHRASING

(See also: Empathy, Emotions, Metaphors and similes, Questions, Self-awareness, Summaries and 'moving interviews forward')

When you paraphrase you attempt to restate, in a fresh way, the main part of what someone has said without adding any of your own ideas, feelings, interpretations, etc. The tone is slightly questioning without being a question, and your aim, in Rice's phrase, is 'to unfold rather than package experience' (Rice, 1974, p.305). The most basic form of paraphrase is 'You feel ... [emotion] because of...'

A key element in paraphrasing is being in close emotional contact with your client and also clearly separate: neither overidentifying (sometimes called 'fusing') nor being coolly distant. Davenport and Pipes (1990) suggest the analogy of swimming close to a deep powerful whirlpool: 'the challenge is to be close enough to the emotional energy to understand what the client must be experiencing without getting swept down into the action oneself' (p.139). Drowning with the client is not helpful, nor is viewing from too far away.

Paraphrasing is an art as well as a skill and therefore can be carried out technically well with poor results, or technically poorly with excellent results (or, of course, both skilfully and artistically, or neither). However, even technical paraphrases can be effective in the sense of encouraging clients to explore and clarify and allowing you to check your understanding.

A key practical question is 'how often do good counsellors paraphrase?' The answer is that it depends, but Rogers (e.g. 1987) believed in frequent checks, and Gendlin (1981, p.19) suggested an *average* of every five or ten sentences. Gendlin's suggestion can be treated too literally! It is a guideline, not a rule, and its merit lies in being concrete about the term 'frequent'. Gendlin makes another specific suggestion about frequency: 'Don't let the person say more than you can take in and say back. Interrupt, say back, and let the person go on' (p.20). If you dislike the word 'interrupt' in this suggestion, you might like to try replacing it with 'contribute'.

A flexible approach is also needed in choosing when to use your client's words in a paraphrase. Sometimes a word or phrase used by your client is very significant to them and can be included by you (or noted for later).

Further guidelines

The following guidelines are intended to help you check on and refine your own paraphrasing, not to replace the artistic element. They are the equivalent of 'instructions' on practising or reviewing a backhand or a golf swing. The guidelines are organised in four sections: purposes, paraphrasing well, paraphrasing less well, and some subtle aspects.

The purposes of paraphrasing

- To help clients to listen to themselves and to clarify what they mean, feel and think (usually by putting it into words).

- To help clients to make more sense of what they're troubled by and therefore increase their sense of perspective and control.
- To help you to listen and to communicate in a concrete way what you've understood and what you haven't, and that you are trying to understand.
- To communicate acceptance and respect.

How do you know when you're paraphrasing well?

Your client is more likely to:

- say more, and go further 'inside' (may become more focused and intent) or
- sit silently, relieved that they've been understood and accepted (may become more relaxed).

And less well?

Your client is more likely to:

- try to paraphrase what you've said
- speak more superficially and continue to do so
- become tense, confused or annoyed ('I've just said that') or
- agree in a desultory way.

Some subtle aspects of paraphrasing

- Good paraphrases tend to emphasise those emotions that are clearly expressed or implied and to capture something of your client's experience.
- Simple words seem to capture meanings best (perhaps through discouraging intellectualising).
- Perhaps most important is helping your client find the words that feel right to him or her.
- Pausing after clients have recognised or clarified an emotion gives them the space to feel it more, and perhaps also to feel a sense of relief that someone has really listened.
- Paraphrasing may also increase clients' sense of responsibility for their reactions.
- If you have understood (or think you've understood) only part of what your client has said, paraphrase that part, and add that you don't understand the rest.
- Pause before you paraphrase or during a paraphrase, and trust yourself to find words which are good enough or better.
- Try including a *little* of your client's emotion or emotions in the way you say the paraphrase.

PATTERNS

(*See also*: Brief counselling, Change, Drama triangle, Emotions, Feelings, Psychological type, Thoughts)

People can learn from experience, modifying and adapting their reactions and responses to similar situations. However, there is also a tendency to repeat the same response and develop a fixed way or pattern of thinking, feeling or behaving in certain situations. Examples are living with or marrying compulsive gamblers or drinkers, clashing with authority figures, and taking a particular stance such as victim, persecutor or rescuer, or earth mother or psychotherapist. Patterns are dysfunctional when they have a compulsive, 'taking over' quality, and when the person is upset and baffled by them.

The most influential patterns may be those established as ways of coping with difficult or problematic situations in early childhood, but patterns can develop at any time in life. Patterned responses can become rigid, compulsive and out of awareness or otherwise dysfunctional. It can be very difficult to abandon the familiar and relatively comfortable, albeit problematic, patterns of behaviour. Patterned behaviour can be used to explain how psychological problems are perpetuated or maintained. Freud used the concept of 'repetition compulsion' to explain resistance to change (Ryecroft, 1985). This seems to describe a phenomenon similar to that of patterns of behaviour.

One of the goals of counselling is to enable clients to identify dysfunctional patterns and seek more flexible or alternative options when the original behaviour is no longer useful or necessary. Beitman (1990) argues that 'pattern search' is the central process goal of the middle stage of all counselling. Co-counselling (Evison and Horobin, 1988) and other models of counselling actually use the term pattern to describe psychological problems and dysfunctional behaviour, and most (if not all) models address the phenomenon as the target or focus of change. A key issue in counselling, regardless of the truth of the associated theory, is the most efficient route to change for all or most clients. Some counsellors normally try simpler, quicker methods first – thought-stopping or assertiveness training, for example – and help clients to explore early relationships only if necessary.

PEER SUPERVISION

(*See also*: Supervision)

Peer supervision is most appropriate for experienced counsellors and is probably best done in a small group. Each person takes a turn at presenting a case or theme for discussion by the group and is given the opportunity to explore particular aspects, as in standard supervision groups. Other group members can be supportive and challenging, and offer alternative ways of thinking about particular issues.

A supervision group should be small enough, and meet often enough, to enable each member to have adequate time for case presentation. A group of four might need to meet every week for about two hours. Peer supervision in pairs, using a reciprocal model, can also be very useful.

The advantages of peer supervision groups include the opportunity to hear how others meet and overcome difficulties, to share ideas and information and to practise being supportive and constructively challenging. Disadvantages include the fact that groups can find themselves short of time to include everyone fully, and that sometimes peer groups become collusive and find it difficult to be challenging. One way to overcome this second problem is for the group to meet periodically with an 'outside' facilitator to review its practices and the relationships that have built up among group members (Horton, 1993, p.24).

The group can also review itself. Hawkins and Shohet's (1989, pp. 56–72) six modes of group supervision can be used for this. They focus respectively on clients, counsellor interventions and strategies, what the counsellor is 'carrying' from a session, the relationship between counsellor and client, parallels between what is happening in the supervisor and in the counselling and what is stimulated (emotions, values, images) in the members of the group by a particular presentation. A seventh mode, multicultural factors, can be added to this framework. A group using the framework may discover that, for example, it is neglecting one or more of the modes.

PENCIL AND PAPER EXERCISES

(*See also*: Challenge, Experiments by clients, Homework)

Some clients find eye-to-eye/face-to-face contact threatening, especially when talking about some issues, and may find it easier to focus on a form of writing or drawing shared with the counsellor. 'Paper and pencil' exercises can represent or summarise in words, diagrams or pictures what the client is saying, or be a way for the counsellor to explain or challenge. The entry on life space diagrams gives a detailed example of an elaborate paper and pencil exercise.

PERSECUTOR

See: Drama triangle

PERSONAL COUNSELLING FOR THE COUNSELLOR

Different approaches to counselling disagree on how necessary it is for counsellors to have their own counselling, especially as part of their training (Dryden and Thorne, 1991). Most forms of psychodynamic counselling make it a requirement that trainee counsellors have extensive personal counselling, other approaches advise or strongly recommend but do not require it, and some regard it as fully optional. Andrews *et al.* (1992, p.571) argue that 'the unique needs of the individual student or client would be violated by insisting on a single modality of uniform length', for example, 40 sessions of personal therapy.

In 1998 the BAC introduced a new therapy criterion for Individual Counsellor Accreditation. This requires counsellors to have completed a minimum of 40 hours of personal counselling or an 'equivalent' experience of being 'in the client role' that is consistent with their core theoretical model. This may include – it is a matter of arguing a case – co-counselling for example, which would obviously cost much less than 40 of hours counselling (about £1000 at 1998 prices).

The benefits of personal counselling include:

- Improved emotional and mental functioning and a more complete understanding of personal dynamics and interpersonal conflicts and issues.
- Avoidance or alleviation of emotional stress and professional burnout, which are inherent risks in counselling others.
- The ability to resolve or cope better with particular problems related to current life stress (and experiences on counsellor training courses)
- Socialisation in the client role: what it is like to be a client, in particular becoming aware not only of how counselling can help but also of the difficulties clients sometimes have in making the best use of counselling.
- Provision of first-hand opportunity to observe and experience clinical methods.

However, there is no clear evidence for a relationship between mandatory personal counselling in training and clinical effectiveness (Bergin and Garfield, 1994; Macran and Shapiro, 1998). Obviously it depends partly on the counsellor's level of psychological functioning. Sometimes personal problems get in the way of effectiveness as a counsellor, but counselling others may re-stimulate the counsellor's own problems and undergoing personal counselling could temporarily exacerbate the difficulty in counselling others.

In training, it is important to find a counsellor who uses a similar model of counselling to the one you are studying.

PERSONAL GROWTH FOR THE COUNSELLOR

(*See also*: Journal, writing a, Personal counselling for the counsellor, Physical activity, Professional development, Self-awareness, Stress)

Counsellor training courses almost always contains a significant component of personal growth as an explicit component. Any BAC-accredited course, for example, has to show how the personal growth needs of participants are catered for in the course design, in addition to any requirement for personal counselling. Definitions of personal growth or personal development vary (Johns, 1996), but here we assume it to include any activity (including personal counselling) that enables you to develop more self-awareness and self-understanding, clearer perception of self and others, more openness to experience and less defensiveness. We also include a commitment to challenging personally held prejudices and cultural and social stereotypes. Dryden *et al*. (1995) describe four areas for self-development in training: self-structure, self in relation to others, self in relation to clients and self as learner.

The personal growth element of training is crucial for person-centred counsellors, and the personal development objectives are 'daunting' (Mearns, 1997 p.x). This is because congruence, or authenticity, plays such a critical role in person-centred counselling and demands a lifelong commitment to a continuing process of increasing self-awareness. In the psychodynamic tradition, personal growth and development is equally crucial because of the need to minimise the effects of counter-transference in counselling.

Once a counsellor's training is complete (whether or not it has included periods of personal counselling) there is still a need to attend to continuing personal growth and development. In many places it would be considered unethical (or at least unprofessional) for a counsellor to believe that no further development on their part was necessary. For example, if a BAC-accredited counsellor decides to apply for re-accreditation (which is required every five years), she or he has to show how they have taken care of personal growth and professional development needs during the previous five years.

There are many activities that can legitimately be considered as appropriate for personal growth. What you choose to do will depend on your approach to counselling and your individual circumstances. In our experience people have found some combination of the following activities helpful, although this list is not exhaustive:

- Keeping a personal journal, which is more than just a record of events but explores your own feelings and learning.
- Being part of a network or support group that encourages personal exploration.
- Going on short courses, conferences and workshops to keep up with developments in your field
- Reading.
- Researching and writing.
- Undertaking further formal study.
- Being in a personal growth group.
- Exploring particular aspects of counselling or counselling with specific client groups (survivors of childhood abuse, etc).
- Learning how to manage personal stress better.

You might also consider developing aspects of yourself that you have hitherto neglected, such as your spiritual development (if you have an interest in this). Exploring the many forms of meditation can help you to deal with areas of confusion or anxiety. The more 'body oriented' approaches to meditation, like some forms of yoga or T'ai Chi Chuan suit some people. You might also consider developing your creative and artistic sides (if you feel these have been neglected) by taking art classes, writing poetry, dancing, listening to or playing music, for example.

Similarly, some attention to physical fitness and/or the adoption of a more healthy lifestyle (if you need it) might also be considered as a contribution to personal development if it enables you to give better attention to your clients.

Whatever you choose to do, it is important that you feel challenged and stimulated, and that what you do helps you question the assumptions about yourself that affect the way you relate to your clients and others. Holding the notion that you are fully trained and have no need for further personal work is likely to result in your practice becoming stale and lacking creativity. Rogers' idea of the person as someone continually in a process of becoming more fully functioning (Rogers, 1961) is helpful whatever your counselling approach.

PERSONALITY

See: Psychological type, Theories

PHYSICAL ACTIVITY

(*See also*: Stress)

Some counsellors and clients survive well without coming close to the current main recommendation for exercise, which is to accumulate about 30 minutes of 'low intensity' activity per day. This means walking fairly briskly or its equivalent, rather than getting sweaty and out of breath (Wimbush, 1994). If you do want to excercise, it is generally best to become more active *gradually and comfortably*, with more than 30 minutes a day or more rigorous exercise giving a reserve of fitness and greater protection against some illnesses (Wimbush, 1994; Seligman, 1995). Other fairly standard pieces of advice are to remember that rest (at least one day a week) matters too, to find a form of exercise that suits you and that you enjoy, and to increase the amount of exercise you do gradually – and that 'gradually' varies for different activities (though it is probably best to base this on your own self-awareness rather than on an external criterion like number of minutes). See the book by Schlosberg and Neporent (1996), which is a good reference, despite its brash title, and Fiennes (1998).

POST-TRAUMATIC STRESS DISORDER (PTSD)

(*See also*: Abuse, Anger, Anxiety, Assessment, Crisis Counselling, Depression, Emotions, Panic attacks, Psychodiagnosis, Stress, Thoughts)

PTSD was formally recognised in 1980 by the American Psychiatric Association.

The criteria in DSM-IV (Frances, 1994) for PTSD are as follows:

1. The client must have experienced or witnessed a serious threat to life or physical well-being.
2. The client must re-experience the event in some way.
3. The client must persistently avoid stimuli associated with the trauma or experience a numbing of general responsiveness.
4. The client must experience persistent symptoms of arousal.
5. Symptoms have lasted for at least a month
6. Delayed onset takes place when symptoms do not appear for six months or more.

'Post trauma stress' (PTS) is the term given to those who experience destabilisation – the natural sense of disturbance and upset – following a traumatic incident (Scott, 1997), which could range from being mugged to armed combat. About 1% of the population of the UK suffer from PTSD and about half of these people go on to develop a chronic form of the disorder (Scott and Stradling, 1992). There is debate about eliminating the word 'disorder' or changing it to 'syndrome' as 'disorder' suggests a failing or weakness in some way.

Understanding the diagnostic criteria of PTSD in DSM-IV can be useful in providing a common language when communicating with other professionals. However, although DSM-IV is useful for identifying PTSD following classic traumatic experiences it has its limitations. DSM-IV is 'classification by committee' and the definitions that are finally agreed are the best compromises that could be reached at the time of publication. This means, for example, that trauma following childbirth would not qualify under the current criteria (McMahon and Doggart, 1997) even though the client may be manifesting many of the signs and symptoms associated with PTSD, and the counsellor would use the same counselling strategies as with a client whose traumatic incident did fit the diagnostic criteria.

Many clients with PTSD are also angry, anxious and/or depressed, so it is quite likely that the counsellor will be working with a variety of problems. As with any extreme case, it is important to be very clear about how you are working and why. A variety of approaches may help the client – e.g. a peer support group, anxiety management groups, relaxation classes. A client might also find that they are unable to cope with their everyday life as they could before, which adds a further burden. Depending on the severity of the trauma, there may be a variety of topics to deal with. What is traumatic is not always obvious (Scott, 1997).

Clients who present with various forms of emotional abuse from childhood could also be suffering from PTSD. In the case of sexual or physical abuse the cause may be quite clear, but there is no clear knowledge of what a child, particularly at preverbal stages, sees as traumatic. For some clients the precipitating stressor is only the last in a long series of stressful circumstances and very often the final stressor is quite minor in intensity. For these clients the term 'prolonged duress stress disorder' might be more appropriate (Scott, 1997).

It is important that counsellors working with trauma receive informed supervision of their work: secondary trauma can easily occur if the counsellor is not properly supported and debriefed (McMahon and Doggart, 1997).

The main general principle for coping with psychotraumatic stress is to 'work through' it rather than pressing on or coping in silence. The three checklists below are condensed from Buyssen (1996).

What you can do for yourself

- Try to focus on what happened.
- Allow time for the natural healing process.
- Alternate confrontation with distraction.
- Talk (and/or write) about what happened.
- Ask for and accept support.
- Expect some people to be more understanding than others.
- Resume work as soon as possible, but stay in the background.
- Be more careful than usual.

When to call in professional help

- When your emotions are too much, and you feel chronically tense and empty.
- When symptoms – e.g. lack of appetite, nightmares – do not disappear.
- When one or more of the three main elements of psychotrauma – re-experiencing, denial and inappropriate arousal – persists.
- When, after a month, you are still not able to enjoy anything.

Helping others

- Keep in contact.
- Let the other person talk: they may well need to go over the event several times.
- Occasionally say what you understand the other person to be saying.
- Be patient, both with the person and with the process of recovering.
- Offer to do the things with them that you normally do with them.

The rest of the original checklist is mainly 'Don'ts', but if you do the above and not much else, you will avoid these.

POWER

(*See also*: Abuse, Assertiveness, Boundaries, Contract, negotiating a, Counselling, Endings, Expectations, clients', Furniture, Immediacy, Multicultural counselling, Questions, Respect, Role conflict, Sexual attraction, Trust)

In most counselling relationships, the counsellor has more power than the client: counselling takes place in the counsellor's room, counsellors may be seen as an expert or authority, they know more about counselling than the client, clients disclose far more about themselves than counsellors do, and clients are often in a particularly troubled and vulnerable period of their lives.

An imbalance of power makes abuse more likely, and can be an obstacle to the trust and clear communication at the heart of most approaches to counselling. Most counsellors try to reduce the power imbalance and to support clients' responsibility and autonomy. Listening hard to the client is deeply respectful in itself, and so is the process of negotiating a contract. The general principle is to be aware of differences, or perceived differences, in power and to discuss them with the client if they're getting in the way of counselling (see Immediacy).

PREPARATION FOR BEING A CLIENT

See: Contract, negotiating a, Expectations, clients'

PRESENTING CLIENTS

See: Supervision, presenting clients for

PRESENTS FROM CLIENTS

(*See also*: Assertiveness, Boundaries)

There seems to be nothing inherently wrong with accepting gifts from clients from time to time, particularly as tokens of appreciation when counselling is coming to an end, for example. The occasional small gift need not be any cause for concern, and can be enjoyed, but the client who is forever bringing or sending unwanted or expensive gifts can be a problem. Inappropriate gifts are a challenge to boundaries, and your client may be in counselling partly because he or she is confused or unaware about appropriate boundaries; accepting gifts from such clients can create further problems.

It can be difficult to refuse a gift. Some people can be very hurt or embarrassed by a refusal, so it needs to be done with great sensitivity. Moreover, gifts have different significance in different cultures. It may be better to risk hurt or embarrassment by confronting the issue directly, but how you do this will depend on the approach you take generally to counselling. In psychodynamic counselling, a client offering a gift may be thought of as exhibiting transference, and you will deal with this in the same way you deal with all forms of transference. A person-centred counsellor might appreciate the sentiment behind the gift, but want to express his or her own mixed feelings about accepting it. Whichever form of counselling you prefer, it is better to incorporate the 'gift giving' into the counselling directly than to ignore the significance it may have, particularly if it happens often.

PRIVACY

(See also: Confidentiality, Violence and its prevention)

Counselling is essentially a private activity, not only in the sense that it is confidential but also in that it needs to take place in a private setting. An effective counselling relationship can be established only in a non-threatening environment in which the client feels safe and secure. Clients need to feel that they can talk about deeply personal and emotional issues without any risk of being disturbed, overheard or seen by others.

In many modern buildings with lightly constructed or poorly insulated partition walls it is easy to hear doors banging and people talking and laughing or answering the telephone. This can be distracting at best, and could increase a client's anxiety at a time when they already feel vulnerable. They need to feel that nobody will overhear them or suddenly come into the room. While you might have no, or only very limited, choice where the counselling takes place, it is possible to take some steps to enhance the feeling of privacy:

1. Put a clear 'PLEASE DON'T DISTURB' notice on the door.
2. Ensure that the telephone is turned off or that calls will be automatically redirected.
3. Make sure that clients sit where they cannot see or be seen by people passing by any window. Net curtains for windows and translucent self-adhesive sheets for glass door panels can help with this. If fire regulations require that the glass panels can be seen through, you can leave a small gap, covering it temporarily when you are counselling.
4. Inform other users of the building, especially of the corridor and adjacent rooms, of your need for absolute privacy and seek their cooperation. If it is impossible to avoid hearing other people outside the room, it might help clients to tell them that other people are working in the building but that they will not disturb you.
5. Avoid having clients waiting immediately outside the counselling room.

PRIVATE PRACTICE

(See also: Administration, Business, Marketing)

Working as an independent counsellor used to be something of a taboo topic. Feltham (1993) challenged some of the myths: 'I have found the difficulties in earning sufficient money from counselling real, enduring, numerous and rarely openly discussed' (p.165). Among the numerous difficulties and issues of private practice are:

- Using separate premises versus working at home.
- Working alone or in a group practice.
- How to turn away highly disturbed or violent people.
- The effects on children and partners of trying to be quiet, of meeting a client on the way in or out, and of knowing that clients are regularly given your uninterrupted time.
- Tension between ethical practice and the need for an income.

McMahon (1994) and Syme (1994) provide clear, detailed discussions.

PROCESS

(See also: Contract, negotiating a, Hidden agendas, Interpersonal process recall, Parallel process, Self-awareness)

The term 'process' is widely used in counselling to refer to how something functions rather than the content or task, as in the following:

Personal process is the functioning of an individual. When a counsellor is unable to empathise, it is sometimes referred to as 'the counsellor's process getting in the way'.

Group process also refers to what is happening under the surface. For example, a decision is required but one member of the group has a need to control, another wants to impress someone else in the group and a third fears being asked to do more work. All these 'hidden agendas' affect the way a group works. Some groups explore the process, although in meetings it is usually the task which is uppermost. Sometimes the task cannot proceed because the process gets in the way.

PROFESSIONAL DEVELOPMENT

(See also: Accreditation, British Association for Counselling, British Psychological Society, Personal development, Research, Supervision, United Kingdom Council for Psychotherapy)

Professional development includes the following activities:

- Basic and further training.
- Supervision, required throughout a counsellor's working life in the UK and, increasingly, in other countries (Bond, 1993a).
- Membership of professional bodies such as the BAC.
- Taking part in workshops, conferences etc.

- Reading books and journals.
- Counselling for oneself.
- Accreditation, which can be gained through various paths, including the BAC Accreditation Scheme, Association for Student Counselling Scheme, UKCP National Register, BPS Chartered Counselling Psychologist, etc.

More experienced practitioners may develop their work through diversification. Ivey *et al.* (1987, p.336) suggest a simplified version of Morrill's cube model for classifying counselling and related activities. The essence of the model can be represented along three dimensions of intervention, each with separate stages. The stages are developmental: later stages are different, not superior.

1. **Target:** (a) Individual (b) Group (c) Organisation.
2. **Purpose:** (a) Remedial (b) Preventive (c) Developmental.
3. **Approach:** (a) Direct service (b) Consultation and training (c) Research and materials.

Most people start counselling by offering a direct service to individual clients. Their work tends to be remedial. Counsellors may at some point want to shift the target of their efforts from individuals to couples, families, groups or organisations. They may also be interested in moving from remedial into more psychoeducational work. Social skills, relaxation and assertiveness training are all examples of interventions with a positive, preventive and developmental purpose. The approach to counselling may also develop, from working directly with clients to consultation, counsellor training, training of trainers, supervision, research, writing, broadcasting or the production of audiovisual curriculum materials.

PROFESSIONALISM, DEVELOPMENT OF

(*See also*: Accreditation, British Association for Counselling, British Psychological Society, United Kingdom Council for Psychotherapy)

Counselling, unlike traditional professions such as medicine and law, has no statutory body controlling standards of training and practice. Three principal organisations are involved: the BAC, the UKCP and the Counselling Division of the BPS. The UKCP published its national register in 1993 and the BPS Counselling Division, established in 1994, means that there are now Chartered Counselling Psychologists. The BAC, which has a much more catholic representation, holds legal and financial responsibilities for the management of the UK Register of Counsellors, and has well established schemes for the accreditation of counsellors, supervisors, trainers and training courses. For many people these schemes spearhead professionalism.

The idea of professionalism has not received a unanimous welcome. There remain strong feelings of ambivalence, if not unequivocal opposition. Some people dislike the whole idea of the professional as someone who earns money for doing what others do for pleasure, sense of duty or intrinsic interest (Charles-Edwards *et al*., 1989). They reject the tendency to mystify and regulate what they see as a fundamental human process that should be available to all. They resent what they see as the setting up of a closed shop or protection racket and strongly deny the assumption that 'non-professionals' necessarily lack skills or experience.

However, it is hard to see how the advancing wave of professionalism within the BPS, UKCP or even within the BAC can be stopped, or indeed whether it should be. Perhaps the key issue is whether what is primarily in the interests of the professional counsellor is necessarily to the ultimate benefit of clients (Baron, 1996).

PSYCHODIAGNOSIS

(*See also*: Assessment)

The best known systems of psychodiagnosis are listed in ICD-10, the World Health Organization's International Classification of Diseases, and DSM-IV, the American Psychiatric Association's Diagnostic and Statistical Manual of Mental Disorders (Comer, 1998; Brammer *et al*., 1993). Some counsellors, such as Shlien (1989), regard these systems as a form of evil.

Some of the advantages of psychodiagnosis are as follows:

- It suggests strategies and methods that have been shown to be effective with similar problems.

- It provides a framework for research and for the development of a body of knowledge about various patterns of disorder and their treatment.

- Many practitioners find themselves working in mental health agencies where they are required to make diagnostic classification of client problems. In the USA, this is increasingly being linked to health insurance.

- A classification system enables practitioners and researchers to communicate more easily. It is not necessary to list every one of a client's symptoms in order to discuss the client with a supervisor or colleague. A diagnostic category is sufficient to give a general picture of the kinds of difficulty the client is experiencing, which can be elucidated further by individual detail.

Criticisms of psychodiagnosis include:

- Diagnosis often places meaningless and poorly defined labels on clients.

- Labels can become self-fulfilling prophecies if the label is perceived as coming from an 'expert' and is interpreted as a statement about the client's general behaviour. Clients can then more easily avoid taking responsibility by 'acting into' the identified symptoms and accepting the patient role.

- Clients diagnosed with particular disorders can be viewed and treated in stereotyped ways by practitioners, friends, relatives and even the clients themselves for a long time after the disorder has disappeared.

- Practitioners can become preoccupied with a client's history and neglect current attitudes and behaviour, losing sight of the client's individual and unique experience.

- As diagnosis has been associated historically with pathology, there is a danger that counsellors will be preoccupied with pathology and underestimate or exclude clients' strengths and resources.

- There is a risk of gender role-socialisation influencing diagnosis. For example, women socialised into being emotionally expressive and putting the needs of others ahead of their own are vulnerable to being diagnosed in particular ways (e.g. histrionic or dependent). Men socialised into being more distant rather than engaging with others may be seen as paranoid or antisocial. In this way diagnosis may reflect the potential for seeing as pathological those aspects of behaviour that are normative for women/men who have been well socialised.

- Sociocultural influences result in people from particular cultural/ethnic groups being vulnerable to inaccurate diagnosis.

- An emphasis on diagnosis can encourage client dependence on experts.

- Practitioners need to be adequately trained to use the various systems which still have relatively low reliability and validity.

- The use of psychodiagnosis can appear on the surface as eminently scientific and objective, thus heightening the mystique of professionalism and investing practitioners with authority.

PSYCHOLOGICAL TYPE

(*See also*: Good counsellors, Theory)

Psychological type is a theory of personality developed by Myers (1980) from some of Jung's ideas. She suggests 16 'kinds of people', describing all 16 primarily in terms of strengths and potential strengths. The evidence for the theory is good, especially its relationship with the 'big five' factor theory of personality currently dominating personality research (Bayne, 1995a). For a broad perspective on personality, see McAdams (1995) and Winter and Stewart (1995) or one of the many text books – e.g. Pervin and John (1996), Winter (1996).

Type is relevant to counselling in several ways:

1. As an approach to elements of the counsellor's self-awareness.
2. As a way of understanding and accepting four major ways in which clients' personalities vary.
3. As a type theory; that is, going beyond the four major ways to suggest how each person's personality is organised.

4. As an approach to personality development and self-esteem: different types have different patterns of development and find self-esteem in different experiences.

The psychological type of each client can be relevant to many aspects of counselling – for example, when:

- negotiating a contract (e.g. the types tend to have different expectations of counselling)
- being empathic and accepting
- challenging (if appropriate) and
- helping clients set goals or take action (if appropriate).

Type theory suggests that each person prefers, and is more comfortable with, some ways of experiencing and behaving than others. Table 9 lists these preferences and their implications for clients' behaviour, in counselling and generally. The table does not take type development, or other factors affecting behaviour, into account.

The implications for counselling of the tendencies listed in Table 9 follow fairly directly – e.g. if you're an introverted counsellor with an extraverted client, you might consider being more active or at least discussing this with your client (Bayne, 1999). The general principle here is the standard one of discussing relevant aspects of your relationship; for example, using the skill of immediacy to say 'I wonder if you're finding it difficult when I don't speak?' A second general principle is to counsel mainly in your own way but to adapt to clients a little. An alternative view here is that counsellors can learn to 'talk 16 types' (Provost, 1993, p.24), but this may ask most counsellors to be too versatile. Provost also states that 'Although counselors can build rapport by mirroring clients' types, this does not mean that counsellors should become the client's type. Counselors must be themselves and work from their own strengths' (Provost, 1993, p.26)

Psychological type theory (e.g. Provost, 1993) suggests that each counsellor, depending on their psychological type, is likely to be most comfortable and effective in different schools, styles, stages and skills of counselling. For example, counsellors of one psychological type will tend to be more skilled at observing non-verbal cues than at detecting themes; counsellors of the opposite type will tend towards the reverse pattern; counsellors who find that support comes 'naturally' may find challenging more difficult, and vice versa; some types are more comfortable with exploration (tending to neglect action), others with action (tending to neglect exploration) (Bayne, 1995a). However, there is a marked bias in counselling generally towards preferences for 'feeling' (dealing with people) and 'intuition' (inferring meanings). This does *not* mean that other types should avoid counselling: all psychological types can be good counsellors, but with different patterns of strengths and comfort.

Myers (1980) is a key source on psychological type. Provost (1993) and Bayne (1995a,b, 1999) discuss type and counselling. Provost's book is mainly a set of brief case studies, on counselling someone of each of the types. Because type theory is concerned with general personality characteristics it has been widely

Table 9

Behaviour associated with preferences (from Bayne, 1998a)

People who prefer	Tend to
Extraversion	Be more active
	Be less comfortable with reflection
	Be optimistic and energetic
Introversion	Be more at ease with silence
	Be less comfortable with action
	Be more private
Sensing	Be concrete and detailed
	Like a 'practical' approach
	Not see many options
	Be uncomfortable with novelty
Intuition	Take a broad view
	Jump around from topic to topic
	See unrealistic options
	See lots of options
	Overlook facts
	Like novelty and imaginative approaches
Thinking	Avoid emotions, feelings and values in early conversations
	Need rationales and logic
	Be critical and sceptical
	Want to be admired for their competence
	Be competitive
Feeling	Focus on values and networks of values
	Need to care (e.g. about a value, a person or an ideal)
	Be 'good' clients or patients
	Want to be appreciated
Judging	Fear losing control
	Find sudden change stressful
	Need structure
	Need to achieve
	Work hard and tolerate discomfort
Perceiving	Avoid decisions
	Need flexibility
	Avoid discomfort

applied – for instance in education (Lawrence, 1997), careers (Martin, 1995) and relationships (Jones and Sherman, 1997). It also has more complex levels of application (Myers, and Kirby, 1994; Quenk, 1996). To confirm or discover your own psychological type, the best method is to complete the Myers–Briggs Type Indicator, with skilful feedback (Carr, 1997).

QUESTIONS

(*See also*: Challenge, Empathy, Paraphrasing, Summaries and 'moving interviews forward')

In searching for an answer or way to help the client, it can be tempting to take a traditional medical role and ask a series of diagnostic questions. This can easily set up a pattern of question and answer, leading to other questions and more answers, with the questioner controlling the direction of the exploration and holding on to the power in the relationship. This type of interaction does little to establish a warm and positive climate in which clients are encouraged to take responsibility. Yet sometimes questions are useful in counselling. As Benjamin, writing about what he refers to as his 'battle' with the use of the question, says: 'I meant to dethrone it but not drive it out' (1969, p.90).

One system for categorising questions is as follows:

1. Open questions (e.g. 'Tell me about...?') allow freedom of choice of response and are useful for most openings or exploration within the client's frame of reference.

2. Closed questions (e.g. 'Would you like a drink?') usually have a correct and/ or short response. They are useful for obtaining single facts, but limit or control the response.

3. Probe questions (e.g. 'What happened next?') are intended to follow up or expand on initial response. They are the 'what, when, where, why and how' questions, useful in checking information or gathering more detailed and concrete information.

4. Hypothetical questions (e.g. 'What do you think might happen if he walked into the room now?') invite clients to imagine their reaction to hypothetical situations and are useful in encouraging them to consider new ideas or to anticipate or rehearse their reactions.

5. Leading questions (e.g. 'Surely you don't believe that?') usually invite the expected or desired answer and are seldom, if ever, useful in counselling.

6. Multiple questions (e.g. 'Have you lived there long? Do you like it?') involve two or more questions at once and tend to be confusing or answered only in part.

Egan (1990) suggests that the intervention following a question should *never* be another question. It is helpful to reflect on whether the question you are about to ask will inhibit or further the flow of the session and in what way the answer will help you to help the client or whether it will merely satisfy your curiosity. Very brief questions – 'And you?' 'And?' 'But?' (each of which is also a challenge) – can occasionally be useful, but generally we suggest asking very few questions. For detailed discussion of types of question etc. see Dillon (1990).

QUESTIONS (PERSONAL) ASKED BY CLIENTS

(*See also*: Assertiveness, Boundaries, Self-disclosure by counsellors, Trust)

Clients sometimes ask personal questions like 'Are *you* married'?, 'Do you like football?', 'Have you been depressed?' How you answer depends to some extent on your model of counselling and the particular circumstances, including how much you're taken by surprise! A general factor to take into account is the client's emotional state: whether she or he is feeling vulnerable and insecure, or curious and challenging. One option for dealing with such questions is to give a brief, direct answer and immediately return the focus to the client. For example, 'Yes, I am. Does it make a difference to you?' or 'No, I haven't. Would you feel more understood or optimistic if I had?'.

Another possibility, though one that runs the risk of sounding like a stereotypical psychoanalyst, is to say something like 'I find that an interesting question for you to ask. Can you say what lies behind it?' or – more bluntly – 'What's the statement behind that question?' If you have a sense of what lies behind the question, you can reflect that to the client, who may not want a literal answer but is saying something about him- or herself or their attitude towards you. The underlying question, as with criticisms of you as being too young, lacking relevant experience, etc. to be a counsellor, may be 'What are you like?' or 'Can I trust you?', so you might say, for example, 'No, I'm not HIV positive but I've spent some time learning about it, and I want to understand what it's like for you.'

QUIET CLIENTS

(*See also*: Beginnings, Contract, negotiating a, Contraindications for brief counselling, Difficult clients, Experiments by clients, Pencil and paper exercises, Rapport, Reluctant clients, Silence, Trust)

There are many reasons for clients being quiet: they may be reluctant, resistant or stuck, they might not know what is expected of them, they may be a quiet person, or may be reflecting. The most important point seems to be whether the silence is beneficial to the client. He or she might need time to adapt to you, to trust you, to think, or to summon up the courage to take responsibility for themselves. It is for you to establish whether the client has a problem with silence and, if so, why. It is also for you to establish that clients know what is expected in the session and if they really want to be there at all. At least initially, some clients find face to face contact threatening. 'Pencil and paper' and other exercises can be a gentle way of respecting and coping with this reaction.

RAPPORT

(*See also*: Beginnings, Congruence, Contract, negotiating a, Core conditions, Empathy, Multicultural counselling, Psychological type, Readiness to change, Referral, Trust, Working alliance)

Rapport is implied by such metaphors as 'in tune', 'being on the same wavelength' and 'a meeting of minds'. It is an intuitively compelling but vague idea. Establishing rapport with a new client is an important part of the initial stages of counselling. One technique is to copy, to some extent, the way each client speaks, uses visual images, and so on. This is too mechanical and contrived for some tastes, and could be experienced by clients as a form of mimicry. It could also conflict with being congruent and natural. However, rapport is easier to establish if your way of speaking and the language you use is not completely at odds with that of your client, and some accommodation to another person is itself a natural part of communication.

In the initial stages of counselling you will be concentrating on listening to and understanding your client, and this includes being aware of your client's way of expression and language. It is possible to maintain your own natural and spontaneous 'way of being' while remaining sensitive to your client's manner and mood. The important thing is to take your time, and 'tune in' to your client gradually without trying to force rapport before either of you are ready: rapport develops with trust.

RAPPROCHEMENT

See: Common factors, Integration and eclecticism

READINESS TO CHANGE

(*See also*: Assessment, Contraindications for brief counselling, Expectations, clients', Furniture, Multicultural counselling, Working alliance)

Some people take to counselling much more easily than others. Counselling cannot begin until people recognise their need to change and until they are at least some way towards committing themselves to change.

Prochaska and DiClemente (1984) suggest the following four-stage model for assessing how ready a person is to change:

1. **Precontemplation:** in this stage people see little or no point in counselling, at least for themselves. They are 'reluctant clients', who have usually been persuaded by friends or relations to try counselling. They are clearly sceptical and doubt the value of counselling, even though they might admit that they would like things or people around them to be different. Reluctant clients tend to drop out quickly. The counsellor can check whether the client sees themselves as in this stage and the implications.

2. **Contemplation:** people recognise that they have a problem and are thinking seriously about what they might do about it. They are not fully committed to the idea of counselling, but tend to be open to exploration and willing to talk about themselves and their problem. Some versions of the model include a preparation stage here, the meaning of which is as it sounds. See the entries on beginnings and expectations.

3. **Action:** at this stage, people have tried different ways of coping with their problems. They have some understanding of themselves, the nature of the

problem and often have clear ideas about what they want to do. People in this stage are genuinely prepared to commit themselves to counselling, but may be impatient to move forward rather than to explore and clarify.

4. **Maintenance:** in this stage people tend to have already made significant changes in their lives. They may have had previously positive experiences of counselling and be fully committed to its value. They seek counselling at this stage to reinforce earlier gains and to develop new strategies and coping skills to prevent the recurrence of problems and to find more positive ways of living.

Dryden and Feltham (1992) argue that counsellors need to be able to recognise the stage of readiness to change of their client. They warn that difficulties will be caused by attempting to apply a single therapeutic approach to all clients, irrespective of the stage they are in. Several factors appear to contribute to higher levels of client readiness – these include positive and realistic expectations of counselling and/or the counsellor, intellectual curiosity, willingness to self-disclose, feeling liked by the counsellor, flexible attitudes and defence systems, openness to new perspectives, high level of commitment to counselling, comfortable physical surroundings and a sense of the counsellor as aware of and sympathetic to any cultural and ethnic differences. Counsellors in general prefer to work with young clients (Brammer *et al.*, 1993), and this can contribute to clients feelings of being liked and therefore to their readiness to change.

RECORD KEEPING

(*See also*: Administration, Confidentiality, Note taking, Sued, being, Suicide)

The BAC do not at present (1998) require or recommend that counsellors keep records, although Bond (1993a) thinks they will at some point. Arguments for keeping records include:

1. Writing them helps to organise your thoughts and feelings (though this is an argument for writing rather than for keeping what you write).
2. Records are an aid to memory and therapeutic planning.
3. Records provide evidence of any change.
4. Records provide evidence of care and professional responsibility.

More formally:

1. To monitor progress: main purpose underpinned by other objectives that follow.
2. To record content: aide-memoire for the next session and for supervision sessions, to help identify key issues/themes/patterns and to facilitate referral.
3. To facilitate reflection on your interventions/responses, your feelings, thoughts, sense of self in the relationship with your client and what is going on in the relationship.

4. To develop clinical formulation or assessment: what is going on for the client – nature, origin and ramifications of client's problem.

5. To develop a therapeutic plan: articulating sense of direction and purpose, plans, objectives/goals, strategies, obstacles and ways forward, target of change, focus.

6. To identify issues for supervision: what you want to discuss in supervision, start recording issues you want to explore.

7. To demonstrate responsibility: to provide evidence of professional and ethical responsibility (this is essential in difficult/problematic circumstances).

The arguments against keeping records include:

1. Avoiding problems of confidentiality and security.

2. Record keeping takes time.

3. Clients may wish to see the records (Bond, 1993a, pp.165–167).

What might matter more than the arguments listed above is your model of counselling. How much do you need to remember, and how much would your clients like you to remember? If you do keep records, Bond's discussions of the issues such as who has access to records, their use in court, their content and format, where and how they are kept, and how long to keep them, are likely to be useful (1993a, pp.167–179).

The BAC Code of Ethics and Practice (British Association for Counselling, 1998) states that counsellors should ensure that records of the client's identity (name, address, telephone number etc.) are kept *separately* from any case notes and that arrangements must be made for safe disposal of client records, especially in the event of the counsellor's incapacity or death. It is important to remember that computer-based records are subject to statutory regulations regarding the clients' right of access to their records (see Jenkins, 1997).

REFERRAL

(*See also*: Boundaries, Contraindications for brief counselling, Endings, First impressions, Values)

You will not be the best available counsellor for every client or every type of problem, and this could become apparent at any stage of counselling. However, you and your clients can experience a whole range of emotions about referral. While it can bring a sense of relief and hope, referral can also be disruptive and disappointing. Clients can feel hurt, rejected and reluctant to start again with someone else, or that counselling is not for them anyway. Those who have been passed on from one mental health agency to another may come to believe that their problem is too big for any counsellor and that they are beyond help. Other clients in similar situations feel powerless and become very angry. Referrals in the early stage of the relationship are likely to be less emotionally fraught for both client and counsellor.

The following are some of the circumstances in which it is ethically responsible and appropriate for you to make a referral or to consider a referral:

1. The client wishes to be referred.

2. The client needs longer-term work, an open-ended contract, or more frequent sessions than you have available or, if you work for an agency, are possible within the constraints of the agency's policy.

3. You feel overwhelmed by, do not understand or have insufficient training or experience to deal with the presenting problem.

4. The presenting problem is one for which other more appropriate or specialist agencies exist. At a later or action-planning stage of counselling it becomes apparent that the client needs more specialist advice, information, longer-term counselling, or practical help.

5. The client persistently fails to respond to your counselling and may be helped more effectively by someone else.

6. The client needs medical attention. For example, Daines *et al.* (1997) recommend referral to a general practitioner for unusual headaches, shortness of breath, fatigue and chest pain. For persistent angina (tight, gripping pain in chest, back or arms) they recommend sending for an ambulance (pp.45–46).

7. The client shows signs of severe mental illness and is not able to continue without intensive care and support.

8. There is, in your view, a real risk of harm to the client or others.

9. You or the client are leaving the area to live somewhere else.

10. You experience a very strong negative reaction to a client or there is a clash of personalities.

11. You discover that you and your client share a close relationship.

Whenever the possibility of referral arises a decision should be made with the client, although the initial suggestion may come from you. The process can be brief or take weeks or longer, and you may wish to serve as a 'bridge' and provide short-term supportive counselling. Facilitating any referral involves a number of tasks to ensure as far as possible that clients feel generally positive about it.

- Checking that the agency or individual will be able to accept the referral.

- Helping clients explore, and perhaps resolve, any emotional blocks towards the agency or referral.

- Working towards bringing clients' perceptions of the problem close enough to that of the referral agency for the referral to 'take'.

- Explaining the nature of the help that might be offered and perhaps encouraging the client to consider accepting the help.

- If necessary, helping clients make their own approach or application.
- Reviewing what has been achieved with the clients, and exploring what still needs to be achieved and how the referral agency could contribute to this.
- Anticipating and exploring ways of coping with possible differences and potential difficulties in starting work with someone else.
- Letting clients know that referral doesn't end your care and concern.

In order to increase the number of options and establish an efficient referral system you should develop your own personal contacts and resources file, listing people in a variety of occupations – lawyers, osteopaths, psychiatrists, but particularly counsellors and psychotherapists with different strengths and specialisms from your own. Lazarus gives some subtle examples of the matching involved, e.g. referring to somebody who 'has a way with certain words'. He also suggests a form of words for referring a client when you are 'stuck': 'I think we need a second opinion here, I am missing something; I have a high regard for my colleague so and so, and would recommend that you see him or her' (Dryden, 1991, p.32).

In addition to listing the nature of the help offered by an agency or individual, it is useful for your resources file to contain full information on each agency – for example:

- name of the contact person, telephone number and address
- whether they offer a 24-hour service, drop-in or appointment system
- scale of fees charged, if any, or if financial assistance is available
- probable waiting time
- how the referral can be made and by whom
- whether they offer a telephone service
- whether they send information or publications
- theoretical orientation of counsellors
- training and supervision of counsellors
- code of ethics to which counsellors subscribe
- whether the agency offers individual and/or group counselling.

REFERRAL LETTERS

(*See also*: Administration)

A referral letter is a means by which one professional person communicates with another. Referral letters to the counsellor may contain detailed information about the client or might simply consist of a single-line statement. Although a referral letter could contain important and relevant information, it is also possible that the referrer has a very different picture of the client than the one the counsellor subsequently forms (McMahon, 1997).

PRIVATE AND CONFIDENTIAL

Dr A
10 December 1998

Dear Dr A,

Re: Mr John KILKER, 115 Rexford Lane, London, SE3 7OP, Dob: 7/5/60.

Mr Kilker came to see me following a hold-up at the fast-food restaurant at which he works. We have met for three sessions and I have his permission to contact you.

Mr Kilker appears to manifest many of the signs and symptoms commonly associated with post-traumatic stress disorder. The hold-up took place some three months ago and since that time Mr Kilker has experienced considerable changes in both his physical and psychological condition.

He suffers from regular panic attacks (up to ten a day of varying intensity), sleeps very little and experiences nightmares when he does, has lost over two stone in weight, has intrusive thoughts and images of the event, is tearful and 'low' in mood and is very frightened of what the future holds. He has withdrawn from all social contact, has been unable to return to work and has been avoiding leaving the house wherever possible. I asked Mr Kilker if he ever thought of self-harm and it would appear that he is not suicidal.

Although Mr Kilker's employers have been very sympathetic he is aware that they cannot remain sympathetic indefinitely.

I have used the three sessions that we have had to normalise the feelings Mr Kilker is experiencing and to help him understand the signs and symptoms associated with post-traumatic stress. Although Mr Kilker has found our sessions useful, we have discussed the limits of my competence and the need for him to receive more specialised help. I have therefore asked Mr Kilker to make an appointment to meet you once you have received this letter.

If you require any further information please do not hesitate to contact me.

Yours sincerely

Counsellor

c.c. John Kilker

Figure 3

An example of a referral letter (adapted from McMahon and Doggart, 1997)

A counsellor could be called upon to write a referral letter on behalf of a client. If this is the case, here are some simple guidelines:

- Mark the letter and accompanying envelope 'Private and Confidential' as a way of respecting client confidentiality.
- The client needs to be informed that the letter is being written and, wherever possible, his or her permission obtained for contact to be made. The form the referral letter will take should be discussed with the client.
- Provide the client's full name, address and date of birth as this leaves less room for error in securing, for example, patient notes.
- Include all relevant information (e.g. client's problems) as discussed with the client.
- Differentiate between fact and opinion.
- Keep sentences and paragraphs short – remember the reader (e.g. doctor, voluntary agency, housing department, etc.)

(McMahon, 1997; Warren-Holland, 1998). An example referral letter is shown in Figure 3.

REFLECTION OF FEELINGS

(*See also*: Core conditions, Emotions, Empathy, Feelings, Paraphrasing)

Most counsellors would associate 'reflection of feelings' with Carl Rogers and client-centred counselling, but it is now widely used and part of the range of methods or techniques within almost all approaches to counselling. Reflection of feelings is a way of communicating empathic understanding, but Rogers (e.g. 1987) became increasingly concerned that it was being misrepresented as a simple and rather mechanical technique. For him empathy was not a matter of 'reflection' in the way a mirror reflects, which he thought was a rather passive process. Rather, he was trying to establish the extent to which his understanding of his clients was accurate, and his responses contained the unspoken question 'Is this the way the world feels to you at the moment?' Rogers' preferred terms, later in his life, were 'testing understanding', or 'checking perceptions', where he tried to emphasise the active process involved in both gaining deeper empathic understanding and communicating it.

REGULARITY OF SESSIONS

(*See also*: Boundaries, Contract, negotiating a, Power, Working alliance)

Some clients appreciate being offered the same day of the week, and the same time of day for their counselling sessions. This has at least three possible advantages. First, you may be seen as consistent and reliable, which will help you establish trust with your client, especially at the beginning of counselling. Second, your client may be able to arrange for time away from work or home more easily, especially if childcare arrangements are necessary. Third, it might help to maintain the working alliance as purposeful and concentrated. On the other hand, some clients and counsellors need flexibility, and short 'bursts' of counselling with gaps may help some clients change more effectively.

RELATIONSHIP BETWEEN COUNSELLOR AND CLIENT

See: Common factors, Core qualities, Counselling, Empathy, Psychological type, Rapport, Trust

RELAXATION, PHYSICAL

(*See also*: Imagery, Stress)

Physical relaxation is an obvious way of coping with stress, both immediately and preventively. Two ten-minute sessions of progressive relaxation a day seem to have a beneficial and cumulative effect (Seligman, 1995). However, sometimes attempting to relax is itself stressful. Lazarus and Mayne (1990) discuss such factors as fear of losing control, competitiveness and lack of patience. A flexible approach helps. Some people prefer a well-lit room, others a dark one, some respond best to several two or three-minute sessions, and so on (Lazarus and Mayne, 1990).

RELUCTANT CLIENTS

(*See also*: Avoidance, Denial, Difficult clients, Empathy, Expectations, clients', Information giving, Quiet clients, Readiness to change, Referral)

Clients can see counselling as a luxury or a necessity, but want, at least in part, to be there. They may also see it as an admission of failure, or an indication that they are losing their sanity, and therefore could be wary of attending. Moreover, some clients are coerced into coming by others, e.g. family or an institution. Children nearly always attend at the insistence of others. The reasons for a client's reluctance need to be clarified – they may be anything from lack of information to a deep-seated fear – and clients must be reassured that their needs come first. Queries must be answered; confidentiality assured. Some clients like to know about codes of ethics. Good use of listening skills, empathy and information giving are all central to responding well to reluctant clients. However, reluctant clients (as distinct from clients who are resistant to change) often drop out of counselling. See Egan (e.g. 1998) for further discussion.

RESCUING

See: Drama triangle

RESEARCH

(*See also*: Journals, academic and applied)

Research can be helpful in two ways: first, its existence makes critical thinking and concern for evidence more likely, second, useful studies have been carried out and there will be more. The following is an example of a potentially useful piece of research. Clarke and Greenberg (1986) compared the effectiveness of two kinds of intervention aimed at helping clients with decisions: one (problem-solving) intended to help clients change their way of thinking, the other (the Gestalt two-chair method) focused more on emotions. The study was thus also relevant to theoretical issues, particularly controversy about the relative importance of thoughts and emotions.

In the study, four counsellors trained in the two-chair method and four trained in problem-solving each saw four clients, all of whom were volunteers facing a 'difficult, personal decision'. There was also a 'waiting list' group (a group that received no counselling). The research design had many good methodological points, e.g. the eight counsellors were equally experienced in and positive about their own approach, and the sessions themselves were taped so that they could be rated for actual use of the two approaches. You may at this point like to predict the result.

Both methods reduced indecision more effectively than being on the waiting list, and the two-chair method was more effective than problem-solving. The authors discussed the strengths and limitations of their study, but perhaps the main point is that although they were doing what most counsellors do anyway – comparing different methods to help them decide which is 'best' – they were doing it in a more systematic and explicit way.

Barkham (1993b) discusses some examples of research findings useful to counsellors but suggests 'it is likely that practitioners will continue to be disappointed' (p.141), though his own reviews (e.g. 1990, 1993a,b, 1996) are clear and practical. Barkham's comment about disappointment raises two issues: the role of evidence in counselling practice, and the complex relationship between reading counselling research and theory and being an effective counsellor. On the first issue, research on counselling is not close to replacing each counsellor's judgement, and may never be close. However, judgements should be as informed as is reasonably possible, for obvious ethical and also legal reasons (see entry on being sued). In psychiatry, proponents of 'evidence-based medicine' (EBM) recognise that it is unrealistic to expect practitioners to keep up with the two million papers published in 20 000 medical journals each year (Geddes and Harrison, 1997).

Geddes and Harrison contrast two positions on EBM. Critics of EBM caricature its opponents as 'evangelists who fail to appreciate the complexity of everyday medical practice and who overlook the wisdom of experienced clinicians' (p.220). Advocates of EBM view the critics as 'Luddites who have an overvalued opinion of their clinical acumen'. Between these positions is the question of how best to apply EBM, taking into account such problems as disagreements about interpreting research results and the risk that EBM might be used as an excuse to cut services (Geddes and Harrison, 1997). In particular, there is the risk of finding 'certainty' where it doesn't exist. 'EBM, if used well, maximises the evidence but does not necessarily reduce the fuzziness – the danger is that we assume it does' (Anderson, 1997 p.226).

On the more general issue of the relationship between reading the counselling literature and being an effective counsellor, McLeod (1997) argues that reading can increase 'cognitive flexibility', a desirable characteristic in counsellors. However, it is also possible to read too much and become too theoretical or find it difficult to communicate directly. The literature can be 'a place of irrelevance, illusion, even of danger' (p.162).

Lewis (1993) gives a useful perspective on reading research papers. He argues that the term 'research' is a very loaded one, and best interpreted as 'finding out' rather than anything mysterious. He then discusses ways of getting closer to formal research – he takes the conventional journal paper apart – how to evaluate it, and how to use it. Leong and Austin (1996) provide a clear, calm guide to carrying out research, with lots of practical tips and a respect for all phases of research, including ideas, dealing with journal editors and reviewers, and writing.

For the formal researcher, Bergin and Garfield's handbook (1994) is essential, even though it often exemplifies why practitioners tend to ignore research. A much wider range of research methods is gradually becoming more accepted by the major journals and textbooks (see, for example, Robson, 1993; Sanders and Liptrot, 1993, 1994; McLeod, 1994). Good attempts have also been made to reduce the terror of statistics, both specifically for counsellors (Liptrot and Sanders, 1994) and generally (Diamantopoulos and Schlegelmilch, 1997).

RESISTANCE

See: Avoidance

RESPECT

(*See also*: Acceptance, Counselling, Core conditions, Warmth)

Respect, also referred to as acceptance and warmth, is considered by most approaches to counselling to be a highly desirable characteristic of the counsellor. Its essential quality is that it is as non-judgemental and unevaluative as possible. Respect is not the same as 'liking' or 'feeling affection', and it is not an instruction to counsellors about how they should feel for their clients; rather, it is a lack of judgement of a client's present way of being, and an acceptance that positive change is possible, even for clients whose behaviour may at present be very destructive towards self or others (Rogers, 1961; Mearns and Thorne, 1988; Merry and Lusty, 1993; Merry, 1995).

RESTIMULATION

See: First impressions, Patterns, Transference

ROLE CONFLICT

(See also: Boundaries, Brief counselling, Confidentiality, Counselling, Effectiveness, Power, Self-awareness, Stress)

For some people counselling is part of a wider professional role. For example, some teachers and nurses offer counselling as one of several ways in which they respond to the needs of others. It is not easy to maintain boundaries between different helping roles with the same person, but many helping professionals are able to achieve this. They seem able to build on their existing relationships, established through their other roles, and offer valuable counselling.

Provided that the distinction between counselling and any other form of helping is explicit, there doesn't seem to be any ethical objection to someone offering counselling to the same person with whom they have, or have had, another role relationship. However, role conflict (as the term suggests) does tend to create some difficulties, five of which are discussed briefly below:

1. **Internal conflict.** It can be very difficult and professionally demanding for the same person to be the expert in one role – with in-depth knowledge of a particular field, efficient and skilled in performing tasks *for* others – and then to switch roles and provide a helping relationship in which the responsibility is on the client to work through and come to terms with painful and emotional aspects of their life.

2. **Expectations.** Clients are also asked to adapt. In the role of the patient, for example, they can justifiably expect a nurse to know some answers and to be able to make some things better but, in the role of the client, they find they can no longer expect things to be made to happen for them in the same way. You may then be faced with their hostility or disappointment, and in turn might doubt your own ability as a counsellor. Clearly this is a difficulty that any counsellor might face at some time with any client, not just those who are having to switch roles with the same person. Nevertheless, role conflict can intensify the problem, and it can be very hard and often discouraging to deliberately resist a client's expectation of us to be someone who has the answer.

3. **Power.** Perhaps anyone who sets themselves up to help others in any professional helping role, not just as a counsellor, will automatically become 'superior'. Neutrality in any helping role, including counselling, is probably a myth. The very fact that counsellors place themselves in the position of offering help puts them in a potentially powerful position over the one who temporarily accepts that help. This can feel good and be very seductive. It is important that counsellors recognise this aspect of the counsellor–client relationship so that it can be appropriately controlled and used (Egan, 1990) or put aside as far as possible (Rogers, 1987).

4. **Individual needs.** Relatively little is known about why people become counsellors. The decision may reflect a special need to help others and to be needed. This source of satisfaction from counselling is quite ethical, unless clients are exploited. A safeguard against this is for counsellors to ensure that their personal lives meet most of their needs sufficiently. Counsellors must monitor what is going on for them and be aware of the ways in which they might misuse their relationships with clients.

5. **Pressure of work.** Professional helpers tend to be very busy. Within the current ethos of quality control and accountability, there is a pressure to get things done as quickly and efficiently as possible so that more can be done for more people. Employers expect results. The difficulty for counselling is that it takes time – sometimes weeks or months – to establish an effective working relationship with clients and allow them to explore and work through their problem and find the best way of coping effectively. It is very tempting to tell clients what to do, what to think and feel in order (on the surface) to manage or resolve their problems quickly. Counselling doesn't work like this, but it can be difficult (especially for someone who offers counselling as one of several ways of helping) to put these pressures aside.

ROOM

See: Furniture, Non-verbal communication

SAFETY

See: Violence and its prevention

SELF-AWARENESS

(*See also*: Assertiveness, Drama triangle, Emotions, Feelings, Immediacy, Interpersonal process recall, Journal, writing a, Metaphors and similes, Patterns, Psychological type, Thoughts, Values)

All the 'core qualities' and many of the skills of counselling require at least a reasonable degree of self-awareness, in the sense of awareness of your own thoughts, emotions, sensations, intuitions, intentions, fantasies, images. If we become clearer about ourselves in this 'inside' sense, we can:

- be clearer with other people
- detect signs of stress earlier
- have more information on which to base decisions
- be more ourselves
- maintain a balance between over-involvement (with consequent stress) and too great a detachment.

Three senses of the term 'self-awareness' are distinguished in Figure 4. First, inner self-awareness, as defined above. Second, self-knowledge, which refers to relatively stable aspects of inner self-awareness, such as talents, values, interests and personality traits. Third, outer self-awareness, which refers to awareness of your own behaviour, and of how it tends to be interpreted by others.

Counsellor education and training focuses on all three senses of self-awareness, because they all have an impact on counselling. Inner self-awareness provides personal experience, especially emotions, intuitions and insights. Self-knowledge affects your judgements of others, and their judgements of you. Outer self-awareness may need to be referred to, e.g. 'I frowned then because...' or 'I was being flippant. There is a serious point there too...'

The idea that we can become more aware of our emotions through counselling, or other ways of focusing attention inwards, applies to the other elements too, and

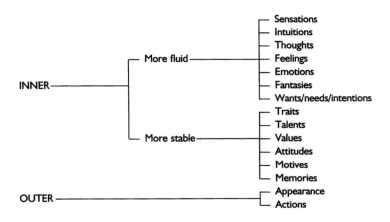

Figure 4

A model of self-awareness

to patterns of emotional responses to people and events, e.g. the drama triangle. There are of course numerous approaches to increasing self-awareness (e.g. Bond, 1986; Dickson, 1987; Merry and Lusty, 1993).

SELF-DISCLOSURE, BY COUNSELLORS

(*See also*: Answerphone, Challenge, Congruence, Crisis, for the counsellor, Furniture, Immediacy, Questions (personal), asked by clients, Self-awareness, Trust)

Three senses of self-disclosure can be distinguished: historical revelation (e.g. 'I've been jealous too'), expression of 'here and now' reactions (e.g. 'I'm feeling stuck'), and non-verbal (e.g. furniture, facial expression). The first should be rare in counselling, although occasionally it is very helpful, the second is a normal part of some approaches to counselling, and the third is almost inevitable.

Self-disclosure in the historical revelation sense can be a useful model for clients who find talking about themselves difficult. Your client may also trust you more. The risks, however, are substantial. In particular, the client may be baffled and perhaps try to help you. It follows that your purpose in self-disclosure should be clear to both you and your client, and that you should be direct, brief and relevant.

SEXUAL ATTRACTION

(*See also*: Assertiveness, Boundaries, Codes of ethics, Immediacy, Self-awareness, Transference)

Of clients for counsellors

Clients often enter counselling at a time when they feel most vulnerable (after the breakdown of an important relationship, for example) and in particular need of understanding and warmth. It is not surprising, therefore, that clients sometimes become sexually attracted to their counsellors, especially when they feel accepted and valued.

Occasionally, clients make sexual suggestions or advances to their counsellors. Some forms of counselling, particularly psychodynamic counselling, view this as a form of 'transference' (having feelings for the counsellor which originate in, and belong to, past relationships). Whatever the theoretical explanation, it is most important to hear and acknowledge such feelings, but never directly to act on them. It is best to respond with a gentle but firm 'No', and to do this in such a way that your client will not feel rejected as a person.

A brief explanation in terms of ethics and boundaries is also likely to be appropriate; then of course it is a matter of listening to your client's reaction and (again, if appropriate and consistent with your approach to counselling) disclosing some of your reactions. To give a rather clinical perspective, you are demonstrating the difference between expressing feelings on the one hand and acting on those feelings on the other.

Of counsellors for clients

(*See also*: Abuse, Boundaries, Immediacy, Power)

The counselling relationship can be very special and close. Counsellors may feel great warmth and love for their clients, and sometimes feelings of sexual attraction. This is not a matter of shame or even regret. However, it is important both to acknowledge these feelings and not to act on them directly. Acknowledging them may mean talking about them with someone you trust, perhaps a supervisor or supervision group, though this may feel risky. Some approaches to counselling suggest sharing your feelings with your client: this may, in some circumstances, be sound advice, but we suggest caution and (perhaps in supervision) a role-play first.

Becoming sexually involved with a client is always unethical, though defining 'sexual' can be a problem (Russell, 1993). It is most important to protect the integrity of the counselling relationship, to be sensitive to and caring of the needs and feelings of your client, to protect and value the professional nature of the counselling activity, and to be true to your own professional, ethical and moral standards. Bond (1993d, p.111) argues that the priority of your concerns should be the client, professional issues and the counsellor, in that order.

The ethics of sexual involvement with an ex-client are more arguable. Russell (1993) argues, on the basis of models of loss and grief, for a six-month period before ex-clients (not counsellors) make contact socially, and current opinion seems to be moving towards a 'cooling off' period, depending on such factors as the length and nature of the counselling relationship (Bond, 1993a,b,d). The idea of imposing an absolute ban does not do justice to the possibility of love between counsellor and ex-client, rather than an exploitative relationship or a misuse of power. Bond's final point gets to the heart of the debate within the BAC: 'The regulations will need to be appropriately protective of clients' interests but without infantilizing them or ignoring their right to act autonomously once the counsellor–client relationship is truly ended' (Bond, 1993b, p.107). But, as he earlier points out, some counsellors believe that some or all counselling relationships are never ended.

The BAC Code of Ethics and Practice for Counsellors (British Association for Counselling, 1998) states that counsellors 'remain accountable for relationships with former clients ... Any changes in relationship must be discussed in counselling supervision' (B.5.3), and that 'Counsellors who belong to organisations which prohibit sex with all former clients are bound by that commitment' (B.5.4.).

SHORT-TERM COUNSELLING

See: Brief counselling

SHOULDS

See: Thoughts

SILENCE

(*See also*: Empathy, Immediacy, Paraphrasing, Questions)

Silences – pauses, intervals, moments of tension – *can* be very caring and effective, depending on the *kind* of silence. Some silences are 'working' ones; your client is trying to clarify or disentangle something. Others are natural breaks; there is nothing more to say about something, at least for the moment. These silences can be very peaceful. Other silences are lost, rejecting or hostile; your client has had enough or is stuck. The best option here is probably to try to be (gently) empathic, for example by saying 'You seem very fed up with this?' or 'You're finding it difficult to talk about?' If you can't tell from the context or the client's expression what is going on, you could say something like: 'We've been quiet for some time. I'm not sure what's happening...'

SMOKING

(*See also*: Boundaries, Stress)

If you don't smoke and you don't like smoking, you have a right to establish as part of the 'contract' with your clients that they don't smoke during sessions. Provided that your clients know beforehand that they cannot smoke, they will decide whether to continue with you or not. Most people who smoke will be able to accept a 'no smoking' agreement.

In the same way, if you smoke and would like to smoke during the sessions (or in the room between sessions), it is a good idea to discuss this with your clients before the counselling starts. Some people are allergic to tobacco smoke, or become very physically distressed by it; others don't mind at all. Some even enjoy tobacco smoke, even when they don't smoke themselves. If you are not a heavy smoker, you will probably be able to smoke with some clients and not others, but remember that the smell of stale tobacco smoke is disliked by many people, even when no-one is smoking at the time. It tends to linger on clothes and curtains.

Smoking is an addiction, and some people can find it intensely uncomfortable, even painful, to go without it for very long, especially if they become emotional or distressed. The best overall principles therefore seem to be being clear about your attitude to smoking with your clients, and doing your best to respect the needs of both you and your client.

If you work in an organisation, you may be asked to advise, or take part in, steps to limit or ban smoking there. The current position appears to be that courts expect reasonable employers to take action to eliminate passive smoking by employees. All workplaces in Europe are required to provide separate rest rooms for smokers and non-smokers, or to ban smoking completely. People who smoke may be offered counselling, and might feel victimised and angry, especially if policies are implemented crudely (Batten, 1992).

STATUTORY REGISTRATION

(*See also*: Accreditation, Professionalism, United Kingdom Register of Counsellors)

Registration by statutory legislation can take many different forms. It can be compulsory (i.e. practitioners cannot practice unless they are registered) or voluntary. Parliament may provide the necessary minimal framework for a profession to manage or regulate itself or the framework could be detailed and prescriptive, depending upon the perceived need for and terms of the legislation. Statutory registration often amounts only to protection of the professional title – i.e. people may practice and offer the relevant services but may not use the professional title unless they are registered.

At present (1998) the UK Register of Counsellors is a voluntary (non-statutory) register, although some form of statutory registration is being considered for the future. While some counsellors are strongly opposed to any form of statutory registration, others see it as the only way to establish counselling as a profession.

The purpose of statutory registration is usually expressed in terms of 'establishing standards to protect the public or consumer' but it also provides a profession with legal protection supported by accreditation or entry procedures and requiring adherence to codes of ethical and professional practice.

STRESS

(*See also*: Journal, writing a, Self-awareness, Supervision, presenting clients for, Post-traumatic stress disorder, Stress, coping with, Support groups, peer, Thoughts)

The word 'stress' is often used to refer to the situation which causes unwanted bodily reactions. It is clearer if the situation as perceived by the stressed person is called the *stressor* and the word *stress* is used for the effects on the person. Several kinds of stressor have been suggested as relevant to counsellors (Brady *et al.*, 1995; Feltham, 1995b):

- Client behaviours such as depression and talking about abuse.
- Financial instability.
- Psychic isolation – not enough intimacy in the counsellor's personal relationships.
- What Hawkins and Shohet (1989, p.10) call the 'shadow side of helping' – hidden motives for being a counsellor, such as a need for power, or a fear of intimacy.

What is stressful varies from person to person. Mild stimulation for one person is intolerable for another. It is the interaction of the potential source of stress with the perception of the individual, plus their attitude and physiological vulnerabilities, that matters. Stress is therefore a body–mind–body interaction: the receptors of the body receive the stimuli, the mind interprets them and the body reacts to these interpretations.

Stress is not entirely negative; some stressors can be beneficial (for example, by lessening boredom), stress may help a person to face up to themselves, to sort out their lives and develop new talents. Some stress, if looked at positively, can be exciting, although looked at negatively it would be anxiety-provoking. The mental attitude is important in the way we regard potential stress.

When a person is overstressed, their thinking, emotions, and the body are likely to be affected. Thoughts often become more negative. Some people become anxious, others angry and yet others depressed, but in all these moods there are usually associated negative thoughts about self, others, or a particular situation. At the same time, the autonomic nervous system stimulates the body to produce signs of stress and, again, these vary between individuals. The heart rate becomes faster, the breathing more shallow, the digestive system slows down and muscles tense. Often a person feels tired but unable to sleep; in others the opposite is true and they sleep too much. All these changes can make the person irritable or ill, and he or she might turn to unhealthy sources of comfort, e.g. too much food, smoking.

STRESS, COPING WITH

(*See also*: Assertiveness, Boundaries, Emotions, Journal, writing a, Physical activity, Post-traumatic stress disorder, Relaxation, Self-awareness, Supervision, Support groups, peer, Thoughts)

Often it is hard to realise that you are overstressed. It is only when they become ill that most people realise something is wrong, and even then they may regard the illness as something outside their control. The first step in overcoming stress is often to understand its nature. After this, it is a matter of seeing which of the three components of stress you can most readily or usefully alter: the stressor, your mind or your body.

The stressor can be altered, modified or eliminated, but sometimes just help in understanding it may be beneficial. Counselling or therapy, particularly cognitive therapy, silent prayer or meditation, may help to sort out negative thoughts, attitudes and perceptions and so generally improve your mental state. For your body, exercise, relaxation and breathing exercises can all be beneficial. It is advantageous if you use coping strategies for both your body and your mind; if they are relaxed and in harmony, you are better able to cope with the stressors of life.

Effective coping with stress involves:

- noticing your own *early* signs of too much stress, and taking action, then

- finding strategies that suit you, and using a variety of strategies.

For discussion of strategies see Bond (1986), Burnard (1991), Rosenthal (1993), Fontana (1989), Palmer and Dryden (1995) and Bayne (1998a). For straightforward neck and back exercises (after checking with your general practitioner), see McKenzie (1983, 1988).

As in counselling, small steps and gradual change are more likely to succeed for most people. Reading about the 'successes' and 'failures' of other counsellors can be very helpful (e.g. Yalom, 1989; Mearns 1990a, b). It may also help to believe – really believe – that in counselling and the health professions generally, there is always more to do, and that it is up to each of us to set our own priorities and boundaries. Proper rest and recovery time is part of being an effective counsellor.

SUED, BEING

(*See also*: Advice, giving, Codes of ethics, Complaints, Insurance, indemnity, Marketing, Referral, Research)

Like all professionals, counsellors are legally required to exercise 'reasonable care and skill' in their work. 'Reasonable' is defined by the profession itself in its codes of ethics, major textbooks and the views of leading practitioners or (in a profession, like counselling, in which there is much disagreement) a subgroup of responsible practitioners within the profession (Cohen, 1992). Cohen further remarks: 'In theory, the courts are entitled to find that an established professional practice is itself negligent; in practice, particularly in medical negligence cases, they have been most reluctant to do so...' (p.12). The professions are trusted by the courts to set and maintain reasonable standards and methods.

The following advice seems clear from Cohen's discussion:

1. Do not guarantee improvement (or non-deterioration) to a client.
2. Do not give advice to clients.
3. Be sure that any information given is accurate and that 'homework' assignments are both legal and ethical.
4. Check your office for physical dangers (slippery floors, sharp edges, etc.) – 'reasonable care' again.
5. Recommend the client sees a doctor if you suspect that his or her emotional problems have a physical cause.

All these actions, apart perhaps from (4), are part of normal professional practice by counsellors. According to Cohen (1992), failure or negligence even for these actions is unlikely to lead to legal action but he emphasises that much of the law in this area is unclear at present. Jenkins (1998) notes an 'enormous increase in civil litigation, and the introduction of conditional fees.' However, Jenkins also sees a significant increase in litigation against counsellors by clients as unlikely, especially if the counsellor works within 'what is accepted to be mainstream practice, as established on the evidence of expert witnesses' (Jenkins, 1998, p.41).

An interesting possibility is that 'mainstream practice', which is obviously very diverse in counselling, may at some time include the notion of 'empirically validated'. Counsellors who failed to use effective techniques, or to refer appropriately, would then be more open to legal action.

Jenkins (1997) gives a comprehensive introduction to legal matters in relation to counselling England and Wales. He provides guidelines and information on such issues as data protection law, insurance, complaints, counselling children and record-keeping. He also discusses the probable effects of European law on counselling.

SUICIDE

There are many myths about suicide (Comer, 1998). For example:

- It isn't true that people who talk about suicide never commit it. People who commit suicide often give clues or definite warnings about their intention.
- People who attempt suicide are not necessarily fully intent on dying. Most are undecided about living or dying and sometimes 'gamble with death', leaving it to others or 'fate' to save them. They may not be aware of their motives.
- Apparent improvement doesn't mean that the risk of suicide is over. Many suicides occur some months after apparent recovery from a suicidal crisis and when the person has the energy to act.
- People are not 'suicidal people' as such; they are people who want (or think they want) to kill themselves, but are suicidal only for a limited time.
- People who commit suicide don't necessarily have a mental disorder, but do tend to be extremely depressed.

People who threaten to commit suicide are typically in a state of overwhelming anguish, highly emotional and ambivalent, absorbed by their problems. They frequently experience rejection or loss and hostility towards self and others. They tend to think in unusually constricted ways that lead them to see suicide as the only logical answer to their problems.

Guidelines for intervention

Approaches to helping people who threaten suicide vary according to whether the help is primarily preventive or crisis intervention (i.e. after suicide has already been attempted). A client mentioning suicide must be taken seriously and the possibility talked about with the client straight away. Some clients, however, only hint at suicide, so it is necessary to listen carefully for clues and confront the client gently; 'It sounds like you feel life isn't worth living for you and you want to end it.' If they question whether there is anything to live for, acknowledge the truth of this for them, and ask if they will give you a chance to listen to them, talk about their feelings and find out if there *is* anything for them to live for.

Most approaches to preventing suicide suggest various tasks and stages, and assume that the counsellor will be relatively active and directive.

1. Establish a positive relationship.
2. Clarify the problem.
3. Assess the risk.

   (a) Precipitating factors: identify possible stressful events and assess whether the level of stress is chronic or acute, recent, episodic or longer term.

   (b) Symptoms: assess the severity of symptoms and whether there has been any sharp, noticeable and sudden onset, e.g. severe depression, withdrawal, delusions, hallucinations, etc.

   (c) Suicide plan: assess the degree of detail and clarity of any plan. Does the client know when, where and how they intend to kill themselves? In particular, how specific is the intended timing and how lethal and realistic is the proposed method?

   (d) History of suicide or depression.

   (e) Client's resources: assess the nature and level of social support and the client's ability to make use of it. Explore the client's view of what other people think of them. A lack of sympathy or understanding can increase the risk of suicide.

4. Form a plan of action. Try to help the client see the temporary nature of the crisis and to recognise possible alternatives to suicide. Counsellors are typically more active/directive than usual, offering guidance and suggestions. Although many clients will view themselves as helpless most will have some strengths and resources, e.g. being employed. Initial plans need to be short-term – identifying any potential 'low' spots in the day and ways of coping differently with them. Some counsellors negotiate a 'no-suicide pact' in which clients promise not to attempt suicide before the next counselling session, or before contacting the counsellor.

The strategy you choose depends partly on the degree of suicide risk. If there is a high risk that a client will actually commit suicide it might be necessary to refer him or her for treatment, hospitalisation, inform their general practitioner, friends or relatives. Such action could mean breaking confidentiality. In this instance counsellors normally try to encourage the client to take the particular course of action for themselves; failing that, they ask the client's permission or agreement, and in the last resort simply tell the client what they are going to do before they do it. It can be helpful for the counsellor to tell the client that they don't want to carry the responsibility of the knowledge alone.

Most counsellors dealing with seriously suicidal clients should contact their supervisor as soon as possible. It is also essential to keep detailed case notes of the assessment, decisions or action taken with supporting evidence, together with times and dates – i.e. to act in a considered and professional way. See Bond (1993a,c) for further discussion.

SUITABILITY OF CLIENTS FOR BRIEF COUNSELLING

See: Assessment, Contraindications for brief counselling

SUMMARIES AND 'MOVING INTERVIEWS FORWARD'

(*See also*: Challenge, Concreteness, Counselling, Intuition, Paraphrasing, Questions)

A summary of what your client has said should help to clarify what they mean, feel and think, and to make more sense of it. In addition it may increase your client's sense of control and hope, or reduce feelings of being overwhelmed. Summaries need to be tentative (they could be wrong in content or emphasis), and have a flavour of 'This is where we are so far, in outline, so where next?' 'Where next' may be further exploration, a focus on one problem or aspect of a problem or the end of counselling. Gilmore (1973) discusses ways of offering clients a way forward: for example, you might add the question 'Is there one of these you'd like to talk about first?' to your summary (they may choose differently from you!). Or you might use a hunch: 'Perhaps your main worry is...' or 'What seems to be most important is...' Alternatively, you might suggest focusing first on something which seems relatively straightforward (Gilmore, 1973).

A further variation is to add a hypothetical question to your summary. Gilmore (1973) calls this 'requesting a contrast'. For example, you might say in the preliminary summary 'You're unhappy about your work, especially whether you can cope with your boss's bullying. You'd love to be fitter and sleep better. And you're worried about being late for work, both because it lets your colleagues down and because being on time matters to you.' (Pause for your client to respond if he or she wishes.) A 'contrast' for this client would be to add: 'Suppose you were sleeping well. Do you think any of your other problems might look different?'

Requesting a contrast works sometimes very well: it helps a client clarify a present feeling or focus on a key point. The risks, though, are also potent: it can look like (or become) premature problem-solving (the instant solution) or lead to a general speculative discussion. Again, how you say something, and your attitude and general approach, are central – and there is a strong artistic element: timing, how you speak, and the quality of the relationship between you and your client all play a part.

A final variation is to ask your clients to summarise.

SUPERVISION

(*See also*: Codes of ethics, Freewriting, Multicultural counselling, Peer supervision, Process, Supervisors, BAC accredited, Tape-recording, Transference)

In the UK, all counsellors are required to discuss their work regularly with a third party, the supervisor (cf. Feltham, 1996). Supervision is primarily for addressing the needs of clients, but it is also to support the counsellor. In addition the relationships between counsellor and client and counsellor and supervisor, and the supervisor's 'process', all need to be kept in mind (Figure 5). A useful resource to work with, as it shows much of what actually happened in the session, not just what is reported, is a tape of a counselling session.

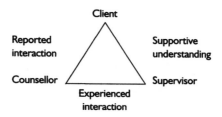

Figure 5

The process of supervision

Supervision is preferably carried out by someone who does not have another role (e.g. line manager) with the counsellor, and who therefore can concentrate solely on the counselling. The BAC Code of Ethics and Practice for the Supervision of Counsellors covers the nature of supervision, issues of responsibility, issues of competence, the management of supervision work and confidentiality.

Hawkins and Shohet (1989) distinguish several modes of supervision that may be used together or at different times, although they say that supervisors often have one preferred area of working. The modes are as follows:

1. Reflect on what the client said and did, avoiding premature theorising.

2. Explore the strategies and interventions used by the counsellor, and possible alternatives.

3. Explore the counselling process and relationship.

4. Focus on the counsellor's counter-transference.

5. Focus on the 'here-and-now' process as perhaps mirroring aspects of the counselling itself ('parallel process').

6. Focus on the supervisor's or supervision group's 'counter-transference.'

A seventh mode is to focus on multicultural factors.

Different ways of carrying out supervision are described in the BAC Code of Ethics for Supervisors:

1. **One-to-one: supervisor–counsellor.** This is the usual form of supervision, in which the supervisor is more experienced than the counsellor and may have attended a supervision course, or is accredited by the BAC as a supervisor.

2. **One-to-one co-supervision.** The time is divided evenly between the two, and they supervise each other. This method is suitable only for experienced counsellors and supervisors.

3. **Group supervision with a supervisor.** There is a range of ways of doing this, from the supervisor working with each individual in turn to the supervisor being the overall facilitator of a group process.

4. **Peer-group supervision.** This is for a group of counsellors of similar experience working with each other.

For further discussion of supervision see Inskipp and Proctor (1989, 1993), Houston (1990), Bond (1993a), Horton (1993), and Inskipp (1996a).

SUPERVISION, NEGOTIATING A CONTRACT FOR

In thinking about a supervisor it may be helpful not to see yourself as a recipient, and supervision as something that is done to you, but rather as a participant and supervision something you do. In this sense you are a consumer and it is worth considering carefully what you want from supervision and negotiating a working agreement with your supervisor. The following guidelines are adapted from Inskipp and Proctor (1993):

Information wanted from the supervisor

- Any vacancies and when (day/time) and fees charged. (This information is usually obtained before the first meeting with the supervisor.)
- Theoretical orientation and training.
- Experience as counsellor *and* supervisor.
- Professional affiliation (code of ethics).
- Sanctions and expectations of ethical and 'good enough' practice.
- Method of payment of fees.
- Preferred method of working – e.g. how to present clients, how to record information about clients.
- Boundaries between supervision and personal counselling for the supervisee.

Information to give to the supervisor

- Your qualifications and experience as counsellor.
- Your theoretical orientation.

- Your professional affiliation (code of ethics).
- Where you see clients (agency/organisation) and how many clients you have.
- Type/range of presenting problems.
- Accommodation/counselling room.
- Any training course requirements.

Issues to negotiate

- Time, place, frequency and length of session.
- Length of contract and regular review sessions.
- Fee and method of payment (when and how).
- Notice required for cancellation of sessions and missed session payment.
- Method of presentation and recording of clients.
- Learning contract – what you want from supervision.
- Any training course requirements.

Your decision

- Can I work with this person as my supervisor?
- Can this person give me what I want from supervision?
- Do I want to have this person as my supervisor?

SUPERVISION, PRESENTING CLIENTS FOR

(*See also*: Assessment, Contract, negotiating a, Crisis counselling, First impressions, Intuition, Process, Working alliance)

Supervision sessions tend to go better when counsellors have spent some time preparing their presentations, and when a contract has been negotiated between counsellor and supervisor about, for example, length of sessions, frequency of sessions, fees, confidentiality and use of tape-recorders. Once this has been done, there must also be clear agreement about how best to use the supervision time.

In presenting a client for supervision it is often useful to decide whether to focus on the entire counselling process or only parts of it, on the client and his or her problems, or on your own sense of effectiveness and well-being. If, for example, you find a particular client difficult or challenging, you might want to present and discuss the difficulties you experience as issues in themselves, rather than specifically talk about a certain client.

We offer two 'schemes' for the presentation of clients. You might choose one or other of them, or a combination of the two, or may decide to develop your own scheme after discussion with your supervisor. The important thing is that both you and your supervisor have a sense of purpose, and have common ground on the kinds of issues or themes that are suitable as case material for discussion.

This goes for both group and individual supervision.

Scheme one

This is a simple series of 'prompts' which offers ways of focusing on your feelings and thoughts about your relationships with your clients. The list is meant as a series of guidelines rather than rules.

1. What do I wish to accomplish through presenting this case?
2. What specific difficulties do I experience with this client?
3. Does this client remind me of aspects of myself and what do I think and feel about those aspects?
4. What does this client hope to accomplish in counselling?
5. What am I doing well with this client?
6. What could I do better with this client?
7. What am I learning about myself as a person and as a counsellor from this client?

Scheme two

Presenting clients: some frameworks for supervision and 'case' study (modified from Horton, 1993).

1. **Identification**
   (a) First name only. Gender. Age/life stage.
   (b) Your first impressions, client's physical appearance.

2. **Antecedents**
   (a) How the client came to see you – e.g. self-referred.
   (b) Context – e.g. agency, private practice, hospital clinic.
   (c) What you knew about the client before you first met. How you used this information. Any existing relationship with the client and possible implications.

3. **Presenting problem and contract**
   (a) Summary of presenting problem.
   (b) Your initial assessment. Duration of problem. Precipitating factors (i.e. why the client came at this point). Current issues.
   (c) Contract – frequency, length and number of sessions.

4. **Questions for supervision**
   (a) Key issues.

5. **Content**
   (a) Description of the client in Gilmore's (1973) framework:
   - work – significant activities, interests

- relationships – significant people
- identity – feelings and attitudes towards self
- further possible elements are the implications of cultural, economic, social, political and other systems, and the client's early experiences, strengths and resources, beliefs, values, hopes, fears and fantasies.

(b) Problem definition:

- construct a picture of the client's view of the present problem
- what would the client like to happen? How would the client like things to be?

(c) Assessment – how you account for and explain the presenting problem:

- any patterns/themes connections?
- which theoretical concepts or models apply? Hunches? New perspectives?

(d) Counselling or therapeutic plan:

- direction or focus for future work?
- criteria for change?
- review and/or formulate plan(s).

6. Process

(a) Strategies and interventions:

- what strategies and interventions have you used?
- what was your intention?
- what was their impact on the client?
- what alternative strategies are there?

(b) Relationship:

- what was happening between you and the client? Reframe the relationship; try a metaphor
- what was happening within the client (transference)?
- what was happening within you (counter-transference)?
- what changes have there been in the relationship?
- evaluate the 'working alliance'.

7. Parallel process

(a) What is happening between you and the supervisor?

(b) Any parallels with you and the client?

8. Critical incident analysis

(a) Description:

- what did the client say and do at the particular point?
- what did you say and do?

- how did the client respond?
- what was happening within you?

(b) Analysis:
- what was happening within the client?
- what was going on between you and the client?
- intention and impact of interventions/responses.
- what hunches/hypotheses did you have at the time? And now?
- review.

9. **Listening to aspects of covert communication**

(a) What was happening within you?
- how well did you listen to your own emotional response to a client?
- you may be aware of your feelings first and thoughts later, or the reverse.
- what did the client do and say to make you feel the way you did?
- what does the client want from you and what sort of feeling is she or he trying to arouse in you to get it?

(b) What was happening within the client? Observe and reflect back when appropriate:
- changes in voice quality, which might indicate an inner focus on something that is being seen or felt differently
- idiosyncratic words or phrases
- aspects of content you don't understand; perhaps the client doesn't either
- encoded statements about other people or situations which may, at some level, actually be about the client: e.g. client says: 'It upset me to see the little dog was alone.' A reformulation might be: 'Seeing the dog gave you a sense of desolation and rejection. Something about loneliness worries you' (Rice, 1980, p.144). Reformulations can be practised almost as a game in supervision
- disguised communication. Anything said about something out there *may* be about you and/or the counselling relationship (Langs, 1982)
- non-verbal communication: e.g. silence, gazing into space, posture.

Supervisors, BAC accredited

All counsellors in the UK are required to undergo regular supervision so that they can discuss their work. Many experienced counsellors are also supervisors, and some of these have been assessed in the BAC Accreditation of Supervisors scheme. This involves submitting a curriculum vitae with details of educational background and professional qualifications, counselling experience, training in supervision, supervision experience and reasons for requesting recognition. A tape of a supervision session is also required, with commentaries by both the supervisor and the supervisee. If all of these items reach the required standard, the supervisor is invited to a *viva voce* examination, where they supervise another applicant and also act as supervisee.

SUPPORT

See: Empathy, Common factors, Frameworks, Respect

SUPPORT GROUPS, PEER

(*See also*: Boundaries, Contract, negotiating a, Stress)

The following ideas about peer support are adapted from Bond (1986) and Nichols and Jenkinson (1991). There are three sections: aims, guidelines and practical issues.

Aims

The main purposes of peer support groups are:

- to offer support to each member of the group by, for example, listening carefully to them, and
- to receive support yourself.

Good support has been shown to reduce stress and lessen the risk of mental and physical illness (e.g. Duck, 1998), although of course other methods are also effective. Support groups are not encounter groups, for therapy, or for attempting to solve other people's problems. They are for each person to talk as openly as they comfortably can about important concerns and worries.

Guidelines

1. Confidentiality is vital. A strict interpretation is agreeing not to discuss what happens in your group outside the group with anyone, not even with another group member or the person concerned.

2. Bond (1986, Chapter 6) distinguishes between several kinds of support. The most relevant for peer support groups are listening (pp.158–170), sharing factual information, sharing personal information, advice and encouragement (pp.147–151).

3. The section on pitfalls in giving and receiving support (Bond, 1986, pp.173–176) may also be useful. Pitfalls include refusing support when you need it, feeling obliged to take unnecessary support, and choosing the wrong kind of support.

4. At the end of each meeting, review what is going on in the group, your reactions and if you would like to change anything.

Practical issues

- How many people? (3–6.)
- How often will you meet? (No accepted right amount. Weekly?)
- For how long? (Try an hour? And an initial contract of, say, six meetings?)
- How will you structure each session and allocate time?
- Do you want one of the group to be the leader? Or take turns? Or ...?
- Where will you meet?
- When will you meet? (If you meet irregularly who will arrange meetings?)

If your group goes well and you feel ambitious for it, try reading the book by Nichols and Jenkinson (1991).

TAPE-RECORDING

You may want to tape-record your sessions with some clients, for training or supervision purposes or as a means of self-monitoring. The most obvious ethical principle involved is to consult the clients beforehand and for their permission to be freely given. This means telling them what the recording is for, who will listen to it and what will happen to the tape once it has been used, and listening hard to the client's reaction. If the client gives their permission initially, check again at the end of the session.

Many clients have no objection to being recorded but some are very uneasy about it, and their wishes should be respected. Sometimes clients appreciate knowing they can switch off the tape at any point, and this possibility should be part of your agreement before recording begins. Another option for dealing with an uneasy client is to give the tape or a copy of it to your client after you have finished with it, or to ask them to bring a blank tape to record the session on. If you do this, you might also want to suggest that the client waits a few days before listening to it, discussing where and how they will listen to the tape and the possible effects it could have. You may also want to discuss confidentiality (whether anyone else will hear the tape).

Dryden (1983) discusses two obstacles to recording sessions for supervision: 'over-concern for clients' and problems with operating tape-recorders. On the first he argues that clients are not psychologically damaged by being recorded, that the concern expressed by some counsellors about clients reflects their own anxiety. When faced with a supervisee whose tape-recorder isn't working, Dryden recommends asking them what it would be like for them to present an audible tape for supervision.

On a practical note, a small, unobtrusive tape-recorder is probably better than a bulky one and 120-minute tapes mean no interruption of the usual 50-minute session. Very good small recorders can now be bought quite cheaply, but most interviews benefit from an additional, external, microphone placed between you and your client.

Tapes *must* be kept securely. It is good practice to write on the tape such details as date, session number, and when it should be destroyed.

TAPES, SELF-HELP

See: Books, self-help

TEA AND COFFEE

See: Drinks/refreshments

TEAMS, MULTIDISCIPLINARY

(*See also*: Confidentiality, Group counselling, Note taking)

Counsellors may work as part of, or in liaison with, a multidisciplinary team. Such teams are usually a group of workers involved in the care of an individual. For example, a client with a history of psychiatric disorder may have a psychiatrist, a social worker and a psychologist involved in their care. A hospice is another example of a multidisciplinary team in action. Similarly, residential drug projects may have more than one worker involved in the care of a resident and many counsellors now find themselves part of a multidisciplinary team when they work in general practices.

There are a number of issues to consider when working as part of a multidisciplinary team. First, the boundaries related to individual roles need to be defined, understood and agreed so that each person involved in the team understands the needs of the other team members and the work each will be undertaking with the client. Second, confidentiality must be considered. For the counsellor working as part of a team this means considering what information is to be made available to the team and what should remain confidential between the client and counsellor. It also means being clear with the client about the parameters of confidentiality, and this in turn has an impact on the type of notes taken and their storage, including access.

Multidisciplinary teams fall into two groups. Group one is hierarchical in nature; the team is lead by one worker who has more status and control over client care than the rest of the team. Group two takes a more holistic view about client care; although the team may be led by one worker the client's needs are given primary importance over and above the status of the workers.

For a brief practical introduction to groups at work, see Kwiatkowski and Hogan (1998).

Telephone Counselling

(*See also*: Brief counselling, E-mail counselling, Non-verbal communication)

Telephone helplines have been in existence for some time. The Samaritans, probably the most well known, started in 1953. Counselling agencies and private practitioners have always used the telephone to provide information about their service, receive client referrals and to arrange for crisis intervention work and follow-up interviews. The telephone is an essential facility for maintaining a counselling practice. However, it was not until the mid-1990s that telephone counselling, involving no face-to-face contact for the entire therapeutic contract, began to emerge as an acceptable mode of practice. Since 1997 it has been possible to count some telephone counselling work towards the required number of counselling hours for BAC Individual Accreditation.

Telephone counselling is usually conducted by fully qualified counsellors. It has a number of issues in common with face-to-face counselling, including the need to adhere to ethical codes of practice and to establish explicit contracts concerning the date, time length and frequency of sessions. Contracts tend to be relatively brief – often one to six, and seldom more than 20, sessions. In telephone counselling it is also important to clarify who calls whom and for the client to have access to a telephone in a quiet and private place.

The most obvious difference between telephone counselling and face-to-face counselling is the absence of visual information (and the related assumptions and prejudices). However, voice tone, pitch and accent will all contribute to the impressions the client and counsellor form of each other. Some telephone counsellors negotiate with clients to exchange photographs, but others prefer to work without any visual clues. The relative anonymity of telephone counselling may mean less opportunity for distraction and a more focused relationship. It may therefore demand more effort and concentration and be more tiring. It is also easier for clients to end a session simply by putting the phone down, and clients may have different expectations of telephone counselling than they do of face-to-face counselling (Rosenfield, 1997; Sanders, 1996).

Telephone counselling is especially useful for crisis work and for clients who are ill or have limited mobility, and it obviously saves the time and cost of travelling. As with most brief or time-limited counselling, it is often necessary to work in a more focused way on specific issues, drawing on explanatory concepts and techniques from a variety of theoretical orientations. Telephone counsellors tend to be integrative or systematically eclectic in their approach.

Most telephone counselling operates on a freephone service. However, Rosenfield (1997) points out that it is possible to purchase a premium-rate tariff line and the difference in cost between that and a regular or standard line may constitute all or part of the counsellor's fee. If this is done it is ethical to inform the client of the likely cost per session. The counsellor's number may appear on the client's itemised telephone bill, which may be seen and/or paid by someone other than the client. Counsellors who call their clients can use the 141 block to withhold their number. It might also be useful for telephone counsellors to become familiar with other technological advances such as the 'anonymous call reject' to prevent unwanted calls.

Useful source: Telephone Helplines Association (1997) *Telephone Technology: Guidelines for Helplines* London: THA.

THEORETICAL SCHOOLS

(*See also*: Integration, Theories)

The proliferation of models of counselling has been well documented (e.g. Newman and Goldfried, 1996). Although there are many individual therapeutic approaches, most of the talking therapies fall within one of the four major theoretical schools: psychodynamic, humanistic, cognitive–behavioural and transpersonal. A theoretical school is one which has a unique underlying theory of personality and human motivation. Each therapy that falls within such a school shares the philosophy, or at least key aspects of that philosophy.

Table 10

Four theoretical schools: some key concepts

School	Views on human personality and motivation
Humanistic	Fulfilment, growth, process, reflectivity, self as organism and experiencing (McLeod, 1996b)
Psychodynamic	Predetermination, the dynamic unconscious, defences (Burton and Davey, 1996)
Cognitive–behavioural	Interaction of physiology, cognition, behaviour and emotion (Scott and Dryden, 1996)
Transpersonal	Angst, authenticity, open-ended, spirituality (Spinelli, 1996)

Counsellors fall into two broad categories: some are purists, preferring to follow the dictate of one therapy within one theoretical school of thought, others prefer to work in an eclectic or integrative manner mixing the concepts and skills of more than one therapeutic approach (Norcross and Grencavage, 1989). Some therapies are created by mixing specific aspects of two or more differing therapies making an independent therapeutic approach – e.g. cognitive analytic therapy (CAT), which aims to integrate skills and beliefs from the cognitive and psychodynamic schools (Ryle, 1995).

For trenchant reviews of 12 theories – psychoanalytic, Adlerian, existential, person-centred, gestalt, interpersonal, emotional flooding, behaviour, cognitive, systemic, gender-and-culture-sensitive, and integrative and eclectic – see Prochaska and Norcross (1994).

THEORIES

(*See also*: Common factors, Frameworks, Integration and eclecticism, Theoretical schools)

Relatively little has been written on the nature of theories of counselling, and to date there has been no thorough examination of what actually constitutes an adequate theory of counselling, although there are of course numerous theories and approaches. One question which arises is: do theories of *personality* provide adequate theoretical underpinning for counselling practice?

Personality is usually understood to represent those characteristics of a person that account for consistent patterns of behaviour. Although they recognise that all people are similar in some respects, theories of personality are particularly concerned with the ways in which people differ from one another. Pervin and John (1996) suggest that personality theories seek to explain the what, how and why of personality: stable characteristics, and possible genetic and environmental determinants of these characteristics, and motives. A theory of personality might help counsellors understand the extent to which a particular emotional state is characteristic of a client, how it developed, why it is experienced in certain circumstances, the way it is expressed, and if (and how) change is possible. However, the link between theory and practice is often unclear.

Nelson-Jones (1985, p.131) suggests four elements of a theory of counselling:

1. An indication of basic assumptions.
2. An explanation of how functional and dysfunctional feelings, thoughts and behaviour are acquired.
3. An explanation of how they are perpetuated or sustained.
4. Practical suggestions for changing and modifying dysfunctional feelings, thoughts and behaviour that are internally consistent with the preceding elements.

This analysis is very similar to the 'elements of personality' theory as outlined by Pervin and John (1996). Those approaches to counselling that place little, if any, importance on the origin of psychological problems would be found lacking as a theory if the elements are accepted. However, there are problems with this idea: Nelson-Jones isn't explicit about the kind of basic assumptions, and the practical component is vague, providing no guidelines on the type or nature of practical suggestions for change and no criteria for internal consistency.

Mahrer (1989) offers a different view. He argues that a theory of psychotherapy (or counselling) is *not* the same as a theory of personality. Its components are different, as are the issues and questions with which it deals, even though he recognises that it may imply or give birth to a theory of psychotherapy. He identifies seven components of a theory of psychotherapy:

1. Useful material to be elicited from the client.
2. How to listen and what to listen for.

3. Explanatory concepts to describe the client's presenting problem and targets for change.

4. Therapeutic goals and direction of change.

5. General and more specific principles of change.

6. Strategies, techniques and procedures.

7. Description of what strategies to use under what circumstances or conditions.

Many other theorists also draw a sharp distinction between theories of personality and theories of counselling or psychotherapy (e.g. Frankel, 1984; Franks, 1984; Goldfried, 1982). In the context of integration and eclecticism, Beitman (1990) says that counselling is a practical endeavour, intended to help people change, and therefore its theories must be connected to practical goals. Beitman is critical of all the efforts to develop theories of personality and the emphasis placed on explanatory frameworks of the origin of psychological difficulty. He argues that theories of counselling must pay greater attention to the process of change and the factors maintaining psychological difficulty.

There is currently a lot of interest in the integration of theories of counselling. However, without a clear analysis of what constitutes a theory it is difficult to know what it is that is being integrated. While there remains no consensus on a template for the analysis of a theory, four constituent elements of a comprehensive model of counselling emerge from the literature (Horton 1998).

1. **Personal belief system.** This is the philosophical element that describes the basic assumptions underpinning the other elements. It is typically concerned with (1) world view – an individual's unique way of making meaning or construing reality and (2) the counselling relationship and process.

2. **Formal theory.** This is concerned with human nature and development. It may provide explanations of how both normal (or functional) and abnormal (or dysfunctional) thoughts, feelings and behaviours are acquired and how they are perpetuated. Alternatively, it may describe the position taken on the need for such explanatory frameworks. Explanations of the origin of psychological problems are not always seen as useful or relevant. Formal theory may emphasise the importance of social or cultural factors and identify targets or levels of change.

3. **Clinical theory.** This is the functional theory that explains what counsellors do and why they do it. It would typically include some account of the general principles and mechanisms of change, the counselling process and how it develops, the nature and function of the therapeutic relationship and clinical procedures such as assessment, therapeutic goals or tasks, contracting etc.

4. **Therapeutic operations.** This describes core skills and strategies. Bond (1995, unpublished work) illustrates the relationship of these elements in Bond's pond, a pictorial metaphor. The four elements are levels of water. At

the bottom of the pond is the personal belief system in dark, murky and often stagnant water – yet Bond says that 'it contains rich and fertile soil, living creatures, flora and fauna and the unregenerate sludge and detritus of our own culture.' The formal and clinical theories are the next levels of water, with therapeutic operations as the clearly visible water on the surface of the pond. This is what counsellors actually do with clients to implement the other theoretical elements.

THERAPEUTIC ALLIANCE

See: Working alliance

THOUGHTS

(*See also*: Assertiveness, Behaviour, Books, self-help, Challenging, Cognitions, Depression, Emotions, Interpersonal process recall, Self-awareness, Theoretical Schools, Values)

Some counsellors and theories of counselling emphasise the role of thoughts – especially irrational self-defeating thoughts and underlying irrational beliefs – in troublesome emotions and behaviour (e.g. Moorey, 1996; Barker, 1992; Dryden, 1995). A central idea in this approach is that when we repeatedly tell ourselves something like 'I must not make mistakes' we are likely to become upset and demoralised and, as a consequence, engage in harmful or self-defeating behaviour (Scott and Dryden, 1996). In therapies such as cognitive–behavioural, multimodal and rational emotive behavioural therapy a distinction is made between negative automatic thoughts (e.g. 'I must not make a mistake') and underlying irrational beliefs (e.g. 'I must not make a mistake otherwise I am a failure') (Beck and Freeman, 1990; Lazarus, 1989; Dryden and Yankura, 1995).

To avoid this self-defeating harmful pattern, the following steps can be taken:

1. Identify the negative automatic thought.
2. Challenge it.
3. Replace it with a more realistic thought.
4. Act on the new thought.

For example, suppose you catch yourself or a client believing 'I should be able to do everything well', and see this as explaining or at least contributing to feeling incompetent, upset and anxious. You can help to dispute this thought by creatively using one of three types of disputation strategies (Ellis *et al.*, 1997).

1. **Empirical:** 'Where is the evidence that you must do everything well?'
2. **Logical:** 'Just because you do something badly, how does it logically follow that you are a bad person?'

3. **Pragmatic:** 'How does believing that you must do everything well help you feel better?'

Having disputed the negative thoughts the next step is to replace the self-defeating thought with a more realistic one. For example: 'I would prefer to do everything well but I do not have to', 'I would prefer to do everything well, however it is not the end of the world if I don't'. The last step is to reinforce and consolidate the new thinking through action. The client might have been avoiding studying for fear of not doing well and as a result of this analysis now signs up for a course.

This approach to changing thoughts is consistent with the assertiveness approach to rights. The list of rights in the entry on assertiveness contains negative thinking by implication – e.g. 'People ought to respect me' or 'I mustn't make mistakes and it is catastrophic if I do.' However, it is important to find each person's own variations.

Counsellors may have their own specialised irrational beliefs, e.g. 'I must be effective with all clients and client problems', 'Rogers or Ellis would help this client', 'Because I'm a counsellor, I shouldn't get stressed, tired, depressed, or anxious'. A general principle is to treat 'musts' and 'shoulds' not as absolutes but as *preferences*. For example, 'I should be effective with all clients' now becomes 'I would prefer to be effective with all clients; however there is no law of the universe that says I must.' Unmet desires are seen as regrettable rather than deeply upsetting.

There are many differing types of cognitive interventions. For example, bibliotherapy and bibliotraining (the use of self-help books, manuals, videos and audiotapes), identifying thinking errors such as 'all or nothing thinking', using constructive self-talk, the deserted island technique, cost–benefit analysis, problem solving training and thought stopping (Palmer and Dryden, 1995).

Thought stopping is perhaps one of the most well used of the cognitive interventions as many people find themselves with unwelcome and unwanted thoughts. There are several techniques that can be employed in thought stopping, all of which require repetitive practice. Two of these techniques are given below.

1. The client is asked to think of an unwelcome thought and then to visualise a 'STOP' sign. Once this has happened the client should try to replace the unwanted thought with a more realistic or pleasant thought or image.

2. The client is asked to wear an elastic band around his or her wrist and to flick the band when an unwanted thought happens. The sensation induced can distract the client from the thought.

Some people are repelled by this kind of technique, seeing it as 'brainwashing' and superficial; others see the techniques as using imaginative power for self-control and as worth trying for their economy, keeping other approaches in reserve.

TIME BOUNDARIES

(*See also*: Boundaries, Endings, Sexual attraction, Stress)

There is considerable agreement among counsellors that it is part of your professional responsibility to be ready to start a session on time, but less agreement about when to end. Some counsellors believe they should be careful to end within 30–60 seconds of the appointed time, and that this should be done without an apology, simply stating to the client that the time is up (Langs, 1982). Others have a more flexible approach, ending each session when it feels appropriate to do so within the time constraints and circumstances for both counsellor and client. They argue that a rigid adherence to boundaries is based on little more than convention. Most counsellors, however, feel that it is important to try to bring a session to a natural close near to the time originally agreed with the client.

There are strong arguments in favour of paying attention to ending on time. Maintaining time boundaries by starting and ending each session promptly can symbolise containment, 'holding' and reliability and provide a client with a sense of security and safety. Only if you keep reasonable time boundaries can your clients learn to use the time that is available. It is quite common for clients to start talking about a significant issue, or to make an apparently throw-away comment, towards the end of a session. This may be a test of their own courage or of your reaction in the relative safety of the limited time available, knowing at some level of awareness that it is possible to avoid taking the issue too deeply, at least in that session. Alternatively, it may be an attempt to manipulate you to spend more time with them.

A small clock behind the client allows you to say when there are only five or ten minutes left and in this way begin to work towards ending and avoid an abrupt halt. Especially with brief counselling, it can be useful to conclude a session with some form of review. You can summarise what has been achieved and what needs to be discussed further or invite your client to do so.

At the end of some sessions a client may still be very distressed. Some counsellors remain silent, giving the client a few moments to recover. They believe that it is the client's responsibility to deal with their own distress and that he or she must learn to deal with it in their own way. Other counsellors prefer to offer an attention-switching or celebratory exercise (Evison and Horobin, 1983) to help their clients gain composure. An ideal situation would be to allow clients to sit quietly in another room until they feel ready to leave. In many settings, however, this is not possible.

TIME MANAGEMENT

See: Assertiveness, Boundaries, Stress, Values

TOUCH

(*See also*: Crying, Kissing, Non-verbal communication)

Touch can be interpreted as caring, patronising, threatening, sympathetic, dominant, sexual, intimate or afraid. Like most non-verbal communications, it is ambiguous. The ambiguity is reduced, but probably not eliminated, by knowing the kind of touch, the cultural context, the situation, and the people involved.

A hug is sometimes a very unhelpful thing to do, because it can block awareness of feelings. It can be more useful to talk about a desire to touch than to initiate it. However, touch is also a very basic way of making contact (perhaps especially when it is not done as a technique), so you should be clear about your own attitudes to touch and role-play reactions to being touched by a client.

It can also be revealing to ask for feedback about your handshake (probably from candid friends or colleagues). Intensity of shake can be seen quite differently by the two people involved: bonecrusher, dead fish, or in between? Duration of handshake can affect impressions too. And both qualities – intensity and duration – seem relatively easy to check and change.

TRANSFERENCE

(See also: Counselling, Counter-transference, Empathy, First impressions, Immediacy, Supervision)

Transference is the displacing of an emotion or attitude from one relationship to another. In psychoanalysis it is more specifically transferral by the client of their feelings and attitudes towards members of their family (usually parents or guardians) to the counsellor. Indicators include inappropriate reactions e.g. too intense, inconsistent or ambivalent. The counsellor is idealised, imitated or hated (Jacobs, 1988; Stewart, 1992). Freud developed the idea of using transference to discover more about the deeper emotional state and early conflicts of clients. An alternative approach is to try to prevent its development and, if it does develop, to challenge it, separating yourself from the person your client would like to believe you are. Empathy reduces transference, and transference is an important factor in only a few relationships, unless counsellor or therapist neutrality deliberately encourages it.

TRANSITIONS

See: Loss

TRUST

(See also: Boundaries, Contract, negotiating a, Contraindications for brief counselling, Empathy, Multicultural counselling, Questions (personal), asked by clients, Respect, Transference)

Although some clients are very trusting right from the start, development of trust is usually a gradual process. Clients will have had mixed experiences of previous relationships. Some will have been let down very badly, and for these people trusting you will naturally take some time. Once counselling is under way, clients may test you by revealing things about themselves, or by asking you questions.

Fong and Cox (1983 p.164) identify six ways in which clients test for trust. They suggest that behind each statement or question the client has a hidden and sometimes unconscious motive or a 'real' question (indicated here in parentheses after each test).

1. Requesting information about the counsellor's personal experience, circumstances or knowledge, e.g. 'Are you married?' (Can you understand me? [if you have not had a similar experience])

2. Revealing, often unexpectedly and out of context, a potentially embarrassing secret e.g. 'My brother masturbates with me' (Can I be vulnerable with you?)

3. Asking the counsellor a favour, e.g. 'Can I borrow that book?' (Do you think I am honest and reliable?)

4. Saying something bad or negative about him- or herself, e.g. 'I always make a mess of things.' (Can you accept the real me?)

5. Inconveniencing the counsellor in some way, e.g. 'Could I use your phone before we start?' (Do you have consistent limits?)

6. Questioning the counsellor's motives, e.g. 'I bet it is hard to listen to other people's problems all day.' (Do you really care for me?)

It is important to take these tests seriously and to show that you can be trusted by being non-judgemental. You might not want to answer, or think it inappropriate to answer some direct questions put to you by clients, but these situations can also be seen as opportunities for you to respond to the real issue or underlying motive. If a counsellor misreads the situation and sees the client's questions as defensive, resistant or even hostile and responds accordingly or only at a surface level, the process of developing trust may be delayed or fail.

TYPE

See: Psychological type

UNITED KINGDOM COUNCIL FOR PSYCHOTHERAPY (UKCP)

The UKCP grew out of the first psychotherapy conference organised by the BAC at Rugby in 1982. Annual meetings were held between 1983 and 1989. The UK Standing Conference for Psychotherapy was inaugurated in 1989 with the formal adoption of a constitution and the election of officers and council members. The name was changed in 1993 to the UK Council for Psychotherapy. The UKCP has a federal structure in which similar kinds of psychotherapy member organisations are grouped together in sections, the largest of which are the Analytic and Humanistic and Integrative sections. Applications for full membership may be made by organisations significantly involved in the practice or teaching of psychotherapy. There is no individual membership. As 'Friends of the Council', the BAC is in a special category of its own.

The essential aims of the UKCP are stated as the protection of the public by the promotion of appropriate standards for training, research, education and the practice of psychotherapy. The UKCP is clearly concerned with safeguarding and promoting the interests of the profession and its practitioners. It intends to set up appropriate structures as the representative body for psychotherapy in the UK. In 1993 the UKCP launched its first national register of psychotherapists.

UKCP
167–169 Great Portland Street
London WIN 5FB
UK
Tel: 0171 436 3002

UNITED KINGDOM REGISTER OF COUNSELLORS (UKRC)

The UKRC was set up in 1997 following a developmental period of four years. There is no statutory regulation for counsellors, and the register is intended to provide a national and recognised standard for self-regulation. Thus, the purpose of the register is to inform and protect the public and those who consult or refer to counsellors, and to promote safe and effective professional practice and accountability through a system for the recognition of counselling qualifications and experience.

The UKRC is managed by the BAC, which has legal and financial responsibility for the register. A Registrar and Executive Committee (UKREC) responsible for the operation and development of the register.

There are two forms of registration:

1. **Registered Independent Counsellor:** this is open to individual counsellors, paid or unpaid, who are accredited by the BAC or Confederation of Scottish Counselling Agencies (COSCA) and who satisfy additional criteria. Alternative entry routes via accreditation by other professional bodies will be introduced. In 1998 there were over 1200 Registered Independent Counsellors.

2. **Registered Sponsored Counsellor:** organisations in the BAC and COSCA (organisational members) may apply to become Register Sponsoring Organisations (RSOs) and may then sponsor their counsellors for registration while the counsellors work for them. Registration will cease when the counsellor leaves that RSO. The UKREC recognises that there is a very wide variety of counselling services, which serve diverse categories of

client presenting problems, use a variety of theoretical approaches and are delivered through different modalities. RSO practice managers have responsibility for these and related issues. However, the procedures and conditions for becoming a RSO require rigorous and exacting standards, including annual monitoring. Registration through sponsoring organisations started in January 1998.

Application forms to become a Registered Independent Counsellor can be obtained from:

UKRC
PO Box 1050
Rugby
Warwickshire, CV21 2HZ
Tel: 01788 568739
Fax: 01788 546809.

UNCONDITIONAL POSITIVE REGARD

See: Respect

VALIDATION, OF COUNSELLOR EDUCATION/TRAINING COURSES IN THE UK

(See also: Accreditation)

Public organisations such as universities, colleges and institutes of higher education usually have some form of internal board or academic standards committee to validate their courses. They subject courses to often rigorous procedures, annual audits and reports from external independent examiners as well as to more extensive triennial reviews and major revalidation events every five or six years. Procedures vary, but validation events, often lasting a whole day, involve a panel of internal people not involved with the course or the department in question, together with external advisers who have knowledge and experience of counselling.

The panel and advisers interview the staff team and consider substantial documentation on the background of the course, selection and admission criteria and procedures, course organisation and structure, staff CVs and, for each module or component of the course, the aims and objectives, methods of teaching and learning, content and methods of assessment and indicative reading. The usual academic criteria are employed and, although panels will take recommendations from the external expert advisers, they very seldom (if ever) require the course to satisfy professional criteria, e.g. for clinical supervision.

Managers of courses run by colleges, institutions and nowadays even private organisations are increasingly seeking university validation. Some also look to outside professional organisations for validation.

VALUES

(*See also*: Acceptance, Assertiveness, Contract, negotiating a, Multicultural counselling, Stress, Self-awareness, Trust)

One emphasis in counselling is to help clients clarify their values, i.e. what is most important (and what is least important) to them. Someone who is relatively clear about their values is more able to make decisions, and perhaps less stressed (at least about values and decisions) as a result. If a client decides, for example, that being fit is less important at this time in her life than, say, having a larger house, then she can use her time and energy accordingly.

The assumptions here are that it is not possible to do everything well, that there is always more to do, that priorities need to be chosen, and that values are a good basis for choosing them. A further assumption is that it is desirable for values to be reflected in behaviour. Each person decides, deliberately or by default, whether to act on their values sufficiently or not.

Some key questions about values are:

- What are your main values?
- Do any of your values conflict with each other?
- Do you act on your main values?
- Do you want to act *more* on any of them more?
- If you do, what will you do less of?
- How do your values affect other people?

Clients are likely to become aware of their counsellor's values on a number of issues, however neutral she or he tries to be, and you might need to be explicit about one or more of your values either before or during counselling. For example, a counsellor and client may have different values about sexuality, abortion or assertiveness. Such differences can be discussed sensitively, preferably with awareness of multicultural factors, and a decision made about whether or not to continue counselling.

For discussions of values in counselling, see Corey and Corey (1993, Chapter 4), and Bergin and Garfield (1994, pp.12–14).

VICTIM

See: Drama triangle

VIDEO

See: Tape-recording

VIOLENCE AND ITS PREVENTION

(*See also*: Anger, Assertiveness, Empathy, Furniture, Paraphrasing, Touch)

Although the risk of violence during counselling is small, preventive steps are worth while.

1. Whenever possible, avoid working in a building alone with a client, especially in the evenings or in buildings away from a main public thoroughfare. If you are working alone, maintain a strict appointment service and do not operate a drop-in clinic. If possible tell the caretaker that you will be working alone and when you expect to finish, but certainly inform a colleague or friend.

2. If you make a home visit, inform a colleague or friend where you are going and the time you expect to return.

3. Have a telephone readily accessible and consider having an alarm or 'panic' button installed in your counselling room. Carry a personal security device in situations in which you feel vulnerable.

4. If you suspect danger it may be advisable to cancel the appointment or, if actually working with a client, to bring the session to a close.

5. When working with a client of the opposite sex, try to ensure that someone of the same sex as the client is within calling range.

6. Take particular care with arrangements to work with any clients who have a history of acting out any form of violence or aggression.

7. Some counsellors consider it advisable and good practice to avoid any form of physical contact with a client apart from a handshake.

8. Arrange the counsellor and client chairs equidistant from the door, so that you both have equal access. If the counsellor's chair is nearer the door the client could feel trapped or closed in.

9. Calmness *and* empathy; sometimes calmness alone infuriates someone further.

Davies (1988) also considers the role of attitudes – e.g. 'I must never run away' – and what he calls 'second-order skills' such as the ability to take personal responsibility for your safety (an aspect of assertiveness) and the ability to analyse aggressive incidents. At an organisational level, there should be a system for recording and following up violent incidents, and support for those attacked. e.g. counselling, paid leave or help with legal action. See Breakwell (1997) for a detailed discussion of managing and preventing violence.

VISUALISATION

See: Imagery

WARMTH

(*See also*: Emotions, Love, adult romantic, Multicultural counselling, Paraphrasing, Psychological type, Readiness to change, Respect, Sexual feelings)

Being warm and affectionate are the opposite of being distant or aloof. They imply a liking for people and a caring approach, especially to people who are distressed or confused. Warmth, however, is not necessarily something you will always feel or feel equally for every client, and some clients are likely to experience you as warmer than others. Warmth, like trust, is often a developing process rather than something established immediately, as the expression 'to warm to somebody' implies. It helps if you have an open and inviting attitude towards your clients when you first meet them, allowing yourself time to get to know them and for them to get to know you.

Excessive warmth can be as much of a problem as no warmth at all. Some clients may feel overpowered or uncomfortable if you are overly warm towards them. It can be very difficult for clients to express angry feelings towards you, for example, if you allow your natural warmth to spill over into being over-protective or over-friendly. Similarly, clients can feel reticent about expressing what they think of as their negative aspects if they feel they risk withdrawal of your affection. This might have very strong echoes of the past for many clients. Some clients prefer a formal, businesslike approach.

WORKING ALLIANCE

(*See also*: Contract, negotiating a, Core conditions, Counselling, Rapport)

Jacobs, a psychodynamic counsellor, writes: 'The working relationship that exists between counsellor and client (sometimes known as the working alliance) is essentially one of adult meeting with adult, not simply as two equal human beings, who share the problems of living, but also as two people who meet to work together on a problem or set of problems. Individual counselling involves an implicit agreement between two adults (counsellor and client) to cooperate in trying to understand certain less adult and less mature aspects in one of them' (Jacobs, 1988, p.99). This definition reflects (1) the psychodynamic emphasis on insight rather than goals, and (2) the fact that counselling is dedicated to a particular set of purposes, and isn't simply a problem-sharing exercise between two people who have the same needs from a relationship. This sense of purpose needs to be communicated by all counsellors, whatever their approach to counselling. It also needs to be accepted by clients. The initial interview, if handled properly, can go a long way towards establishing a purposeful and concentrated atmosphere in which you work together on the concerns of the client.

WRITING

(*See also*: Freewriting, Journals, academic and applied, Professionalism, development of, Research)

We would like to encourage practitioners to consider writing up their ideas for professional journals. One obstacle to this is the myth that writers find writing easy – most rewrite many times, and regard writing as (at least in part) a punishing process. However, writing also helps clarify thoughts and may help others, and there are techniques to try when inspiration fails – such as freewriting, reading your material aloud (or – this is particularly brave – asking someone else to), writing a detailed outline, writing as if to a friend. Becker (1986) Boice (1994, 1997), Elbow (1997), Bayne (1998b) and MacMillan and Clark (1998) offer views, research findings and advice on writing.

Boice's recommendations include those listed below. His general approach is to make writing more enjoyable, and as a result more productive. His research shows clearly that the strategies work well. However, Boice did not consider individual differences (e.g. psychological type) and each strategy is likely to suit some people more than others.

1. Write little and often. Boice specifically recommends 'brief, daily sessions' of ten minutes to an hour.
2. Take at least as long to make notes, play with them, organise them, as to write, rewrite and edit.
3. Check for tension while you write (say every few minutes) and relax if necessary.
4. Aim for an average of one to two and a half pages in an hour.
5. Rewrite several times.

ZEST, MAINTAINING

See: Assertiveness, Burnout, Journal, writing a, Referral, Self-awareness, Stress, Supervision, Support groups, peer

REFERENCES

Adams, K. (1990) *Journal to the Self: 22 Paths to Personal Growth*. New York: Warner Books.

Adams, J., Hayes, J. and Hopson, B. (Eds) (1976) *Transition: Understanding and Managing Personal change*. London: Martin Robertson.

Allinson, T., Cooper, C.L. and Reynolds, P. (1989) Stress counselling in the workplace. The Post Office experience. *The Psychologist*, 2(9), 384–388.

Anderson, I. (1997) Psychiatry: evidence-based but still value-laden. *British Journal of Psychiatry*, 171, 226.

Andrews, J.D.W., Norcross, J.C. and Malgin, R.P. (1992) Training in psychotherapy integration. In J.C. Norcross and M.R. Goldfried (Eds) *Handbook of Psychotherapy Integration*. New York: Basic Books.

Angus, L.E. (1996) An intensive analysis of metaphor themes in psychotherapy. In J.S. Mio and A.N. Katz (Eds) *Metaphor: Implications and Applications*. Mahwah, NJ: Lawrence Erlbaum.

Aronson, E. (1999) *The Social Animal*, 8th ed. New York: Freeman.

Barker, C. (1985) Interpersonal process recall in clinical training and research. In F.N. Watts (Ed.) *New Developments in Clinical Psychology*. Chichester: BPS/Wiley.

Barker, P.J. (1992) *Severe Depression. A Practitioner's Guide*. Cheltenham: Stanley Thornes.

Barker, P.J. (1997) *A Self Help Guide to Managing Depression*. Cheltenham: Stanley Thornes.

Barkham, M. (1990) Research in individual therapy. In W. Dryden (Ed.) *Individual Therapy: A Handbook*. Milton Keynes: Open University Press.

Barkham, M. (1993a) Research and practice. In Dryden, W. (Ed.) *Questions and Answers on Counselling in Action*. London: Sage.

Barkham, M. (1993b) Understanding, implementing and presenting counselling evaluation. In R. Bayne and P. Nicolson (Eds) *Counselling and Psychology for Health Professionals*. Cheltenham: Stanley Thornes.

Barkham, M. (1996) Quantitative research on psychotherapeutic interventions: methodological issues and substantive findings across three research generations. In R. Woolfe and W. Dryden (Eds) *Handbook of Counselling Psychology*. London: Sage.

Baron, J. (1996) The emergence of counselling as a profession. In R. Bayne, I. Horton and J. Bimrose (Eds) *New Directions in Counselling*. London: Routledge.

Barrett-Lennard, C.T. (1993) The phases and focus of empathy. *British Journal of Medical Psychology*, 66, 3–14.

Batten, L. (1992) Stubbing out passive smoking. *Personnel Management*, **August**, 24–27.

Bayne. R. (1995a) *The Myers–Briggs Type Indicator. A Critical Review and Practical Guide*. Cheltenham: Stanley Thornes.

Bayne, R. (1995b) Psychological type and counselling. *British Journal of Guidance and Counselling*, 23(1), 95–106.

Bayne, R. (1998a) Looking after yourself. In R. Bayne, P. Nicolson, and I. Horton (Eds) *Counselling and Communication Skills for Medical and Health Practitioners*. Leicester: British Psychological Society.

Bayne, R. (1998b) Psychological type (the Myers–Briggs). In R. Bayne, P. Nicolson and I. Horton (Eds) *Counselling and Communication Skills for Medical and Health Practitioners*. Leicester: British Psychological Society.

Bayne, R. (1999). The counselling relationship and psychological type. In C. Feltham (Ed.) *Understanding the Counselling Relationship*. London: Sage.

Beck, A.T. and Freeman, A. (1990) *Cognitive Therapy of Personality Disorders*. New York: Guilford Press.

Becker, H.S. (1986) *Writing for Social Scientists. How to Start and Finish your Thesis, Book or Article*. Chicago: University of Chicago Press.

Beitman, B. (1990) Why I am an integrationist. In W. Dryden and J.C. Norcross (Eds) *Eclecticism and Integration in Counselling and Psychotherapy*. Loughton, Essex: Gale Centre Publications.

Beitman, B.D. (1994) Stop exploring! Start defining the principles of psychotherapy integration: Call for a consensus conference. *Journal of Psychotherapy Integration*, 4(3), 203–228.

Benjamin, A. (1969) *The Helping Interview*. Boston: Houghton Mifflin.

Bergin, A.E. and Garfield, S.L. (Eds) (1994) *Handbook of Psychotherapy and Behavior Change*, 4th ed. New York: Wiley.

Bernard, J.M. and Goodyear, R.K. (1991) *The Fundamentals of Clinical Supervision*. London: Allyn and Bacon.

Beutler, L.E., Machado, P.P.P. and Neufeldt, S.A. (1994) Therapist variables. In A.E. Bergin and S.L. Garfield (Eds) *Handbook of Psychotherapy and Behavior Change*, 4th ed. New York: Wiley.

Bimrose, J. (1993) Counselling and social context. In R. Bayne and P. Nicolson (Eds) *Counselling and Psychology for Health Professionals*. Cheltenham: Stanley Thornes.

Bimrose, J. (1996) Multiculturalism. In R. Bayne, I. Horton and J. Bimrose (Eds) *New Directions in Counselling*. London: Routledge.

Bimrose, J. (1998) Increasing multicultural competence. In R. Bayne, P. Nicolson and I. Horton (Eds) *Counselling and Communication Skills for Medical and Health Practitioners*. Leicester: British Psychological Society.

Bloom, J.W. (1998) The ethical practice of Web Counselling. British *Journal of Guidance and Counselling*, 26(1), 53–59.

Boice, R. (1994) *How Writers Journey to Comfort and Fluency. A Psychological Adventure*. London: Prager.

Boice, R. (1997) Strategies for enhancing scholarly activity. In J.M. Moxley and T. Taylor (Eds) *Writing and Publishing for Academic Authors*. London: Bowman and Littlefield.

Bond, M. (1986) *Stress and Self-awareness. A Guide for Nurses*. London: Heinemann.

Bond, T. (1993a) *Standards and Ethics for Counselling in Action*. London: Sage.

Bond, T. (1993b) Counsellor/client sex. In W. Dryden (Ed.) *Questions and Answers on Counselling in Action*. London: Sage.

Bond, T. (1993c) When to protect the client from self-destruction. In W. Dryden (Ed.) *Questions and Answers on Counselling in Action*. London: Sage.

Bond, T. (1993d) Reporting a colleague's misconduct. In W. Dryden (Ed.) *Questions and Answers on Counselling in Action*. London: Sage.

Bond, T. (1996) Future developments in ethical standards for counselling. In R. Bayne, I. Horton and J. Bimrose (Eds) *New Directions in Counselling*. London: Routledge.

Bowlby, J. (1973) *Attachment and Loss, Vol. 2.* New York: Basic Books.

Bowlby, J. (1988) *A Secure Base: Parent–Child Attachment and Healthy Human Development.* New York: Basic Books.

Brady, J.L., Healy, F.C., Norcross, J.C. and Guy, J.D. (1995) Stress in counsellors: an integrative research review. In W. Dryden (Ed.) *The Stresses of Counselling in Action.* London: Sage.

Brammer, L.M., Abrego, P.J. and Shostrom, E. (1993) *Therapeutic Counseling and Psychotherapy,* 6th ed. Englewood Cliffs, NJ: Prentice Hall.

Breakwell, G. (1997) *Facing Physical Violence.* Leicester: British Psychological Society.

Brenner, D. (1982) *The Effective Psychotherapist.* Oxford: Pergamon.

British Association for Counselling (1993a) The complaints procedures – lessons from the past year. *Counselling,* **February,** 14–15.

British Association for Counselling (1993b) The BAC Basic Principles of Counselling. *Counselling,* **August,** 155–156.

British Association for Counselling (1996) *The Recognition of Counsellor Training Courses,* 2nd ed. Rugby: BAC.

British Association for Counselling (1998) *The Code of Ethics and Practice for Counsellors.* Rugby: BAC.

Brock, T.C., Green, M.C. and Reich, D.A. (1998) New evidence of flaws in the Consumer Reports study of psychotherapy. *American Psychologist,* 53(1), 62–63.

Bry, A. (1978) *Visualization.* New York: Harper & Row.

Bugental, J.F.T. and Bugental, E.K. (1980) The far side of despair. *Journal of Humanistic Psychology,* **20,** 49–68.

Burnard P. (1991) *Coping with Stress in the Health Professions.* Cheltenham: Stanley Thornes.

Burton, M. and Davey, T. (1996) The psychodynamic paradigm. In R. Woolfe and W. Dryden (Eds) *The Handbook of Counselling Psychology.* London: Sage.

Buyssen, J. (1996) *Traumatic Experiences of Nurses. When your profession becomes a nightmare.* London: Jessica Kingsley.

Calnan, J. (1991) Handling complaints. In R. Corney (Ed.) *Developing Communication and Counselling Skills in Medicine.* London: Routledge.

Carr, S. (1997) *Type Clarification. Finding the Fit.* Oxford: Oxford Psychologists Press.

Charles-Edwards, D. (1992) *Death, Bereavement and Work.* London: CEPEC.

Charles-Edwards, D., Dryden, W. and Woolfe, R. (1989) Professional issues. In W. Dryden *et al.* (Eds) *Handbook of Counselling in Britain.* London: Tavistock/Routledge.

Clarke, KM. and Greenberg, L.S. (1986) Differential effects of the Gestalt two-chair intervention and problem-solving in resolving decisional conflict. *Journal of Counseling Psychology,* 33(1), 11–15.

Claxton, G. (1997) *Hare Brain, Tortoise Mind: Why Intelligence Increases When You Think Less.* London: Fourth Estate.

Claxton, G. (1998) Investigating human intuition: knowing without knowing why. *The Psychologist,* 11(5), 217–220.

Cohen, K. (1992) Some legal issues in counselling and psychotherapy. *British Journal of Guidance and Counselling,* 20(1), 10–26.

Comer, R.J. (1998) *Abnormal Psychology,* 3rd ed. New York: Freeman.

Corey, G. (1991) *Theory and Practice of Counseling and Psychotherapy*. Pacific Grove, CA: Brooks/Cole.

Corey, M. and Corey, G. (1992) *Groups: Process and Practice*, 4th ed. Pacific Grove, CA: Brooks/Cole.

Corey, M. and Corey, G. (1993) *Becoming a Helper*, 2nd ed. Pacific Grove, CA: Brooks/Cole.

Cormier, W.H. and Cormier, L.S. (1991) *Interviewing Strategies for Helpers*. Pacific Grove, CA: Brooks/Cole.

Cornelius, R.R. (1996) *The Science of Emotion*. London: Prentice-Hall.

Crino, R., Hunt, C., Lampe L. and Page, A. (1994) *The Treatment of Anxiety Disorders*. Cambridge: Cambridge University Press.

Daines, B., Gask, L. and Usherwood, T. (1997) *Medical and Psychiatric Issues for Counsellors*. London: Sage.

Dalton, P. (1992) Chapter 2. In W Dryden (Ed.) *Hard-earned Lessons from Counselling in Action*. London: Sage.

d'Ardenne, P. (1993) Transcultural counselling and psychotherapy in the 1990s. *British Journal of Guidance and Counselling*, 21(1), 1–7.

Davenport, R.B. and Pipes, D.S. (1990) *Introduction to Psychotherapy: Common Clinical Wisdom*. London: Prentice-Hall.

Davies, W. (1988) How not to get hit. *The Psychologist*, 2(5), 175–176.

Deurzen, E. van (1996) Existential therapy. In W. Dryden (Ed.) *Handbook of Individual Therapy*. London: Sage.

Deurzen Smith, E van (1988) *Existential Counselling in Practice*. London: Sage.

Deurzen Smith, E. van (1990) Existential therapy. In W. Dryden (Ed.) *Individual Therapy: A Handbook*. Milton Keynes: Open University Press.

Deurzen Smith, E. van (1992) Counselling psychology in Europe. *Counselling Psychology Review*, 7(3), 5–10.

Diamantopoulos, A. and Schlegelmilch, B.B. (1997) *Taking the Fear out of Data Analysis*. London: The Dryden Press.

Dickson, A. (1987) *A Woman in Your Own Right*, revised ed. London: Quartet.

Dillon, J.T. (1990) *The Practice of Questioning*. London: Routledge.

Dinkmeyer, D. (1985) Adlerian psychotherapy and counseling. In S.J. Lynn and J.P. Garske (Eds) *Contemporary Psychotherapies – Models and Methods*. London: Merrill.

Draucker, C.B. (1992) *Counselling Survivors of Childhood Sexual Abuse*. London: Sage.

Drennan, C. and Rumbold, S. (1998) Working with infertility. In R. Bayne, P. Nicolson and I. Horton (Eds) *Counselling and Communication Skills for Medical and Health Practitioners*. Leicester: British Psychological Society.

Dryden, W. (1983) Supervision of audio-tapes in counselling: obstacles to trainee learning. *The Counsellor*, 3(8), 18–25.

Dryden, W. (1991) *A Dialogue with Arnold Lazarus. 'It Depends'*. Milton Keynes: Open University Press.

Dryden, W (1995) *Facilitating Client Change in Rational Emotive Behaviour Therapy*. London: Whurr.

Dryden, W. (Ed.) (1996) *Handbook of Individual Therapy*. London: Sage.

Dryden, W. and Norcross, J.C. (Eds) (1990) *Eclecticism and Integration in Counselling and Psychotherapy*. Loughton, Essex: Gale Centre Publications.

Dryden, W. and Thorne, B. (1991) *Training and Supervision for Counselling in Action*. London: Sage.

Dryden, W. and Feltham, C. (1992) *Brief Counselling. A Practical Guide for Beginning Practitioners*. Milton Keynes: Open University Press.

Dryden, W. and Yankura, J. (1995) *Developing REB Counselling*. London: Sage.

Dryden, W., Horton, I., and Mearns, D. (1995) *Issues in Professional Counsellor Training*. London: Cassell.

Duan, C. and Hill, C.E. (1996) The current state of empathy research. *Journal of Counseling Psychology*, **43**(3), 261–274.

Duck, S. (1998) *Human Relationships*, 3rd ed. London: Sage.

Egan, G. (1975) *The Skilled Helper*. Monterey, CA: Brooks/Cole.

Egan, G. (1990) *The Skilled Helper*, 4th ed. Monterey, CA: Brooks/Cole.

Egan, G. (1998) *The Skilled Helper*, 6th ed. Monterey, CA: Brooks/Cole.

Ekman, P (1992) Are there basic emotions? *Psychological Review*, **99**(3), 550–553.

Ekman, P. (1993) Facial expression and emotion. *American Psychologist*, **48**(4), 384–392.

Elbow, P. (1973) *Writing Without Teachers*. Oxford: Oxford University Press.

Elbow, P.(1997) Freewriting and the problem: Wheat and tares. In J.M. Moxley and T. Taylor (Eds) *Writing and Publishing for Academic Authors*, 2nd ed. London: Bowman and Littlefield.

Eleftheriadou, Z. (1997) Cultural differences in the therapeutic process. In I. Horton with V. Varma (Eds) *The Needs of Counsellors and Psychotherapists*. London: Sage.

Ellis, A., Gordon, J., Neenan, M. and Palmer, S. (1997) *Stress Counselling*. London: Cassell.

Elton Wilson, J. (1993) Towards a personal model of counselling. In W. Dryden (Ed.) *Questions and Answers on Counselling in Action*. London: Sage.

Ernst, S. and Goodison, L. (1982) *In Our Own Hands*. London: The Women's Press.

Evison, R. and Horobin, R. (1983) *How to Change Your Self and Your World*. Sheffield: Co-counselling Phoenix.

Evison, R. and Horobin, R. (1988) Co-counselling. In J. Rowan and W. Dryden (Eds) *Innovative Therapy in Britain*. Milton Keynes: Open University Press.

Eysenck, H.J. (1952) The effects of psychotherapy: An evaluation. *Journal of Consulting Psychology*, **16**, 319–324.

Eysenck, H.J. (1992) The outcome problem in psychotherapy. In W. Dryden and C. Feltham (Eds) *Psychotherapy and its Discontents*. Milton Keynes: Open University Press.

Falloon, V. (1992) *How to Get More Clients*. London: Brainwave.

Feltham, C. (1993) Making a living as a counsellor. In W. Dryden (Ed.) *Questions and Answers on Counselling in Action*. London: Sage.

Feltham, C. (1995a) *What is Counselling?* London: Sage.

Feltham, C. (1995b) The stresses of counselling in private practice In W. Dryden (Ed.) *The Stresses of Counselling in Action*. London: Sage.

Feltham, C. (1996) Beyond denial, myth and superstition in the counselling profession. In R. Bayne, I. Horton and J. Bimrose (Eds) *New Directions in Counselling*. London: Routledge.

Feltham, C. (1997a) *Time Limited Counselling*. London: Sage.

Feltham, C. (1997b) Challenging the core theoretical model. *Counselling*, 8(2), 121–125.

Fiennes, R. (1998) *Fit for Life*. London: Little, Brown.

Fong, M.L. and Cox, B.G. (1983) Trust as an underlying dynamic in the counselling process: How clients test trust. *Personnel and Guidance Journal*, **November**, 163–167.

Fonagy, P. and Higgitt, A. (1984) *Personality Theory and Clinical Practice*. London: Methuen.

Fontana, D. (1989) *Managing Stress*. London: Routledge/BPS.

Foss, B (1983) *Report for BAC on Accreditation Scheme*. Rugby: BAC.

Frances, A. (Ed.) (1994) *Diagnostic and Statistical Manual of Medical Disorders*. Washington: American Psychiatric Association.

Frank, J.D. (1981) Therapeutic components shared by all psychotherapies. In J.H. Harvey and M.M. Parks (Eds) *Psychotherapy Research and Behaviour Change*. Washington: American Psychological Association.

Frankel, A.J. (1984) *Four Therapies Integrated*. New Jersey: Prentice Hall.

Frankland, A.M. (1996) Accreditation and registration. In R. Bayne, I. Horton and J. Bimrose (Eds) *New Directions in Counselling*. London: Routledge.

Franks, C.M. (1984) On conceptual and technical integrity in psychoanalysis and behaviour therapy. Two fundamentally incompatible systems. In H. Arkowitz and S.B. Messer (Eds) *Psychoanalytic Therapy and Behavior Change: Is Integration Possible?* New York: Plenum.

Gallo, P.S. (1978) Meta-analysis – a mixed metaphor. *American Psychologist*, 33(5), 515–517.

Garfield, S.L. (1992) Eclectic psychotherapy: A common factors approach. In J.C. Norcross and M.R. Goldfried (Eds) *Handbook of Psychotherapy Integration*. New York: Basic Books.

Gawain, S. (1978) *Creative Visualization*. New York: Bantam Books.

Geddes, J.R. and Harrison, P.J. (1997) Closing the gap between research and practice. *British Journal of Psychiatry*, 171, 220–225.

Gendlin, E.T. (1981) *Focusing*, 2nd ed. London: Bantam.

Gilbert, P. (1992) *Counselling for Depression*. London: Sage.

Gilbert, P. (1996) Working with the depressed person. In R. Bayne, I. Horton and J. Bimrose (Eds) *New Directions in Counselling*. London: Routledge.

Gilbert, P. (1997) *Overcoming Depression*. London: Robinson.

Gilmore, S.K. (1973) *The Counselor-in-Training*. London: Prentice-Hall.

Goldfried, M.R. (1982) *Converging Themes in Psychotherapy*. New York: Springer.

Green, H. (1964) *I Never Promised You a Rose Garden*. London: Pan.

Greenberg, L.S. and Safran, J.D. (1990) *Emotion in Psychotherapy*. New York: Guilford Press.

Grencavage, L.M. and Norcross, J.C. (1990) Where are the commonalities among the therapeutic common factors? *Professional Psychology: Research and Practice*, 21, 372–378.

Griest, J.H. and Jefferson, J.W. (1993) *Panic Disorder and Agoraphobias: a Guide*. New York: Dean Foundation for Health, Research and Education.

Griffiths, P. (1998) Rehabilitation counselling. In R. Bayne, P. Nicolson and I. Horton (Eds) *Counselling and Communication Skills for Medical and Health Practitioners*. Leicester: British Psychological Society.

Hall, E. and Hall, C. (1988) *Human Relations in Education*. London: Routledge.

Hallam, R. (1992) *Counselling for Anxiety Problems*. London: Sage.

Hawkins P. and Shohet, R. (1989) *Supervision in the Helping Professions*. Milton Keynes: Open University.

Heap, M. and Dryden, W. (1991) *Hypnotherapy. A Handbook*. Milton Keynes: Open University Press.

Hill, C.E. and Corbett, M.M. (1993) A perspective on the history of process and outcome research in counseling psychology. *Journal of Counseling Psychology*, 40(1), 3–24.

Horton, I. (1993) Supervision. In R. Bayne and P. Nicolson (Eds) *Counselling and Psychology for Health Professionals*. Cheltenham: Stanley Thornes.

Horton, I. (1995) Theory. In W. Dryden, I. Horton and D. Mearns (Eds) *Issues in Professional Counsellor Training*. London: Cassell.

Horton, I. (1998) Principles and practice of a personal integration. In S. Palmer and R. Woolfe (Eds) *Eclectic and Integrative Counselling and Psychotherapy*. London: Sage.

Horton, I. and Bayne, R. (1998) Counselling and communication in health care. In R. Bayne, P. Nicolson and I. Horton (Eds) *Counselling and Communication Skills for Medical and Health Practitioners*. Leicester: British Psychological Society.

Houston, G. (1990) *Supervision and Counselling*. London: Rochester Foundation.

Humphrey, G.M. and Zimpfer, D.G. (1996) *Counselling for Grief and Bereavement*. London: Sage.

Inskipp, F. (1993) Beyond Egan. In W. Dryden (Ed.) *Questions and Answers on Counselling in Action*. London: Sage.

Inskipp, F. (1996a) New directions in supervision. In R. Bayne, I. Horton and J. Bimrose (Eds) *New Directions in Counselling*. London: Routledge.

Inskipp, F. (1996b) *Skills Training for Counselling*. London: Cassell.

Inskipp, F. and Proctor, B. (1989) *Counselling Skills for Supervision* (audiotapes with notes and exercises). St. Leonards-on-Sea: Alexia Publications (also from BAC).

Inskipp, F. and Proctor, B. (1993) *The Art, Craft & Tasks of Counselling Supervision. Part 1. Making The Most of Supervision*. Twickenham: Cascade.

Ivey, A.E., Ivey, M.B. and Simek-Downing, L. (1987) *Counseling and Psychotherapy: Integrating skills, Theory and Practice*, 2nd ed. London: Prentice Hall.

Ivey, A.E., Ivey, M.B. and Simek-Morgan, L. (1997) *Counseling and Psychotherapy: A Multicultural Perspective*, 4th ed. London: Allyn and Bacon.

Jacobs, M. (1988) *Psychodynamic Counselling in Action*. London: Sage.

Jenkins, P (1997) *Counselling, Psychotherapy and the Law*. London: Sage.

Jenkins, P. (1998) From transference to false memory: counsellor liability in an age of litigation. *Counselling*, 9(1), 40–44.

Johns, H. (1996) *Personal Development in Counsellor Training*. London: Cassell.

Jones, J.H. and Sherman, R.G. (1997) *Intimacy and Type. A Practical Guide for Improving Relationships for Couples and Counselors*. Gainesville, FL: Center for Applications of Psychological Type.

Kagan, N. (1984) Interpersonal Process Recall: Basic methods and recent research. In D. Larsen (Ed.) *Teaching Psychological Skills*. Monterey, CA: Brooks/Cole.

Kahn, M. (1991) *Between Therapist and Client*. New York: W.H. Freeman.

Kahn, M. (1997) *Between Therapist and Client. The New Relationship*, revised edition. New York: W.H. Freeman.

Karpman, S.B. (1968) Fairy tales and script drama analysis. *TA Bulletin*, VII(26), 39–43.

Katz, J.H. (1985) The sociopolitical nature of counseling. *The Counseling Psychologist*, 13(4), 615–624.

Keinan, G., Ben-Zur, H., Zilka, M. and Carel R.S. (1992) Anger in or out, which is healthier? An attempt to reconcile inconsistent findings. *Psychology and Health*, 7, 83–98.

King, S.A., Engi, S. and Poulos, S.T. (1998) Using the Internet to assist family therapy. *British Journal of Guidance and Counselling*, 26(1), 43–52.

Kohut, H. (1987) *The Kohut Seminars on Self Psychology and Psychotherapy with Adolescents and Young Adults*. New York: W.W. Norton.

Kubler-Ross, E. (1981) *Living with Death and Dying*. New York: Macmillan.

Kwiatkowski, R. and Hogan, D. (1998) Group membership. In R. Bayne, P. Nicolson and I. Horton (Eds) *Counselling and Communication Skills for Medical and Health Practitioners*. Leicester: BPS Books.

Lago, C. (1996) Computer therapeutics. *Counselling*, 7, 287–289.

Lakoff, G. and Johnson, M. (1980) *Metaphors We Live By*. London: University of Chicago Press.

Lambers, E. (1993) When the counsellor shares the client's problem. In W. Dryden (Ed.) *Questions and Answers on Counselling in Action*. London: Sage.

Lambert, M.J. and Cattani-Thompson, K. (1996) Current findings regarding the effectiveness of counseling: implications for practice. *Journal of Counseling and Development*, 74, 601–608.

Lancaster, B. (1991) *Mind, Brain and Human Potential*. New York: Element.

Lane, D. (1990) Counselling psychology in organisations. *The Psychologist*, 12, 540–544.

Lang, G., Molen, H. van der, Trower, P. and Look, R. (1990) *Personal Conversations. Roles and Skills for Counsellors*. London: Routledge.

Langs, R. (1982) *Workbooks for Psychotherapists, Vol. II Listening and Formulating*. Emerson, NJ: Newconcept Press.

Lasswell, M.E. and Lobsenz, N.M. (1980) *Styles of Loving*. New York: Ballantine.

Lawrence, G. (1997) *Looking at Type and Learning Styles*. Gainesville, FL: Center for Applications of Psychological Type.

Lazarus, A. (1989) *The Practice of Multimodal Therapy*. Baltimore: Johns Hopkins University Press.

Lazarus, A. and Mayne, T.J. (1990) Relaxation: some limitations, side effects and proposed solutions. *Psychotherapy* 27, 261–266.

Lebow, J.L. (1987) Developing a personal integration: Principles for model construction and practice. *Journal of Marital and Family Therapy*, 13, 1–14.

Lee, J. (1988) Love styles. In R.J. Sternberg and M.C. Barnes (Eds) *The Psychology of Romantic Love*. London: Yale University Press.

Lenson, E.S. (1994) *Succeeding in Private Practice*. Thousand Oaks, CA: Sage.

Leong, F.T.L. and Austin, J.T. (1996) (Eds) *The Psychology Research Handbook*. London: Sage.

Levenson, R.W. and Ruef A.M. (1992) Empathy: A physiological substrate. *Journal of Personality and Social Psychology*, 63(2), 234–246.

Lewis, C. (1993) Making use of research. In R. Bayne and P. Nicolson (Eds) *Counselling and Psychology for Health Professionals*. Cheltenham: Stanley Thornes.

Ley, P. (1988) *Communicating with Patients*. London: Croom Helm.

Liptrot, D. and Sanders, P. (1994) *An Incomplete Guide to Inferential Statistics for Counsellors*. Manchester: PCCS Books.

Locke, D.C. (1992) *Increasing Multicultural Understanding. A Comprehensive Model*. London: Sage.

Loftus, E.F. (1993) The reality of repressed memories. *American Psychologist*, 48(5), 518–537.

Loftus, E.F. and Loftus, G.R. (1980) On the permanence of stored information in the brain. *American Psychologist*, 35, 409–420.

Lord, A. (1989) *Everyone Lives by Selling Something*. Kent: ICON.

MacMillan, M. and Clark, D. (1998) *Learning and Writing in Counselling*. London: Sage.

McAdams, D.P. (1995) What do we know when we know a person? *Journal of Personality*, 63(3), 365–396.

McKenzie, R. (1983) *Treat Your Own Neck*. Waikanae, NZ: Spinal Publications.

McKenzie, R. (1988) *Treat Your Own Back*. Waikanae, NZ: Spinal Publications.

McKinney, K. (1990) Sexual harassment of university faculty. *Sex Roles*, 23(7–8), 421–438.

McLeod, J. (1990) The client's experience of counselling and psycho-therapy: a review of the research literature. In D. Mearns and W. Dryden (Eds) *Experiences of Counselling in Action*. London: Sage.

McLeod, J. (1994) *Doing Counselling Research*. London: Sage.

McLeod, J. (1996a) Counsellor competence. In R. Bayne, I. Horton and J. Bimrose (Eds) *New Directions in Counselling*. London: Routledge.

McLeod, J. (1996b) The humanistic paradigm. In R. Woolfe, and W. Dryden (Eds) *Handbook of Counselling Psychology*. London: Sage.

McLeod, J. (1997) Reading, writing and research. In I. Horton with V. Varma (Eds) *The Needs of Counsellors and Psychotherapists*. London: Sage.

McMahon, G. (1994) *Setting Up Your Own Private Practice*. Cambridge: National Extension College.

McMahon, G (1997) Counselling in private practice. In S. Palmer and G. McMahon (Eds) *The Handbook of Counselling*. London: Routledge.

McMahon, G (1998) Integrative counselling. In S. Palmer (Ed.) *An Introductory Handbook of Approaches to Counselling and Psychotherapy*. London: Sage.

McMahon, G. and Doggart, E. (1997) *Understanding Trauma*. Cambridge: National Extension College.

McMullen, L.M. and Conway, J.B. (1996) Conceptualizing the figurative expressions of psychotherapy clients. In J.S. Mio and A.N. Katz (Eds) *Metaphor: Implications and Applications*. Mahwah, NJ: Lawrence Erlbaum.

McNeilly, C. and Howard, K. (1991) The effects of psychotherapy: a reevaluation based on dosage. *Psychotherapy Research*, 1, 74–78.

Macran, S. and Shapiro, D.A. (1998) The role of personal therapy for therapists: a review. *British Journal of Medical Psychology*, 71, 13–25.

Mahalik, J.R. (1990) Systematic eclectic models. *The Counseling Psychologist*, 18(4), 655–679.

Mahrer, A.R. (1989) *The Integration of Psychotherapies*. New York: Human Science Press.

Mann, J. (1973) *Time Limited Psychotherapy*. Cambridge, MA: Harvard University Press.

Marangoni, C., Garcia, S., Ickes, W. and Teng, G. (1995) Empathic accuracy in a clinically relevant setting. *Journal of Personality and Social Psychology*, 68(5), 854–869.

Marks, I.M. (1986) *Behavioural Psychotherapy*. London: IOP.

Martin, C.R. (1995) *Looking at Type and Careers*. Gainesville, FL: Center for Applications of Psychological Type.

Maslach, C. and Goldberg, J. (1998) Prevention of burnout: new perspectives. *Applied & Preventive Psychology*, 7, 63–74.

Matek, O. (1988) Obscene phone callers. *Journal of Social Work and Human Sexuality*, 7(1), 113–30.

Mearns, D. (1990a) The counsellor's experience of failure. In D Mearns and W. Dryden (Eds) *Experiences of Counselling in Action*. London: Sage.

Mearns, D. (1990b) The counsellor's experience of success. In D. Mearns and W Dryden (Eds) *Experiences of Counselling in Action*. London: Sage.

Mearns, D. (1992) Chapter 6. In W. Dryden (Ed.) *Hard-earned Lessons from Counselling in Action*. London: Sage.

Mearns, D. (1993) Against indemnity insurance. In W. Dryden (Ed.) *Questions and Answers on Counselling in Action*. London: Sage.

Mearns, D. (1997) *Person-Centred Counselling Training*. London: Sage.

Mearns, D. and Thorne, B. (1988) *Person-Centred Counselling in Action*. London: Sage.

Megranahan, M. (1997) Counselling in the workplace. In S. Palmer and G. McMahon (Eds) *The Handbook of Counselling*. London: Routledge.

Mellor-Clark, J. and Barkham, M. (1996) Evaluating counselling. In R. Bayne, I. Horton and J. Bimrose (Eds) *New Directions in Counselling*. London: Routledge.

Merry, T. (1995) *Invitation to Person Centred Psychology*. London: Whurr.

Merry, T. and Lusty, B. (1993) *What is Person Centred Therapy?* Loughton, Essex: Gale Publications.

Mills, C.K. and Wooster, A.D. (1987) Crying in the counselling situation. *British Journal of Guidance and Counselling*, 15(2), 125–130.

Moorey, S. (1996) Cognitive therapy. In W. Dryden (Ed.) *Handbook of Individual Therapy*. London: Sage.

Moos, R.H. (Ed.) (1991) *Coping with Life Crises – An Integrated Approach*. New York: Plenum.

Morley, W.F., Messick, J.M. and Aguilera, D.C. (1967) Crisis, paradigms of intervention. *Journal of Psychiatric Nursing*, 5, 537–538.

Mueller, J. (1983) Neuroanatomic correlates of emotions. In L. Temoshok, C. Van Dyke and L.S. Zegans (Eds) *Emotions in Health and Illness: Theoretical and Research Foundations*. Orlando, FL: Grune and Stratton.

Murgatroyd, S. and Woolfe, R. (1982) *Coping with Crisis*. London: Harper and Row.

Murphy, L.J. and Mitchell, D.L. (1998) When writing helps to heal: e-mail as therapy. *British Journal of Guidance and Counselling*, 26(1), 21–32.

Murray, R. (1997) *Ethical Humanities in Health Care: A Practical Approach through Medical Humanities*. Cheltenham: Stanley Thornes.

Murray, R. (1998) Communicating about ethical dilemmas: a medical humanities approach. In R. Bayne, P. Nicolson and I. Horton (Eds) *Counselling and Communication Skills for Medical and Health Practitioners*. Leicester: British Psychological Society.

Murray, S. (1992) *PPS Practitioner Guide and Reference Book*. Kincardine: PPS.

Myers, D.G. (1998) *Psychology*, 5th ed. New York: Worth.

Myers, I.B. (with Myers, P.B.) (1980) *Gifts Differing*. Palo Alto, CA: Consulting Psychologists Press.

Myers, K.D. and Kirby, L.K. (1994) *Introduction to Type Dynamics and Type Development*. Palo Alto, CA: Consulting Psychologists Press.

Nelson-Jones, R. (1985) Eclecticism, integration and comprehension in counselling theory. *British Journal of Guidance and Counselling*, 13(2), 129–138.

Newman, C.F. and Goldfried, M.R. (1996) Developments in psychotherapy integration. In W. Dryden (Ed.) *Developments in Psychotherapy*. London: Sage.

Nichols, K.A. and Jenkinson, J. (1991) *Leading a Support Group*. Cheltenham: Stanley Thornes.

Norcross, J.C. and Grencavage, L.M. (1989) Eclecticism and integration in counselling and psychotherapy: major themes and obstacles. In W. Dryden and J.C. Norcross (Eds) *Eclecticism and Integration in Counselling and Psychotherapy*. Loughton: Gale Centre Publications.

Novaco, R.W. (1975) *Anger Control*. Lexington MA: Lexington Books.

Ortony, A. and Turner, T.J. (1990) What's basic about basic emotions? *Psychological Review*, 97(3), 315–331.

O'Sullivan, G. (1996) Behaviour therapy. In W. Dryden (Ed.) *Handbook of Individual Therapy*. London: Sage.

Palmer, S. and Dryden, W. (1995) *Counselling for Stress Problems*. London: Sage.

Palmer, S. and McMahon, G. (1997) *Client Assessment*. London: Sage.

Parkes, C.M. (1986) *Bereavement: Studies of Grief in Adult Life*. Harmondsworth: Penguin Books.

Parry, G. (1990) *Coping with Crises*. London: BPS/Routledge.

Patterson, C.H. (1984) Empathy, warmth and genuineness: a review of reviews. *Psychotherapy*, 21(4), 431–438.

Peake, T.H., Borduin, C.M. and Archer, R.P. (1988) *Brief Psychotherapies – Changing Frames of Mind*. London: Sage.

Pedersen, P. (1987) Ten frequent assumptions of cultural bias in counseling. *Journal of Multicultural Counseling and Development*, 16, 36–40.

Pennebaker, J.W. (1993) Putting stress into words: health, linguistic and therapeutic implications. *Behaviour Research and Therapy*, 31(6), 539–548.

Pennebaker, J.W., Colder, M. and Sharp, L.K. (1990) Accelerating the coping process. *Journal of Personality and Social Psychology*, 58(3), 528–537.

Pervin, L.A. and John, O.P. (1996) *Personality: Theory and Research*, 7th ed. Chichester: Wiley.

Pipes, R.B., Schwartz, R. and Crouch, P. (1985) Measuring client fears. *Journal of Consulting and Clinical Psychology*, 53(6), 933–934.

Ponterotto, J.G., Casas, J.M., Suzuki, L.A. and Alexander C.M. (Eds) (1995) *Handbook of Multicultural Counseling*. London: Sage.

Pope, K.S. (1997) Science as careful questioning: are claims of a false memory syndrome epidemic based on empirical evidence? *American Psychologist*, 52(9), 997–1006.

Prochaska, J.O. and DiClemente, C.C. (1984) *The Transtheoretical Approach*. Homewood, IL: Dow Jones Irwin.

Prochaska, J.O. and DiClemente, C.C. (1992) The transtheoretical approach. In J.C. Norcross and M.R. Goldfried (Eds) *Handbook of Psychotherapy Integration*. New York: Basic Books.

Prochaska, J.O. and Norcross, J.C. (1994) *Systems of Psychotherapy. A Transtheoretical Analysis*. Pacific Grove, CA: Brooks/Cole.

Provost, J.A. (1993) *A Casebook: Applications of the Myers–Briggs Type Indicator in Counseling*, 2nd ed. Gainesville, FL: Center for Applications of Psychological Type.

Quenk, N.L. (1996) *In the Grip. Our Hidden Personality*. Palo Alto, CA: Consulting Psychologists Press.

Rainer, T. (1978) *The New Diary*. New York: St Martin's Press.

Rakos, R. (1991) *Assertive Behaviour: Theory, Research and Training*. London: Routledge.

Raphael, B. (1984) *The Anatomy of Bereavement*. London: Hutchinson.

Reddy, M. (1987) *The Manager's Guide to Counselling at Work*. London: BPS/Methuen.

Rice, L.N. (1974) The evocative function of the therapist. In D. Wexler and L.N. Rice (Eds) *Innovations in Client-Centred Therapy*. New York: Wiley.

Rice, L.N. (1980) A client-centred approach to supervision. In Hess, A.K. (Ed.) *Psychotherapy Supervision: Theory, Research and Practice*. New York: Wiley.

Ridley, C.R. (1995) *Overcoming Unintentional Racism in Counseling and Therapy*. London: Sage.

Ridley, C.R. Mendoza, D. and Kanitz, B. (1994) Multicultural training: Re-examination, operationalization and integration. *The Counselling Psychologist*, 22(2), 227–89.

Robson, C. (1993) *Real World Research. A Resource for Social Scientists and Practitioner-Researchers*. Oxford: Blackwell.

Rogers, C.R. (1957) The necessary and sufficient conditions for therapeutic personality change. *Journal of Consulting Psychology*, 21(2), 95–103.

Rogers, C.R. (1959) A theory of therapy, personality and interpersonal relationships as developed in the client-centred relationship. In S. Koch (Ed.) *Psychology: A Study of a Science, Vol. III*. New York: McGraw Hill.

Rogers, C.R. (1961) *On Becoming a Person*. London: Constable.

Rogers, C.R. (1980) *A Way of Being*. Boston, MA: Houghton Mifflin.

Rogers, C.R. (1986) Rogers, Kohut and Erickson: A personal perspective on some similarities and differences. *Person-Centred Review*, 1, 125–140.

Rogers, C.R. (1987) Comments on the issue of equality in psychotherapy. *Journal of Humanistic Psychology*, 27(1), 38–40.

Rogers, C.R. and Sandford, R.C. (1980) Client-centred psychotherapy. In H. Kaplan, B. Sadock and A. Freeman (Eds) *Comprehensive Textbook of Psychiatry, Vol. 3*. Baltimore: Williams and Wilkins.

Rosen, G.M. (1981) Guidelines for the review of do-it-yourself treatment books. *Contemporary Psychology*, 26(3), 190–191.

Rosen, G.M. (1987) Self-help treatment books and the commercialization of psychotherapy. *American Psychologist*, 42(1), 46–51.

Rosenfield, M. (1997) *Counselling by Telephone*. London: Sage.

Rosenthal, R. (1990) How are we doing in soft psychology? *American Psychologist*, 45, 775–777.

Rosenthal, T. (1993) To soothe the savage breast. *Behaviour Research and Therapy*, 31(5), 439–462.

Russell, J.A. (1991) Culture and the categorization of emotions. *Psychological Bulletin*, 110(4), 426–450.

Russell, J. (1993) *Out of Bounds: Sexual Exploitation in Counselling and Therapy*. London: Sage.

Russell, J.A. (1995) Facial expressions of emotion: what lies beyond minimal universality? *Psychological Bulletin*, 118(3), 379–391.

Russell, J. and Dexter, G. (1993) 'Menage á trois'. Accreditation, NVQs and BAC. *Counselling*, November, 266–269.

Ryecroft, C. (1985) *A Critical Dictionary of Psychoanalysis*. Harmondsworth: Penguin Books.

Ryle, A (1995) Cognitive analytic therapy: history and recent developments. In A. Ryle (Ed.) *Cognitive Analytic Therapy*. London: Wiley.

Sanders, P. (1996) *An Incomplete Guide to Using Counselling Skills on the Telephone*, 2nd ed. Llangarron: PCCS Books.

Sanders P. and Liptrot, D. (1993) *An Incomplete Guide to Basic Research Methods and Data Collection for Counsellors*. Manchester: PCCS Books.

Sanders, P. and Liptrot, D. (1994) *An Incomplete Guide to Qualitative Research Methods for Counsellors*. Manchester: PCCS Books.

Sanders, P. and Rosenfield, M. (1998) Counselling at a distance: challenges and new initiatives. *British Journal of Guidance and Counselling*, 26(1), 5–10.

Schlosberg, S. and Neporent, L (1996) *Fitness for Dummies*. Foster City, CA: IDG Books Worldwide.

Scott, M.J. (1997) Counselling for trauma and post traumatic stress disorder. In S. Palmer and G. McMahon (Eds) *The Handbook of Counselling*. London: Routledge.

Scott, M.J. and Stradling, S.E. (1992) *Counselling for Post Traumatic Stress Disorder*. London: Sage.

Scott, J. and Dryden, W. (1996) The cognitive–behavioural paradigm. In R. Woolfe and W. Dryden (Eds) *Handbook of Counselling Psychology*. London: Sage.

Segal, J. (1995) The stresses of working with clients with disabilities. In W. Dryden (Ed.) *The Stresses of Counselling in Action*. London: Sage

Seligman, M.E.P. (1995) The effectiveness of psychotherapy. The 'Consumer Reports' study. *American Psychologist*, 50(12), 965–974.

Shaver, P.R. and Hazan, C. (1988) A biased overview of the study of love. *Journal of Social and Personal Relationships*, 5(4), 473–501.

Sheffield, C.J. (1989) The invisible intruder: women's experience of obscene phone calls. *Gender and Society*, 3(4), 483–488.

Shillito-Clarke, C. (1993) Book review, *Counselling*, August, 219.

Shlien, J.M. (1989) Boy's person-centred perspective on psycho-diagnosis – a response. *Person Centred Review*, 4(2), 157–162.

Sills, C. (1997) Contracts and contract making. In C. Sills (Ed.) *Contracts in Counselling*. London: Sage.

Silove, D. and Manicavasagar, V. (1997) *Overcoming Panic*. London: Robinson.

Spinelli, E (1996) The existential–phenomenological paradigm. In R. Woolfe and W. Dryden (Eds) *The Handbook of Counselling Psychology*. London: Sage.

Stern, R and Drummond, L. (1991) *The Practice of Behavioural and Cognitive Psychotherapy*. Cambridge: Cambridge University Press.

Sternberg, R.J. and Barnes, M.C. (1988) *The Psychology of Romantic Love*. London: Yale University Press.

Stewart, I. (1989) *Transactional Analysis in Action*. London: Sage.

Stewart W. (1992) *An A–Z of Counselling Theory and Practice*. Cheltenham: Stanley Thornes.

Stiles, W.B., Shapiro, D.A. and Elliott, R. (1986) Are all psychotherapies equivalent? *American Psychologist*, 41, 165–180.

Stiles, W.B., Shapiro, D.A. Barkham, M. (1993) Research directions for psychotherapy integration. In J.C. Norcross (Ed.) Research directions for psychotherapy integration: A roundtable. *Journal of Psychotherapy Integration*, 3, 91–131.

Storr, A. (1990) *The Art of Psychotherapy*, 2nd ed. London: Heinemann/Secker and Warburg.

Strong, S.R. (1968) Counselling: An interpersonal influence process. *Journal of Counseling Psychology*, 15, 215–224.

Sutherland, N.S. (1998) *Breakdown: A Personal Crisis and a Medical Dilemma*, new edition. Oxford: Oxford University Press.

Syme, G. (1994) *Counselling in Independent Practice*. Milton Keynes: Open University Press.

Tavris, C. (1984) On the wisdom of counting to ten. Personal and social dangers of anger expression. In P. Shaver (Ed.) *Review of Personality and Social Psychology, Vol.5*. London: Sage.

Tavris, C. (1989) *Anger: The Misunderstood Emotion*, 2nd ed. London: Touchstone Books/ Simon & Schuster.

Templeman, T.L. and Sinnett, RD. (1991) Patterns of sexual arousal and history in a 'normal' sample of young men. *Archives of Sexual Behaviour*, 20, 37–50.

Thorne, B. (1992) Psychotherapy and counselling: the quest for differences. *Counselling*, 3(4), 244–248.

Townsend, R. (1984) *Further Up the Organisation*. London: Hodder & Stoughton.

Trickett, S. (1992) *Coping Successfully with Panic Attacks*. London: Sheldon Press.

Truax, C.B. and Carkhuff, R.R. (1967) *Toward Effective Counselling and Psychotherapy*. Chicago: Aldine.

Usher, C.H. (1989) Recognizing cultural bias in counseling theory and practice: the case of Rogers. *Journal of Multicultural Counseling and Development*, 17, 62–71.

Velleman, R. (1992) *Counselling for Alcohol Problems*. London: Sage.

Walker, M. (1992a) *Surviving Secrets*. Milton Keynes: Open University Press.

Walker, M.(1992b) Chapter 10. In W. Dryden (Ed.) *Hard-earned Lessons from Counselling in Action*. London: Sage.

Walker, M. (1993) When values clash. In W. Dryden (Ed.) *Questions and Answers on Counselling in Action*. London: Sage.

Walker, M. (1996) Working with abuse survivors: the recovered memory debate. In R. Bayne, I. Horton and J. Bimrose (Eds) *New Directions in Counselling*. London: Routledge.

Warren-Holland, S. (1998) Practical ... s. *Counselling*, 9(2), 96–97.

Webb, W.B. (1981) How to or not how t ... *mporary Psychology*, 26, 192–193.

Weinrach, S.G. and Thomas, K.R. (1996) The counseling professions' commitment to diversity-sensitive counseling: a critical reassessment. *Journal of Counseling and Development*, 74, 472–477.

Weishaar, M.E. (1993) *Aaron T. Beck*. London: Sage.

Wheeler, S. (1996) *Training Counsellors. The Assessment of Competence*. London: Cassell.

Wheeler, S. (1998) Challenging the core theoretical model: a reply to Colin Feltham. *Counselling*, 9(2), 134–138.

Whitaker, D.S. (1985) *Using Groups to Help People*. London: Routledge.

Whitmore, D. (1991) *Psychosynthesis Counselling in Action*. London: Sage.

Wimbush, E. (1994) A moderate approach to promoting physical activity: evidence and implications. *Health Education Journal*, 53, 322–336.

Winter, D.G. (1996) *Personality: Analysis and Interpretation of Lives*. Maidenhead: McGraw-Hill.

Winter, D.G. and Stewart, A.J. (1995) Commentary: tending the garden of personality. *Journal of Personality*, 63(3) 711–727.

Woolfe, R. (1990) Counselling psychology in Britain: an idea whose time has come. *The Psychologist*, 12, 531–535.

Woolfe, R., Dryden, W. and Charles Edwards, D. (1989) The nature and range of counselling practice. In W. Dryden *et al.* (Eds) *Handbook of Counselling in Britain*. London: Routledge.

Worden, W.J. (1984) *Grief Counselling and Grief Therapy*. London: Tavistock.

Wortman, C.B. and Silver, R.C. (1989) The myths of coping with loss. *Journal of Consulting and Clinical Psychology*, 57(3), 349–357.

Yalom, I.D. (1986) *Theory and Practice of Group Psychotherapy*, 3rd ed. New York: Basic Books.

Yalom, I.D (1989) *Love's Executioner and Other Tales of Psychotherapy*. Harmondsworth: Penguin.